The Restoration Newspaper
and its Development

This book is a major survey of the English newspaper and the way it developed from 1660 to the early eighteenth century, a crucial period in its long history.

Professor Sutherland's approach is comprehensive and deals with a wide range of topics: the administration of newspapers, the source from which they obtained information, the state and reliability of reporting, the contributions of country and foreign correspondents, and the extent to which papers were able to print political news and express political opinions in a period of government repression. A final chapter provides an account of the chaotic and often dangerous lives of newspaper men and women. The emphasis throughout falls on how much was actually achieved in difficult circumstances, and how often modern developments were anticipated.

The importance of this book lies in the sustained effort to demonstrate how newspapers worked and how they changed; it will become a useful work of reference for scholars of seventeenth and eighteenth-century literature, as well as for political and social historians.

The Restoration Newspaper and its Development

JAMES SUTHERLAND

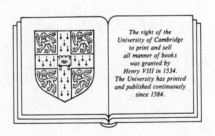

The right of the
University of Cambridge
to print and sell
all manner of books
was granted by
Henry VIII in 1534.
The University has printed
and published continuously
since 1584.

CAMBRIDGE UNIVERSITY PRESS

Cambridge
London   New York   New Rochelle
Melbourne   Sydney

Published by the Press Syndicate of the University of Cambridge
The Pitt Building, Trumpington Street, Cambridge CB2 1RP
32 East 57th Street, New York, NY 10022, USA
10 Stamford Road, Oakleigh, Melbourne 3166, Australia

First published 1986

Printed in Great Britain at the University Press, Cambridge

British Library cataloguing in publication data
Sutherland, James
The Restoration newspaper and its development.
1. English newspapers – History – 17th century
2. English newspapers – History – 18th century
I. Title
072 PN5115

Library of Congress cataloguing in publication data
Sutherland, James Runcieman, 1900-
The Restoration newspaper and its development.
Bibliography: p.
Includes index.
1. English newspaper – History – 17th century.
I. Title.
PN5115.S97 1986 072 86-1295

ISBN 0 521 32613 3

GG

Contents

Preface

The London newspaper was already forty years old when Charles II returned to England in 1660, to reign over his people for the next quarter of a century. During the Civil War there had been a vigorous growth of weekly news-books; that is periodicals in small quarto size of eight pages. I have not dealt with these here because they have been fully treated by Joseph Frank in his lively and well-informed work, *The Beginnings of the English Newspaper* (1960). It is with the next forty years that my own study is mainly concerned. Although I have called it *The Restoration Newspaper*, I have felt free to take account of the small number of newspapers that made a brief appearance in the winter of 1688–9, during the uncertain weeks preceding and following the flight of James II to France, and of the new generation of papers that began to appear in the last five years of the seventeenth century. With the foundation of the *Oxford Gazette* in 1665, the format of the Restoration newspaper was a folio half sheet, printed on both sides in double columns.

The year 1660 did not inaugurate a new age of freedom for the periodical press: the King and his ministers disliked and distrusted newspapers, and did everything they could to get rid of them. A new Licensing Act in 1662 was the first step to their eventual suppression. By the autumn of 1666 the only paper the King's subjects were allowed to read was the official *London Gazette*, and from that they could learn little more than what was happening in foreign countries. By a lucky mischance, however, the reign of Charles II has a special significance in the development of the English newspaper. When, in 1679, the House of Commons introduced a bill designed to exclude his Catholic brother James from the succession, the King prorogued parliament, and on 12 July dissolved it. While this was happening, the Licensing Act, then due for renewal, was left in abeyance with other unfinished business. On 7 July, without waiting to see if the prorogued parliament might not be recalled, Benjamin Harris brought out the first number of his *Domestick Intelligence*, and it was soon followed by a succession of other newspapers. In the next three years from 1679 to 1682 almost forty different papers were published, a few hardly surviving their birth, but others lasting for several months, and some persisting for nearly two years. By the autumn of 1682, however, the government had regained complete control, and, without the introduction of a revived Licensing Act (for the King had now resolved to rule without a parliament), the newspapers were again suppressed.

It is this seminal period from 1679 to 1682, when the newspapers were legally free to appear, although not free from incessant prosecution and interference, that I have chosen for particular study. By taking a close-up view of the newspaper press at this time I have tried to show how it was establishing a pattern for much of its future development; and by treating this period in depth I have had the opportunity to indicate not only how the news was presented from day to day, but also the intense rivalry between papers of a different political complexion, the tricks they played on one another, their quarrels and the personal abuse that at once divided and linked them together. Since complete files of those newspapers are now available only in national and academic libraries (and even there for the most part in microfilm) I have quoted from them fairly liberally for the benefit of the general reader. I have envisaged this book, then, as a contribution to the history of the English newspaper in one of it most formative periods, taking the word newspaper in its usual sense of 'a printed publication containing the news, commonly with the addition of advertisements and other matters of interest'. Two notable periodicals of mainly political comment, *Heraclitus Ridens* and *The Observator*, began to appear in 1681; but although they contain some incidental news and they are cited here from time to time, I have not considered them as newspapers.

At an early stage it became clear to me that it would be impracticable and counter-productive to avoid all references to the newspapers of the early eighteenth century. In the first chapter, which is historical, I therefore thought it desirable to include the more important developments and innovations that took place in the first few decades of the new century, if only because I had occasion in later chapters to refer fairly frequently to the newspapers of that period for purposes of comparison or contrast. In the chapter dealing with foreign news, for example, I could not otherwise have checked the claims occasionally made by seventeenth-century newspapers to have their own foreign correspondents. Three chapters (2–4) are concerned with the domestic and foreign news. They deal with such questions as how the news was collected in London, and how it was obtained from the country districts and from abroad; what part was played by regular correspondents; how far papers took what they published from written news-letters, or stole it from one another; what sort of news interested the seventeenth-century reader, how reliable it was, and how it varied in kind from one newspaper to another. Since many of the Restoration newspapers were politically committed, a separate chapter on the way political issues were handled was clearly required. Here again I have concentrated on the years of political crisis from 1679 to 1682, dealing, *inter alia*, with the danger of publishing any news at all about the proceedings of parliament or the Privy Council, and the need to walk a tightrope between news and comment. I have also indicated some of the innovations in controversial technique devised by newspapers of the early eighteenth century, and some changes in the way that governments dealt with the opposition press. In the final chapter I have endeavoured, firstly, to trace the careers of a number of intrepid newspaper men and women, and the troubles they brought upon themselves by their own indiscretions; and, secondly, to point out the difficulties they had to face in producing papers printed by manual labour on a hand-press, and the extent to which such conditions prevented an orderly presentation of the day's news. In trying to establish the varying responsibility of author, newswriter, printer, publisher and proprietor for what appeared in the newspapers I have at times been forced to fall back on conjecture; but I take comfort from the words of Dr Johnson on a different occasion: 'There is no danger in conjecture, if it is proposed as conjecture.'

In conclusion, I have to add that I am not a professional historian, but I am deeply indebted to historians of the Restoration period, without whose guidance I might often have failed to realise the full significance of some piece of news or some statement in my newspapers. I am aware that I may be reproached for anticipating the use of the terms Whig and Tory by a few years in applying them to Shaftesbury's faction and the Court party before they had become fully current, but I took the chance for the sake of convenience. My main problem with English history in this book has been how to provide as briefly as possible some necessary historical background for the general reader, without over-simplifying or distorting the issues. This is never an easy thing to do, and I would be glad to think I have not set too many scholarly teeth on edge.

CHAPTER 1

Origins and developments

When Charles II returned from exile in 1660, the general air of rejoicing prompted a burst of confidence from John Dryden:

> At home the hateful names of Parties cease
> And factious Souls are weary'd into peace.

But this was either wishful thinking, or an early example of that loyalist propaganda he was later to practise so successfully as poet laureate. The real state of affairs was different. As new laws were put into force and government control was steadily tightened, opposition inevitably increased, and equally inevitably, was driven underground. In such circumstances resistance was still possible; the discontented, the dispossessed, the persecuted and the fanatically faithful believers in 'the Good old Cause' could still find men who dared to print, and others to disperse, their seditious pamphlets. The risks were great and the penalties heavy, but in the early 1660s such pamphlets kept appearing in considerable numbers, and fostered the spirit of opposition to the restored monarchy. The government had foreseen this danger, and in November 1660 the old Cavalier journalist, Sir John Berkenhead, had been appointed official licenser for the press; but he could only deal with such manuscripts as were submitted to him.[1] More effective was another old royalist, Roger L'Estrange, who, on 24 February 1662, became 'Surveyor of the Presses' by virtue of a warrant from Sir Edward Nicholas, one of the two Secretaries of State. This appointment was to be confirmed on 15 August 1663 by letters patent from the King, by which L'Estrange became 'Surveyor of the Imprimerie' and at the same time a licenser of the press.[2]

For L'Estrange it was not only a moral duty to hunt down heretical and seditious publications, it became a pleasure. In the course of the next few years his spies and informers enabled him to raid the premises of many printers, and to arrest his victims in the act. Among those was John Twyn, who was arrested on 27 October 1663, and tried some months later for printing 'A Treatise of the Execution of Justice'. Giving evidence at the trial, L'Estrange told the court that he had set a man to watch Twyn's house, and when at length a message reached

1

him '*that now they were about it as hard as they could drive* (which was about four in the morning)', he went at once with one of the King's messengers and a constable, and after a long delay the door was opened to them. In the interval Twyn and his apprentices had been endeavouring to destroy or conceal the evidence, but L'Estrange found some sheets still wet from the press, and later he obtained the manuscript from which they had been set. In sentencing Twyn to be hanged, drawn and quartered, Lord Chief Justice Hyde told him that he must be made an example for this sort of offence. Two days later, in passing sentence on three other members of the book trade, Hyde again stated the need for 'examples':

The Press is grown so common, and Men take the Boldness to print whatever is brought to them, let it concern whom it will; it is high time Examples be made.[3]

In ferreting out unlicensed publications L'Estrange had behind him a new Act of parliament, usually referred to as the Licensing Act, which came into force on 10 June 1662. This was 'An Act for preventing the frequent Abuses in printing seditious, treasonable, and unlicensed Books and Pamphlets, and for regulating of Printing and printing Presses'. The preamble to the Act makes it clear why the government believed that such legislation was needed: the nation was still suffering from the poison injected into the body politic in the commonwealth days. By 'the general licentiousness of the late times many evil disposed persons have been encouraged to print and sell heretical, schismatical, blasphemous, seditious and treasonable books, pamphlets and papers', thus endangering 'the peace of these kingdoms' and raising disaffection to the King and his government. For the future no book or pamphlet was to be printed unless it was first entered, with full details of its content, in the Stationers Register in London, and unless it 'shall be first lawfully licensed and authorised to be printed by such person and persons only as shall be constituted and appointed to license the same'. Every printer had to put his name to what he printed, and supply the name of the author, if required by the licenser. A further clause provided that journeymen printers should be kept at work: a journeyman printer out of work was the sort of man most likely to turn to illicit printing to earn a living. The penalties for breaking the new law were severe: for a first offence, a suspension for three years; for a second offence, final disablement, together with a fine, imprisonment, or corporal punishment 'not extending to life or limb'.[4]

An important provision was made to ensure that the Act would be effective: warrants might be granted by the principal Secretaries of State 'to search all houses and shops where they shall know, or upon some probable reason suspect any books or papers to be printed, bound or stitched, especially printing houses, booksellers' shops and warehouses, and bookbinders' houses and shops'. It was this clause in the Act that enabled L'Estrange to function so successfully. For the next hundred years the right vested in the Secretaries of State to issue warrants to search for unnamed persons and unspecified books and papers was to remain a source of grievance and controversy. But at last, in 1763, following upon the publication of No. 45 of *The North Briton* and the action brought by John Wilkes against the under-secretary who had authorised the search for and removal of his papers, Lord Chief Justice Pratt declared that, in spite of long precedent, the practice was 'illegal, and contrary to the fundamental principles of the constitution'. In 1766 the House of Commons condemned general warrants.

It is hard for us today to realise that under the Stuarts any criticism of the government could be, and often was in a court of law, interpreted as an attack on the sovereign: on such occasions no real distinction was made between the king's servants and the king himself. On 4 November 1704, for example, John Tutchin was indicted at the Guildhall as 'a seditious person, and a daily inventor and publisher of false news, and horrible and false lies and seditious libels', who made it his business 'the government, and adminstration of justice under our Lady the Queen to traduce, scandalize and vilify, and our said Lady the Queen, her ministers and officers to bring into suspicion, and the ill opinion of her subjects'. Passages were cited from various issues of Tutchin's periodical *The Observator*, in which he had criticised severely the administration of the Navy and the incompetence of its officers, complained that government offices were frequently given to men of title rather than to men competent in business, and hinted openly that the sad state in which the nation found itself was in large measure due to bribery and corruption by 'French gold'. This was strong stuff, and even today no government could afford to ignore such charges. But what is significant is the way in which the Attorney-General practically equated Tutchin's accusations with treason. 'Here is the highest Reflection on the Government imaginable,' he told the court. 'There can be no Reflection on them that are in Office under Her Majesty, but it must cast some Reflection on the Queen who employs them.' If this seems to be stretching the argument too far, it must be remembered that under Queen Anne – and still more under Charles II and James II – ministers were appointed or dismissed at the will of the sovereign, who could thus be said to be more personally responsible for the government of the nation than is so today. At all events Lord Chief Justice Holt made it abundantly clear that criticism of the government of the day by mere journalists was not to be tolerated:

If people should not be called to account for possessing the people with an ill opinion of the government, no government can subsist. For it is very necessary for all governments that the people should have a good opinion of it. And nothing can be worse to any government than to endeavour to procure animosities as to the management of it; this has always been looked upon as a crime, and no government can be safe without it be punished.[5]

On this occasion Tutchin was lucky. He had an able counsel who succeeded in having the trial quashed on a technicality, and the government thought it best to let the charge drop. But any political comment in this period was potentially dangerous, and the more so because no journalist could ever be sure what the government of the day might choose to consider objectionable. Even if he refrained from comment and simply reported what was happening, the newswriter could still be in trouble if, in the government's judgement, some item of news was false, or inflammatory, or a statement of facts that it did not wish to see published. For the greater part of Charles II's reign the periodical press was under strict control, and in the *Gazette* only such news was released as the government thought fit to make known.

So far as news was concerned, steps had been taken to curb 'the general licentiousness of the late times' even before the Licensing Act became law. During the Civil War there had been, on both sides, a remarkable growth of news-books – *Mercuries, Diurnals, Intelligencers, Scouts* and so on – and the various issues that divided the King from his parliament had been fought over in those and in other controversial pamphlets. When the war was over, parliament exercised some censorship of the press, but it was only partially effective, and it was not until 1655 that Cromwell finally clamped down on the news-books. In that year Marchamont Nedham was left in undisputed possession of the field with his two weeklies, *Mercurius Politicus* (Thursdays) and *The Publick Intelligencer* (Mondays), both supervised by John Thurloe, Cromwell's Secretary of State. In the rapidly changing political atmosphere of 1659–60 Nedham took some discreet steps to adapt his news to the new monarchical feeling that was beginning to emerge; but late in March 1660, by order of the Council of State, he was 'discharged from writing or publishing any publique intelligence', and he must have felt it prudent to escape while he could, for soon afterwards he withdrew to Holland.[6]

4

London, however, was still left with two news-books. Since 26 December 1659, Henry Muddiman, a protégé of General Monck, had been writing and publishing *The Parliamentary Intelligencer* on Mondays, and this had been followed on 5 January 1660 by Giles Dury's *Mercurius Publicus*, published on Thursdays. In getting rid of Nedham, the Council of State at the same time authorised Muddiman and Dury to take his place as publishers of the news; and *The Parliamentary Intelligencer* (re-named *The Kingdomes Intelligencer* on 7 January 1661) and *Mercurius Publicus* were allowed to continue after the Restoration, by which time Muddiman appears to have taken sole charge of both news-books. Their official or semi-official status was made clear by the words 'Published by Order'; and until the end of August 1663 they provided the only printed news that Englishmen were permitted to buy or to read. A few short-lived periodicals that had sprung up in the early months of 1660 were finally suppressed by order of the Privy Council on 18 July 1660.[7] The government had shown that it was determined to exercise its authority. While it was still possible for daring men to print unlicensed pamphlets or even books in secret, and for others to sell them surreptitiously, it would have been impracticable to carry on a weekly news-book or newspaper in such circumstances if it were to sell more than a very limited number of copies. Any attempt to 'vend' it openly on the streets would have led at once to the arrest and examination of the hawkers concerned, and in no time at all L'Estrange and his men would have discovered and arrested both printer and publisher.

Henry Muddiman (1629–92) is a notable figure in seventeenth-century journalism to whom justice has only been done in the present century.[8] We know that he matriculated at St John's College, Cambridge, and later became a schoolmaster. In the uncertain months before the Restoration, when General Monck was looking for someone who could give a favourable interpretation of 'the affairs now in agitation in England, Scotland and Ireland', his brother-in-law Thomas Clarges persuaded Muddiman to give up his schoolmastering and write *The Parliamentary Intelligencer*. Muddiman was a highly methodical man, a lucid and easy writer, and an able organiser who soon established a wide range of correspondents. His news-book was only two weeks old when another very methodical man, Samuel Pepys, met him by chance, and recorded his first impressions of the newswriter:

I found Muddiman a good scholar – an arch rogue – and one that, though he writes news-books for the Parliament, yet he did declare that he did it only to get money; and did talk very basely of many of them.[9]

When the two men met, Pepys was not quite 27, and Muddiman a few weeks short of his thirtieth birthday. On this occasion Pepys got his facts wrong: Muddiman was not writing for the parliament, but for Monck. This entry in the famous Diary, however, offers one of the few intimate glimpses we have of Muddiman, who normally kept himself so much in the background that it is surprising to find him being described as an 'arch rogue'.

With his monopoly of the printed news, Muddiman's two news-books could not fail to be profitable. He had, however, a more lucrative source of income in the written news-letters that he sent out to subscribers for almost thirty years. Those must be mentioned here, for in a time of rigid press control they enabled news to be circulated that would never have been permitted to appear in print. The written news-letter, multiplied by professional copyists and sent by post to subscribers, had been established in England by the 1630s; but Muddiman brought it to a point of efficiency, both in its contents and its circulation, that it had never reached before. He began with two great advantages. Early in the new reign he was attached to the office of Sir Edward Nicholas, though what his precise duties were is by no means clear. His biographer seems to acknowledge this uncertainty by stating on one page that Muddiman was 'given the task of organizing the correspondence of the [two] Secretaries all over the kingdom', and on another page that he 'arranged' their correspondence.[10] There is evidence that Muddiman felt free to open the domestic correspondence that reached the two Secretaries, and to make abstracts from it, but that he left the foreign letters unopened. In this way he could obtain information for his two news-books and his private news-letters, and also build up a list of correspondents who might supply him with news in the future. Muddiman sent out his news-letters from his own office at the Seven Stars in the Strand near the New Exchange, but invariably headed them 'Whitehall'. The fact that many of the replies he received are now among the State Papers indicates that he passed them on to the under-secretary in Nicholas's office, Joseph Williamson. Other letters were addressed to the under-secretary, but marked 'For Mr. Henry Muddiman'. That Muddiman was asking for and receiving information from some of the subscribers to his news-letter may be instanced by a reply he received from William Duckett, member of parliament for Calne, beginning: 'Sir. In your last you desired me to acquaint you what nonconformists, papists and others were indicted at quarter sessions . . .' It seems to be a reasonable suggestion that 'some of his correspondents, such as the postmasters, probably obtained their news-

letters at reduced fees on condition of supplying intelligence of what
was happening in the neighbourhood of their homes'.[11] At all events,
by simultaneously serving the government and serving himself, Muddiman built up a large body of subscribers to his news-letter, including
peers and members of parliament, postmasters and country booksellers,
clergymen and doctors, army officers, merchants, innkeepers and
others, mostly living in England, but some in Scotland and Ireland, and
even a few abroad.

His first advantage, then, was his easy access to domestic intelligence; his second, that by an order of Secretary Nicholas he had been
granted free postage not only for his own letters and news-letters, but
for those letters that should be addressed to him. How much this concession was worth to Muddiman is not easy to assess. Most of his
subscribers received one news-letter a week, but to some he wrote
twice, and to others three times a week. The total number of his
subscribers in any given year can only be guessed, but one guess is
'some hundreds'. Since his normal charge for the newsletter service
was £5 a year, and his expenses for copying would not have been heavy
in the reign of Charles II, he must have become a wealthy man.[12]

A writer of news-letters was not immune from prosecution if what
he had written became known and gave offence to the government. But
so long as his letters were sent out privately to the limited number of
gentlemen who could find £5 a year for this personal service, the
government could afford to take the view that was taken over a hundred
years later when William Godwin published his revolutionary work
Political Justice, and was spared from political martyrdom because the
government of the day considered that a book published at three
guineas was not likely to do much harm. As a government servant
Muddiman took care not to circulate news that would be objectionable
to the King and his ministers, and he must gradually have learnt from
experience how far he could go. However, there was still much of
interest that could safely be written, but which it would have been
dangerous, and even illegal, to print. On 25 June 1660 the House of
Commons had ordered that 'no person whatsoever do presume, at his
peril, to print any votes or proceedings of this House, without special
leave and order of this House';[13] and this restriction remained more
or less effective until late in the eighteenth century. The order,
however, related only to printing, and Muddiman and later writers of
news-letters felt able to pass on to their subscribers interesting information about parliamentary proceedings. During the vital debates on the
Exclusion Bill in the two sessions of 1680 and 1681, when the *London*

Gazette ignored the crisis, Muddiman give his readers full reports of what was going on in parliament. On the whole he steered clear of trouble with remarkable success; and when, in 1676, he was summoned to appear before the Privy Council and answer a charge of writing false news, he was able to prove it was not in *his* news-letter that the offending statement had been made.[14]

How many competitors he had in the early years after the Restoration it is impossible to say, for although many news-letters have survived among the State Papers or in private collections, they were not signed, and the compilers of news-letters cannot therefore be identified. (Those in the handwriting of Muddiman's clerks can be recognised by his practice of dating them from 'Whitehall'.) In the years of the Popish Plot, however, the circulation of news-letters notably increased, and several of their writers lost their anonymity by coming within the range of the law. Worse still, from the government's point of view, those newsletters were now circulating in the coffee-houses, and filling men's minds with seditious notions which they freely discussed in public. On 23 December 1675 the King had issued a proclamation for the suppression of coffee-houses (a popular but comparatively recent innovation), on the grounds that 'many tradesmen and others do herein misspend much of their time ... but also for that in such houses divers false, malitious and scandalous reports are devised and spread abroad to the defamation of His Majesty's government'. The unpopularity of this move may have caused the government to think again, for on 8 January 1676 a further proclamation postponed the closing of the coffee-houses till June, but enjoined that the proprietors must give security that they would not allow scandalous papers on their premises. Such warnings usually had an immediate effect, but one that quickly wore off. In September 1677 twenty coffee men appeared before the Council for still having scandalous literature on display, and had their licenses cancelled.[15]

Muddiman, however, continued to send out his news-letters without interference until October 1689. Even when the newspaper press had greatly expanded in the reign of Queen Anne, many gentlemen (more especially if they were politically opposed to the government of the day) continued to subscribe to a private news-letter, partly because in that way they could obtain some news that was not 'fit to print', but also because it was a personal service, beginning politely with the word 'Sir', and giving the recipient the pleasant feeling that he was reading his own private correspondence.

Muddiman's two news-books, *The Kingdomes Intelligencer* and *Mercurius Publicus*, came to an end in 1663, not because they were failing to give satisfaction, but because Muddiman was forced to make way for the newly-appointed Surveyor of the Press. No salary had been attached to the Surveyorship, but, like so many of the King's servants, L'Estrange was to be paid by the emoluments he could gain from his office. He was now granted Muddiman's sole right to print and publish news ('all narratives not exceeding two sheets of paper, mercuries, diurnals'), and also playbills and the advertisements for quack medicines, etc. In addition, he appears to have exacted one shilling a sheet from all the books he licensed. On Monday, 31 August, L'Estrange brought out the first number of *The Intelligencer. Published for the Satisfaction of the People*, an eight-page news-book, increased in June 1665 to sixteen pages, and followed it on Thursday, 3 September with *The Newes*. Both were published 'With Privilege', and the price was 2*d*. Muddiman had been requested to help the inexperienced L'Estrange, and he agreed to do so for a payment of £3 a week, which, on L'Estrange's reckoning, was equivalent to more than half the profits from his two news-books.[16] How far Muddiman placed his unique news service at the disposal of L'Estrange it is impossible to tell, but in the event the agreement did not last for long, and L'Estrange was left to his own devices. He was a man of unbounded confidence, who was not in the least intimidated by the responsibility of providing the nation with all the news it was going to get, and he had an easy colloquial style which must have pleased some of his readers and infuriated others. He was never at a loss for something to say; and if he was sometimes short of news he could always fill his news-books with comment of a kind that was agreeable to the King and his ministers. By his own standards he was doing a good job. But in the summer of 1665 he had to cope with a catastrophe that would have dismayed the best of journalists. With the outbreak of the Great Plague the Court had withdrawn from London, to be followed in due course by many government officials; communications were increasingly disrupted, and sources of news began to dry up. It is to L'Estrange's credit that all through the Plague he stayed on in London and kept his news-books going, but only at the price of an inevitable deterioration in the news he offered. In his address to his readers in the first number of *The Intelligencer* he had promised not to 'vamp' his news (that is, not to serve up stale news as if it were fresh), or to be 'so foul a dealer as to make any man pay twice for the same commodity'. But that, increasingly, was what he was now doing. What had already appeared in *The Intelligencer* was now frequently repeated in *The Newes*, and *vice versa*. The final blow came on 16 November 1665, when, with the Court and parliament both removed to Oxford, the first number of *The Oxford Gazette* was published. L'Estrange did not give up without a struggle; but by the end of January 1666 both his news-books had ceased publication.

The foundation of *The Oxford Gazette* takes us back to the two Secretaries of State, and more especially to Henry Bennet, Earl of Arlington, who had succeeded Secretary Nicholas in October 1662, and to his under-secretary Joseph Williamson, a man with all Muddiman's application to public affairs, and with a determination to channel as much lucrative business his own way as possible. The foreign correspondence that came to Arlington's office passed regularly through the under-secretary's hands, for the easy-going Arlington 'remitted all to his man Williamson';[17] and the under-secretary began to realise that one way to improve his fortunes would be to bring L'Estrange's two rather amateur news-books to an end, and replace them with an official newspaper, which he himself would control, and from which he could derive most of the profits. How far dissatisfaction with L'Estrange's performance as an official journalist played a part in this move to supplant him it is impossible to say; but his colloquial style may well have grated on the ear of a dedicated civil servant, and his tendency to interpret his duties in terms of propaganda (or, as he put it to Arlington, 'to teaze and persecute the whole rabble of the faction'), rather than to deliver the news in a dignified and impersonal manner, may have played a part.

The first step was to get rid of L'Estrange, and here events played into Williamson's hands. With the King and Court and parliament all settled in Oxford, L'Estrange was isolated in the stricken City, and had been working under great difficulty, since, in his own words, 'the plague came into my own family and, in truth, into most of the houses where I had to do'.[18] Williamson must have felt that the time to act had come. On 16 October 1665 L'Estrange received a letter from Oxford, signed by Lord Arlington but no doubt drafted by his under-secretary, suggesting that it might be a good thing for all concerned, L'Estrange included, if he were now to give up writing his news-books. He would, of course, be appropriately compensated:

I take the freedom to propose to you that, if you will relinquish to me your whole right in the composing and profit of the news-book, I will procure for you in recompense of it a salary from his Majesty of £100 per an. which shall be paid through my hands . . . If I tax it too low you must blame yourself for having told me several times that the duty of it is very burthensome to you and the profit inconsiderable.

Quite unprepared for this sudden blow, L'Estrange wrote in shocked surprise to Arlington next day, and again on 19 and 21 October. What must have particularly galled him was the astute estimate of £100 as the appropriate compensation for his giving up the news-books. He had, indeed, when it suited him to stress how much they cost him in time and expense, complained that the profit was inconsiderable; but now he tried to convince Arlington that the profits had remarkably increased: 'I have brought it up to above £500, and even at this instant it is worth £400, when the sale is at the worst' (i.e. owing to the Plague).

There is no record of any reply to L'Estrange's three letters, and perhaps none was sent. Faced with a serious loss of income, L'Estrange appealed directly to the King, and on the whole justice was done: it was ordered that he should receive out of the profits of the *Gazette* the £100 a year already offered him by Arlington, and a further £200 a year from the Secret Service money, together with 'extraordinary expences' for carrying on his work in the discovery of libels.[19]

Meanwhile the experienced Muddiman had been summoned to Oxford to write the projected *Gazette*; on what terms, and whether on a temporary or a permanent basis, we do not know. When the first number appeared, 'Published by Authority', it was, for English readers, a complete innovation, replacing the traditional format of the news-book with a half sheet in folio: a two-page newspaper, set for the first time in double columns, and costing 1*d*. For the rest of the seventeenth century this was to be the normal format for an English newspaper. The word itself took some time to become established. In the 1680s a newspaper was commonly referred to as an 'intelligence'; and even allowing for the conservatism of official English, it is surprising to find a royal proclamation prohibiting in May 1680 the printing and publishing of all unlicensed 'News-Books and Pamphlets of News whatsoever'.[20]

So long as it remained *The Oxford Gazette*, the new government paper was printed by Leonard Lichfield, the printer to the University, and published on Mondays and Thursdays, but a London edition was also printed by Thomas Newcombe. With the return of the King to Hampton Court at the end of January 1666, it became, on 5 February, *The London Gazette*; but, after one more number, Muddiman, whose relations with Williamson had reached breaking point, was replaced by a new editor, Charles Perrot.[21] If Williamson had planned to get rid of L'Estrange so that he could himself obtain a monopoly of the printed news he was to be disappointed. In the order he had made when compensating L'Estrange for the loss of his news-books, the King had provided that they should be 'taken into the offices of the

Secretaries of State', and there were two Secretaries. Worse still, Muddiman now transferred himself to the office of the other secretary, Sir William Morice, and in June 1666 began to publish 'with authority' *The Current Intelligence*, which was in the same format as the *Gazette* and at once became a serious rival to it. The last recorded issue is No. 24 for 23 August 1666, but it may have survived for a week longer. What almost certainly brought it to an end was the Great Fire of London, which broke out on 2 September and burnt for several days, destroying almost everything in its path, including every printing house in the City. The *London Gazette* lost one issue, but reappeared on Monday 10 September with a full account of the catastrophe, printed by Newcombe on a press he had set up in the open air. Muddiman's *Current Intelligence* was not revived: either his printer, John Macock, was less enterprising than Newcombe, or he found it impossible to lay his hands on a printing press, or, as has been suggested, he had come to terms with Williamson.[22]

From now on, for almost thirteen years, the *Gazette* was to remain the sole English newspaper. Concentrating as it did on foreign news, it had little or no popular appeal. Even its foreign news was often scanty, but it was reliable; and when foreign wars made the normal trade routes dangerous to English shipping, the latest news from abroad could be of vital importance to the London merchant. As a modern historian of the *Gazette* has observed, 'It might not say all; but what was said could be taken as correct.'[23] So far as home news was concerned, it was never the policy of the *Gazette* to 'say all', but to say only what the government was prepared to make known. Under the Stuarts, it has been suggested, news was a branch of the royal prerogative.

In 1679, however, the situation suddenly changed, owing to the unexpected lapse of the Licensing Act. The Act of 1662 had been for two years, but it had been regularly renewed, and was due again for renewal in June 1679. In the excitement following upon the Popish Plot in the winter of 1678–9, the King was at loggerheads with the House of Commons, and parliament was dissolved on 24 January 1679. The new parliament, which met in March, proved to be even more recalcitrant. A bill to exclude the King's Catholic brother James from the succession was introduced on 15 May; but Charles stopped its further progress by proroguing parliament to 14 August, and then, before that date was reached, dissolving it. The new parliament, the fourth of his reign, was summoned to meet in October 1679, but was immediately prorogued, and did not commence its first session till October 1680. The Commons at once made up for lost time by rushing through a new Exclusion Bill, but after a tense debate it was defeated in the House of Lords. The Commons continuing to debate ways and means of securing a Protestant succession, the King dissolved Parliament on 18 January 1681. His fifth and last parliament, summoned to meet at Oxford in March 1681, lasted only a week. It was during those years of bitter contention that the nation divided into the two political parties soon to be known as Whigs and Tories. In such a period of almost continual crisis it is not surprising that the renewal of the Licensing Act should have been laid aside for more pressing business; but in any case the King's ministers could have had no confidence that they would succeed in getting the Act renewed by a hostile House of Commons.

At all events, it was not long before the lapse of the Act of 1662 resulted in the appearance of a number of unlicensed newspapers, published, like the official *Gazette*, twice a week. The first to appear, on 7 July 1679, was *The Domestick Intelligence; Or, News both from City and Country*, printed and published by Benjamin Harris. Harris, who now or later had the assistance of Nathaniel Crouch* in writing his paper, was an ardent Protestant Dissenter, and his anti-Catholic and pro-Whig bias soon became blindingly obvious, although each issue carried the reassuring words, 'Published to prevent false reports'. As the title indicated, the emphasis fell on home news. This was not merely because the *Domestick Intelligence* was a popular paper, addressed to readers who would not normally take much interest in what was going on in distant countries: the turn of events in 1678–9 was such that what was happening at home made any other sort of news seem to most Englishmen irrelevant. From Harris they got, whether it was true or false, what they would never have learnt from the *London Gazette*. The *Domestick Intelligence* set the pattern for other popular papers that followed between 1679 and 1682; and although most of them printed some news from abroad, it was perhaps as often as not to fill up a gap in the day's paper rather than to meet any demand from their readers.

Almost at once Harris had competitors, and he was soon to receive an unpleasant shock. On 26 August, when he published No. 15 of his *Domestick Intelligence*, another *Domestick Intelligence* appeared on the streets, apparently identical with his own, except that this one was 'Printed for N.T.'. The man who had played this successful trick on Harris was Nathaniel Thompson, known in the trade as 'Popish Nat', although he himself claimed that he was upholding the Church of England against fanatical sectarians, in other words against men like

---

* For Crouch, see p. 209.

Harris. On 2 September (No. 17) Harris warned the public about the impostor:

There [has] stoln into the World a Nameless Pamphlet, under the Title of the Domestic Intelligence, Upon Tuesday, August 26 last past, said to be No. 16 [i.e. 15], and impudently and falsly referring the People to his last of Elections of Parliament men, though this were the first he ever published. . . .

Harris went on to say that it was supposed to be the work of 'a base and scandalous Person, who has been Tenant to most of the Prisons in and about London, for his great service and diligence in Printing and promoting Popish Books and Catechisms', and that there was 'no Real Domestick Intelligence but what is Printed by Benjamin Harris, who was the first Contriver and Promoter thereof'.

Thompson was more than equal to this challenge. On 5 September (*his* No. 18) he gave his own impudent version of what had happened:

There hath lately dropt into the World an Abortive Birth (some fifteen days before the Legitimate Issue) by a Factious, Infamous and Perjur'd Anti-Christian, a senseless lying Pamphlet by the name of the City and Country News. This is the first of his offspring that ever bore name, the rest being Spurious or Illegitimate (like his Natural Issue) which he either durst not own, or wou'd not bring to the Font to receive the marks of Christianity no more than himself. This Pamphlet-Napper and Press-Pyrat hath cruised abroad since he put up for himself; to make a prize of other mens Copies, to stuff his own Cargo with ill gotten profit, making his business Cheating and Usurpation to Defraud all men; and by Factious Libells to sow Sedition amongst the people . . . Now I leave your selves and all Honest men to be judges whether of the two be the best Intelligence; he having not only stolen from all other Intelligences, but likewise from mine to make up his Senseless Scrowl . . .

Thompson had now had his joke at Harris's expense, and if he had been no more than a practical joker the jest would have ended there. On the contrary, he continued, with the help of Benjamin Claypoole,* to publish his interloping paper regularly till 14 May 1680, changing the title with No. 19 to *The True Protestant Intelligence*, and coming out on the same days as Harris, Tuesday and Friday. Harris, who changed his title on 16 January 1680 to *The Protestant (Domestick) Intelligence*, managed to steer clear of serious trouble until he published an anti-Catholic pamphlet, *An Appeal from the Country to the City*, attacking the Duke of York and advocating the claims of the King's illegitimate son, the Protestant Duke of Monmouth, to the throne. On 5 February 1680 Harris was sentenced to a year's imprisonment, to stand in the

---

* For Claypoole, see pp. 161, 208.

pillory and to pay a fine of £500.* His newspaper, written by Nathaniel Crouch, continued to appear up to 16 April. On 23 April, someone (probably Crouch) began to publish, without any authority from Harris, *The True Protestant (Domestick) Intelligence*, and carried it on until 14 May. Harris, writing from King's Bench Prison on 27 April, was forced to put an advertisement in another newspaper, stating that 'for several weighty reasons' he had given up his *Domestick Intelligence* and had no connection with this one.[24]

It was not long before other enterprising printers and booksellers took advantage of the political crisis to publish their own unlicensed newspapers. Most of these were short-lived; but among those that survived for over a month were Robert Hartford's *Mercurius Anglicus* (10 November 1679 – 15 May 1680), John Smith's *Currant Intelligence* (14 February – 4 May 1680), and *Mercurius Civicus* (22 March – 6 May 1680). All three were less crudely political than the papers of Harris and Thompson, and were addressed to more educated readers. But by the middle of May every paper that had survived till then was suppressed.

Since the House of Commons was unlikely to agree to renewing the Licensing Act, the King had looked for some other way to meet the growing threat to his authority of the unlicensed newspapers. He had therefore consulted the judges to find if his sovereign power extended over the publication of news, and on 5 May 1680 the judges unanimously declared that 'His Majesty may by law prohibit the printing and publishing of all News-Books and Pamphlets of News whatsoever, not licensed by His Majesty's Authority, as manifestly tending to the breach of the Peace, and disturbance of the Kingdom'.[25] Having been told by his judges what he had hoped, and indeed expected, to hear, the King issued a proclamation on 17 May, stating how important it was that the minds of his subjects should not be 'disturbed or amused by Lyes or vain Reports, which are many times raised on purpose to scandalise the Government or for other indirect ends', and how 'of late many Evil-disposed Persons have made it a common practice to print and publish pamphlets of news without licence or authority, and therein have vended to His Majesty's people all the idle and malicious reports that they could collect or invent, contrary to Law, the continuance whereof would in a short time endanger the Peace of the Kingdom'. His Majesty therefore thought fit 'strictly to prohibit and forbid all persons whatsoever to print or publish any news-books or

---

* For Harris's temporary escape from prison in December 1680, see pp. 191–2.

pamphlets of news not licensed by His Majesty's authority'. Anyone contravening this order would be proceeded against with the utmost severity of the law.[26]

It must not be supposed that this was an idle threat. All who were concerned in writing, printing or publishing news in the reign of Charles II were well aware what they could expect if the law was invoked against them. During the next three years many of them were to suffer fines and imprisonment, and in exceptional cases the pillory. Looking back at those chronic law-breakers over a gap of three hundred years, we may make the mistake of giving them more credit than they deserve, but if their motives were sometimes mercenary, we may still admire their indomitable persistence, and their willingness to take the consequences.

For the present, however, the royal proclamation of 17 May 1680 had the effect the King desired. A whole summer and autumn went by without a single newspaper appearing on the streets or in the coffee-houses, always excepting the *London Gazette*. But a change was on the way. On 22 December someone ventured to bring out the first number of *The English Gazette*, which ran twice a week until 12 January 1681. On 28 December Langley Curtiss started another new twice-weekly paper, *The True Protestant Mercury*, and this was to prove one of the most outspoken of the Whig newspapers. On the same day Benjamin Harris, temporarily freed from prison, re-started his *Protestant (Domestick) Intelligence*, and carried it on until 15 April 1681. Those two anti-Court newspapers were joined by a third on 1 February 1681, when Francis Smith began to publish his *Smith's Protestant Intelligence*, which was brought to a sudden end on 14 April by his arrest and imprisonment.

The King's proclamation of 17 May 1680 had clearly become a dead letter with those intrepid journalists. What had happened to make them so willing to take chances? The answer must lie in the changed political situation since the end of October 1680. Charles II's fourth parliament which came into session on 21 October 1680 was so over-whelmingly Whig in composition that it almost disturbed the constitutional balance between King, Lords and Commons. This may be seen not only in the determined way in which it set about securing the Pro-testant succession, but in some of its minor acts and decisions. When, on 30 October, the House of Commons decided to reverse its standing practice and to have its votes and transactions printed daily, the printer they chose to reward with the contract was Francis Smith, a man whom the average Tory regarded as a fountain of sedition. For another of its

16

Protestant friends, Benjamin Harris, the House twice petitioned the King unsuccessfully for a remission of his fine of £500, and finally had him released by sending a secret order to the Marshal of the King's Bench Prison. In such circumstances men like Harris and Smith might be excused for believing that the real power in the nation lay with the House of Commons. And if they were none the less indicted for some offence, there was a good chance that a Whig jury would get them off.[27]

In this gradual revival of the unlicensed newspapers Nathaniel Thompson had been uncharacteristically cautious. He petitioned the King on 23 February 1681 for a licence to publish a weekly newspaper 'not meddling with affairs of State', and claimed that in his previous 'intelligence', which he had discontinued in obedience to the King's proclamation, he had exposed the notorious falsehoods published by disaffected persons in their intelligences and news-books, but although the same persons were now at work again inflaming the people with their false news, he had refrained from resuming his own paper without the royal permission.[28] This attempt of Thompson's to obtain some sort of official status for his paper appears to have met with no response; but on 9 March he revived it with a new title, *The Loyal Protestant and True Domestick Intelligence*, and carried it on, in endless conflict with the Whig papers, until 20 March 1683. Like all the other papers, it came out twice a week, until, on 3 November 1681, Thompson broke new ground by changing to three times a week. In this he had no immediate imitators. On 27 April 1681 there appeared another *True Protestant Mercury*, which became, after four numbers, *The Impartial Protestant Mercury*, and so continued to 30 May 1682.

John Smith now revived his *Currant Intelligence* (30 April – 24 December 1682), and T. Benskin's *Domestick Intelligence* ('impartially related') ran from 13 May 1681 until 16 November 1682. Among the shorter-lived papers starting up in 1682 were Thomas Vile's *London Mercury*, *The Loyal Impartial Mercury* of E. Brooks, *The Loyal London Mercury: Or, The Moderate Intelligencer*, and *The Loyal London Mercury; Or, The Currant Intelligence*. The word 'Protestant' in some of those titles was the sign of a Whig newspaper advertising to its readers that it was against a Catholic succession to the throne. The author of the Tory *Heraclitus Ridens* (8 February 1681) had some facetious remarks on the value of the word for the Whig newswriters: 'Oh it makes 'em sell: I heard a fellow cry Protestant Pears, and another, Hot Protestant Pudding, hot, hot . . .'. It is significant that the Tory Thompson, perhaps because he thought it essential for his circulation, used the word in the title of his new paper, *The Loyal Protestant*. The word

'Loyal' in a title would normally indicate that a newspaper supported the government; but with some papers it might be used as an insurance against possible trouble. Similarly, 'Impartial' was a propitiatory word, intended to suggest the absence of all biased political comment.

To the wholesale flouting of the royal declaration of 17 May 1680, the King and his ministers had no immediate solution. So divided was the nation from 1679 to 1681 that any new attempt to muzzle the press would almost certainly have met with increased resistance. Instead of provoking further confrontation the King now decided to play a waiting game, and he played it with skill and with an unexpected firmness. At some point (the evidence points to early in 1681) the government adopted a new procedure in dealing with the unlicensed newspapers: what suppression could not do might be achieved by humour, banter and ridicule. If we are to believe Roger North, the first suggestion for this sensible course of action came from his brother Francis, at that time Lord Chief Justice of the Common Pleas, who argued that much the best way to deal with seditious publications was 'to set up counter writers, that, as every libel came out, should take it to task, and answer it'. In that way 'all the diurnal lies of the town' would be dealt with quickly, whereas severe punishments inflicted on the printers and hawkers of libels 'would make them but the more inquired after'. His advice was taken, North continues,

and some clever writers were employed, such as were called The Observator and Heraclitus, for a constancy, and others, with them, occasionally; and then they soon wrote the libellers out of the pit, and during that king's life the trade of libels, which before had been in great request, fell to nothing.[29]

Heraclitus Ridens; *Or, a Discourse between Jest and Earnest, where many a True Word is spoken in opposition to all Libellers against the Government* first appeared on 1 February 1681, and continued once a week to 22 August 1682. Its aim, as stated in No. 1, was 'to prevent Mistakes and False News, and to give you a true Information of the state of things, and advance your understandings above the common rate of Coffee-House Statesmen who think themselves wiser than the Privy Council, or the Sages of the Law'. As the title implies, this was a dialogue paper, written in colloquial English, but addressed to readers of some politeness who could appreciate a witty turn of phrase.[30] It was joined on 13 April 1681 by L'Estrange's *The Observator in Question and Answer*, which ran into the reign of James II, ending on 9 March 1687. This racy dialogue paper had a more downright approach than *Heraclitus Ridens*. With its earthy humour, its idiomatic turns of phrase, and its loud appeal to common sense, it was the favourite (perhaps the only) reading to the country squire. So long as the government had L'Estrange it had the best propagandist of the day.

The turning-point for the Whigs came with the short-lived Oxford parliament, when the King transformed what had looked perilously like defeat into victory. On 8 April 1681, eleven days after he had dissolved parliament, he issued *His Majesties Declaration to all His Loving Subjects, Touching the Causes & Reasons that Moved Him to Dissolve the Two Last Parliaments*. This well-timed justification of the King's actions was so ably and reasonably written that one is tempted to see in it the hand of the Marquis of Halifax, the statesman who had persuaded the Lords to throw out the Exclusion Bill in November 1680. Ordered to be read from all the pulpits in England, it obtained the widest possible publicity, and, as events were soon to show, had a marked effect on public opinion.

The King's counter-attack continued with the arrest of Shaftesbury on 2 July 1681 on a charge of treason, and he was sent to the Tower, to answer in due course the bill of indictment. The Whigs were confident, however, that the two Whig sheriffs, whose business it was to empanel the jury, would pick men who could be relied upon not to be browbeaten. On 24 November, when Shaftesbury appeared to answer the indictment, a jury of determined Whigs brought in a verdict of *ignoramus*, and on 1 February 1682 the charges against him were dropped. The King, however, bided his time. If he was ever to feel secure, the City had to be won over and the Whig sheriffs replaced by Tories. In the summer of 1682, by dint of leaning on a weak Lord Mayor, and in the end by a certain show of force, two Tory sheriffs were at last sworn in to office. Among the sufferers from this political reverse in the City were the newswriters. Since the King was now resolved to rule without a parliament, there could be no question of a new licensing act, but from now on control over the press was steadily tightened. In the autumn of 1682 those unlicensed newspapers that still remained were gradually, and at last abruptly suppressed.

What had happened is made clear by a statement in the last number (23 October) of *The Moderate Intelligencer*. This paper had failed to appear on the previous Thursday, and the author now explained why. He had been visited by a messenger of the press and a beadle of the Stationers Company, who told him the press had become so provocative with its scandalous reflections that the government intended 'within a few weeks to suppress all manner of printed news-books'. That this was to be a clean sweep was made clear by the further statement that 'neither side shall have cause to think they have had hard measure in being supprest, because all shall fare alike'. Among the last to give up was the *True Protestant Mercury* of Langley Curtiss, on 25 October. Thomas Benskin carried on his *Domestick Intelligence* and Nathaniel Thompson his *Loyal Protestant* to 16 November, when both papers ceased to appear. In taking leave of his readers Thompson made a virtue of necessity: he had consistently attacked 'those Plagues and Pests of the Nation, the Phanaticks', who had done their best 'to bring into contempt with the Vulgar His most Sacred Majesty . . . and the most Pure and Innocent Religion on the Earth (I mean the ONLY TRUE Protestant Religion now by Law Established)'. He had therefore thought it was his duty to go on publishing his *Loyal Protestant*.

But being now informed that Authority is displeased therewith, I am very willing to desist writing any more, in regard it would be most inexcusable for Me, who have ever writ in defence of *Them* and their *Authority*, now to continue in disobedience to their Just Commands.

The messengers to the press had obviously done their work well. But Thompson was irrepressible. He may have thought the prohibition of 'Authority' could not possibly apply to such a loyal supporter of the government as he was. On 20 February 1683 he started publishing his paper again, but it finally stopped, without any explanation, on 20 March. The unlicensed newspapers had finally been suppressed.

The *Observator* continued to appear with official approval. *Heraclitus Ridens*, however, had already come to an end on 22 August 1682. In his final issue the author explained why he had decided to lay down his paper. He 'did at first take up this way of Scribling purely out of a Sense of Duty and Loyalty, at a time when both were shock'd and well-nigh over-turn'd by the Outrage and Intemperance of a restless and daring Faction'; but now their cause was 'so batter'd, its Friends and Assertors so feeble and out of heart, and their Plots and Carryings-on so manifestly laid open and exploded' that there was nothing left for him to answer.

What this remarkable outburst of newspapers between 1679 and 1682 had demonstrated beyond all possible doubt was the popular demand for more news, a demand that was scarcely met at all by the official *Gazette*. The policy of the King and his ministers had always been to release as little political news as possible, since the more the people learnt what was going on in the seats of power and privilege, the more likely they were to become opinionative, to judge for themselves, to grumble and find fault, and to set themselves up as equal with their superiors. The King had always believed, in the words of one of his favourite divines, that 'the great business of Government is to procure Obedience, and keep off Disobedience'[31]. But for some time now the unlicensed newspapers had been leaking political information to the people, or, worse still, spreading tendentious rumours; and until he could persuade one of his parliaments to renew the Licensing Act there was little he could do about it. In any case the House of Commons had started to nullify his policy of secrecy by releasing the very sort of information he had always tried to withhold from his subjects: in October 1680 and in March 1681, they voted to have their proceedings published daily. On the first of those occasions his Secretary of State, Sir Leoline Jenkins, had argued in the House against this dangerous procedure on the grounds that it was 'a sort of appeal to the people'; only to be answered by Sir Francis Winnington, 'I think it not natural, nor rational, that the people, who sent us hither, should not be informed of our actions.'[32] There was nothing the King could do about this, except to rule without a parliament, and this he had finally decided to do.

In those circumstances it may seem strange that the idea never occurred to the King and his ministers to publish a genuine newspaper, not to take the place of the *Gazette*, but to supplement it. Such a paper could have included the sort of popular non-political news that most of his subjects would have welcomed – murders, highway robberies, fires, storms and other natural disasters; and such political information as it printed could have been presented as the government wished it to appear, but in such a way as to give an impression of impartiality. This would surely have been better than leaving the ill-informed and blundering Nat Thompson to be a self-appointed spokesman for the government. It is true that *Heraclitus Ridens* and the *Observator* were effective enough in answering the Whig opposition, but they were not, except incidentally, newspapers. Although the King was not averse to using what Roger North called 'the employed writers', their business was to controvert, ridicule, and expose the false statements of Whig journalists, not to provide news of public affairs, which could only lead to people meddling in matters that were none of their business. The King had shown great patience – more, he must often have thought, than befitted a king – in containing over several years the steady pressure of Shaftesbury and his Whig faction; but their limiting notion of what a king should be was never his. He had always had a longing to reign as an absolute monarch without having to go cap in hand to his parliaments for money, and without being challenged by defiant statesmen out of office; and now in the last years of his life, with the aid of secret subsidies from Louis XIV, he came very near to realising his dream.

With the accession of James II the Licensing Act was renewed on 2 July 1685 for a further seven years. The new King was no more in love with democracy than his brother. Yet in the end he seems to have realised the value of having a genuine government newspaper, for on 21 February 1688 there appeared the first number of a weekly paper, *Publick Occurrences Truely Stated*, published 'With Allowance',[33] and written by two once notorious anti-Catholics who had now turned their coats, Henry Care and Elkanah Settle. Its semi-official standing may reflect, in a time of increasing difficulty, a need felt by the King and his ministers for a more favourable interpretation of current events than it was fitting for the official *Gazette* to give. Care died on 8 August, but not before it had fallen to him to report the trial of the Seven Bishops, which he played down as much as possible. Settle then carried on alone, but the paper came to an end on 2 October. On 1 October the *Gazette* published a royal proclamation that 'a great and sudden Invasion from Holland' was being planned, and it may well have been considered that in this time of crisis it was no longer safe to allow any but official news to be published. In his final issue Settle was able to report that the Dutch fleet had been badly battered in a violent storm.

When the Dutch fleet set sail for England on 19 October, it encountered another storm, and was beaten back to Holland to re-fit. In England, the *Gazette* carried, on 22 October, a second royal proclamation announcing the great preparations being made 'to Invade and Conquer this our Kingdom', and ordering all horses, oxen and cattle 'which may be fit for Burthen or Draught . . . to be driven and removed by the space of at least twenty Miles from the place where the Enemy shall Attempt to Land'. This was followed one week later by 'A Proclamation to Restrain the Spreading of FALSE NEWS', by writing, printing or other publication.

On 1 November the Dutch fleet set out again, this time with a favourable wind, and sailed down the Channel without encountering the English Navy. On 5 November William of Orange reached Tor Bay, and went ashore unopposed at Brixham. The *Gazette* could not afford to suppress all news of the invasion, and indeed carried a short report of the landing in its issue of 8 November. But for the next month the information released by the *Gazette* was so meagre and so uncertain that only those with access to a news-letter could have any clear idea of what was happening. As the King's authority gradually weakened, and as more and more of his subjects went over to the Prince of Orange, the longing for news increased, and at the same time the danger of being prosecuted for publishing an unauthorised newspaper diminished. On 11 December John Wallis, a London printer, brought out the first number of *The Universal Intelligence*, which was followed one day later by *The London Courant* and *The English Currant*, and on 15 December by *The London Mercury: Or, Moderate Intelligencer*. None of those four papers (all dealing mainly with home news, and appearing twice a week) was licensed.

How great was the thirst for news may be seen from the rather grandiose preamble to the first number of the *London Courant*:

It having been observed, that the greater the itch of curiosity after News hath been here of late, the less has the humour been gratified. Insomuch, that a modest enquiry where his Majesty, or his Royal Highness the Prince of Orange was, or what they were doing, could scarce be resolved, till the news had been exported and imported in a Foreign News-Letter. And further, the Inquisitive after truth having been so baulk't with Sham-accounts of things and characters of Persons, that the Chapter was just the reverse of the Contents, and the Book the Contradictory of the Title; what more acceptable service could be done than to rescue Truth, the Daughter to Time, from the Pretensions of Supposition and Fiction?

The author promised 'with the integrity of an unbyass'd Historian to do Justice to all parties, in representing things as they shall really happen', but he was obviously anti-Catholic and pro-Protestant from the start. At all events, he managed to give his readers a day-by-day account of what was going on: the flight of the Queen with the infant Prince of Wales, the attempted escape of the King, the capture of Lord Chancellor Jeffreys at Wapping, the burning of 'Popish chapels', the arrest of L'Estrange, and of course the steady progress of the Prince of Orange.

But this free-for-all was not to last for long. With the arrival of the Dutch prince in London on 18 December, law and order were quickly restored. On 10 January 1689 the *Gazette* published a proclamation about 'divers False, Scandalous and Seditious Books, Papers of News, and Pamphlets, daily Printed and Dispersed, containing idle and mistaken Relations of what passes', and stating that orders had been given to search all printing houses and 'to apprehend all such Authors, Printers, Booksellers, Hawkers and others, as shall be found to Print, Sell, or Disperse the same', and to have them before the nearest Justice of the Peace, to be proceeded against according to law. This put an immediate stop to the four unlicensed newspapers already mentioned. A fifth, *The Orange Gazette*, which had been appearing since 31 December, stopped with the others, but must have succeeded in obtaining at least semi-official recognition, for it reappeared after a few days' delay on 17 January, carrying the words 'With Allowance'. After a longer stoppage the *London Mercury* resumed on 6 February with similar permission. A new paper, *The London Intelligence*, had carried the words 'With Allowance' since it first appeared on 15 January. The publisher of *The Universal Intelligence* may have decided to take a chance, for his paper reappeared on 13 February without such protection as the words 'With Allowance' afforded, but it survived for only one more issue.

Who 'allowed' the other three newspapers to be published, and whether the authorisation came in each case from the same or a different source, it would be hard to determine. In the uncertain and transitional weeks between the flight of James II in December and the acceptance of the crown by William and Mary on 13 February, verbal permission may have been sought and obtained from some nobleman or statesman who appeared to have the authority to grant it. In any case such permission was soon to lose what validity it ever had. On 21 February the *Gazette* reprinted the proclamation of 10 January, and in all probability the messengers of the press had been on their rounds again before that; for after 18 February three of the four surviving newspapers ceased to appear. For some unexplained reason *The Orange Gazette* held out for almost three weeks more, but on 9 March it too came to an end.

In the reign of William and Mary the Licensing Act remained for some years in force. It was due for renewal in 1693, and although there was now a growing feeling that the Act had outlived any usefulness it ever had, it was extended for a further two years. Only a few weeks before, the muddle-headed Tory Edward Bohun had been duped into licensing a pamphlet called *King William and Queen Mary Conquerors*, the very title of which, in Macaulay's words, had 'set all London aflame', and had resulted in Bohun being removed from the office of licenser and the pamphlet being 'burned in Palace Yard by the common hangman'.[34] In spite of this flagrant exposure of its working, and the opposition of such an influential peer as Lord Halifax, public opinion was not yet ready for the Act's demise. When, however, it came up again for routine consideration in 1695, the House of Commons voted against a renewal.

A conference with the House of Lords now followed, in which the reasons for allowing the Act to lapse were put by Edward Clarke, member of parliament for Taunton and a friend of John Locke, who was largely responsible for drafting them. No resounding claims were made for the liberty of the subject, for such an approach might only have alarmed the more conservative legislators. Instead, attention was drawn in a reasonable way to the objectionable consequences and practical defects of the Act, such as the power to issue a general warrant to search houses 'and to seize upon all books which they shall but think fit to suspect', and the delays and frustration caused to printers and booksellers. Above all, the Act had 'in no wise answered the end for which it was made', which was to prevent the publication of seditious and heretical writings, and was in any case unnecessary, since 'every one being answerable for books he publishes, prints, or sells, containing anything seditious or against law, makes this or any other Act for the restraint of printing very needless'. To those arguments the Lords listened, and common sense prevailed. The Licensing Act was not renewed.[35]

In practical terms, however, the change brought about by the lapse of the Act was far from spectacular, and Macaulay's assertion that 'English literature was emancipated, and emancipated for ever, from the control of the government'[36] would have raised a hollow laugh among those journalists and publishers who continued to be arrested, tried, convicted and sentenced to fines, imprisonment or the pillory for writing what offended the government of the day. What had happened was that after 1695 everyone was free to publish what he pleased – and to take the consequences. In practice the freedom conferred by the lapse of the Licensing Act was conditional on not publishing anything that was held to be 'improper, mischievous or illegal', and that in turn meant anything that might be considered dangerous to 'the preservation of peace and good order, of government and religion'. But ministries come and go, and sentiments that were regarded as seditious under one government might be looked upon as harmless or even laudable under its successor. Some satirical verses written in 1732 put the situation fairly enough:

> In good Queen Anna's days, when Tories reign'd
> And the just liberty of press restrain'd,
> Sad Whigs complain'd in doleful notes and sundry,
> O liberty, O virtue, O my country!
> But when themselves had reach'd the day of grace,
> They chang'd their principles, as well as place.
> From messengers secure no printer lies,

They take compositors, press-men, devils, flies.
What means this change? The sum of all the story's,
Tories deprest are Whigs, and Whigs in pow'r are Tories.[37]

But if newspaper publishing was still a dangerous business, there were those ready to take the risk. Some of the men of 1679–82 were still on hand in 1695. Thompson had died in 1687, but Harris had recently returned from New England, where in 1690 he had published the first American newspaper, *Publick Occurrences, Both Foreign and Domestick*, which was promptly suppressed. Back in London, he brought out on 14 May 1695 *Intelligence Domestick and Foreign*, which, after several changes of title in less than two months (a sure sign that it was not prospering) came to an end.

Three other papers that appeared in 1695 and came out three times a week were to survive into the reign of George II: *The Post-Boy, The Flying Post*, and *The Post Man*. The first of these, which was to become increasingly Tory, was written by Abel Roper, and the second, which was to grow increasingly Whig, by George Ridpath. (By a strange coincidence these two political opponents were to die within one day of each other, Ridpath on 5 February 1726, and Roper the following day.) The *Post Man*, a venture of Richard Baldwin's, which began in 1694 as *An Account of the Publick Transactions in Christendom*, was incorporated with the *Post-Boy* for about six months in 1695, and finally appeared as the *Post Man* on 24 October 1695.[38] It was written by the French Huguenot John de Fonvive, and was for a long time held to be the most reliable, if not the most exciting, of the three papers, concentrating mainly on foreign news.

Those three papers established a pattern for the London newspaper that was to last for over a quarter of a century. They were published on Tuesday, Thursday and Saturday, the three days on which the mails left London in the late evening for all parts of the country. The word 'Post' in their titles now supplanted the older 'Intelligence'. In 1699 there appeared *The London Post* (a new venture of Benjamin Harris, in which Defoe later played some part), and in 1700 *The English Post*, written by Nathaniel Crouch; the first was to last for six years and the second for over nine. Since those two papers came out on Monday, Wednesday and Friday, their news would be two days old before they could be posted to the country by the night mail, and one must assume that they circulated mainly among London readers. On the other hand, by publishing between the post days they might sometimes be first with the news. When, in 1715, Robert Mawson decided to publish a *Supplement* to his Saturday *Weekly Journal* he explained that he had chosen Wednesday because

Tuesday was 'the likelyest Day for the Arrival of the French and Dutch Mails, on which they are due'. In 1722 another journalist gave a fuller picture of the days on which foreign mails could be expected:

The Foreign Mails are due at London every Tuesday and Friday from Holland and France. Every Monday and Thursday from Flanders. Every Monday, Wednesday and Friday from Ireland. And once a Week from Portugal and Spain.[39]

In the days of sail, when the packet boats were at the mercy of contrary winds, he was a rash man who would state with any confidence the days on which the foreign mails would reach London; but if they arrived on the days they were due, the Monday-Wednesday-Friday newspapers might expect to have fresh news from Holland and France in their Wednesday issue and fresh news from Flanders in their Friday issue, which newspapers coming out on Tuesday and Saturday could not publish until a day later. The country reader, of course, would reap no benefit, since (with the exception of a daily delivery to Kent and Colchester) there was no country post leaving London on Wednesdays and Fridays.

The change from publication twice a week in the years 1679–82 to three times a week in 1695 marked a genuine advance. But there are signs that it was not accomplished without difficulty. In format the new papers had not changed: a single half sheet, printed on both sides in double columns. But when the *Post-Boy* first appeared on 14 May 1695 the news was confined to the front page, and the verso was blank. No. 2 has one short advertisement (for a book) after the news, and again the verso is blank. With No. 6 the news at last spills over to page 2; but Nos. 7 and 8 are again one-page issues. No. 9 manages to fill half the second page with more home news than usual; No. 10 just reaches page 2, again by increasing home news; No. 11, with no foreign news at all, but with three advertisements, is back to a single page. The reason for the concentration on home news in the last three of those issues becomes clear with the publication of No. 12 (11 June). This begins: 'Wee have received 12 Flanders Mails, in which upon Perusal I find these Occurrences. . . .'; and the writer then proceeds to a brief summary in 27 lines of the long-delayed news that has just come in. That there had been no time to deal fully with this sudden glut of foreign news becomes clear from the fact that later on that same day *A Postscript to the Post-Boy* was published, giving news that the Duke of Wurtemberg had besieged 'the Fort called Knock, near Furnes, with fourteen Thousand Men on Friday last', and that King William was 'now encamped at Beclaer'. As the weeks passed the *Post-Boy* continued to give its readers short measure. We should perhaps allow something for Abel Roper's inexperience in those early days; yet twenty years later it is not uncommon to find the news in the *Post-Boy* or the *Post Man* covering less than the whole of the first page. The only difference is that by that time the rest of the paper was taken up by advertisements, which not only helped to conceal a dearth of news, but brought the proprietor a considerable revenue.

The *Flying Post* succeeded in filling its two pages from the start. But Ridpath (a Scot) had begun more cautiously with twice-weekly publication, which put him under less pressure for news, and only later (with No. 12) went over to three days a week. From the start, too, he had set out not only to publish the latest news, but to give his readers some editorial comment. His policy was outlined in the first number:

It is thought that it may be a good Service to the Nation, to give a true Account of things as related in France and the Confederate Countries, and also a faithful Account of the most observable Domestick Occurrences with some Remarks tending to discover the Probability or Improbability of the things related, and which way the ballance of publick Affairs in Europe seems to encline, and a short Description of all places of Sieges, Battels, Encampments, &c as far as is needful.

The news in No. 1 begins with 'The Present State of Publick Affairs abroad, as Related in the Confederate Countries', and contains reports dated from Adrianople, Venice, Vienna, Rome, Turin, Brussels and the Hague. The rest of the paper deals with 'The Present State of Affairs as related in France', followed by some 30 lines of 'Remarks'. In No. 3, 'according to our Promise to give a Geographical Description of any Place Besieged', there are accounts of Ceuta (20 lines) and Mellila (8 lines), two towns being blockaded by the Moors. In No. 7 a fairly long abstract from the Paris *Gazette* is followed by an exposure of 'that lying Gazette' by means of reports from Allied sources. Ridpath's editorial remarks were so patently patriotic that they were unlikely to get him into trouble; but comment of any kind in a seventeenth-century newspaper was always open to government rebuke. In the next century it was often their predilection for making remarks that brought the weekly journals of Robert Mawson, Nathaniel Mist and others into conflict with the law.

A word must be said about the 'Postscript' to the *Post-Boy* mentioned above. Sometimes important war news would reach a paper when the sheets had already been run off; and since this news would be stale by the time the next issue appeared two days later, it became a common practice to publish it in a Postscript, a half sheet in folio, set in a larger type and to the full measure (i.e. not in double columns). We know that when Abel Boyer was in charge of the *Post-Boy* he was paid extra for writing postscripts,[40] but this may not have been the general practice. The 'author' of a newspaper, who would probably be on hand until the paper was printed, might have been difficult to contact later in the day. In such circumstances, as Stanley Morison suggested, the person responsible for writing a postscript may have been the printer.[41] On 1 January 1704, De Fonvive, the author of the *Post Man*, announced that he was not responsible for 'any other News but what is printed in the *Post Man*'. At the same time he dissociated himself from written postscripts, which had also begun to appear.

The publishing of separate printed postscripts offered a chance to the unscrupulous to bring out sham versions. On 5 May 1710 the *Post Man* stated that the publishing of counterfeit postscripts was so much in fashion that in future all its own would be printed on paper watermarked in the margin with the words 'The Post Man'. This may have had the desired effect; but in the ill-lit streets of London it would have been hard to detect the watermark when buying the postscript from a hawker. On 29 February 1712 a sham postscript to Roper's *Post-Boy*, announcing the death of Louis XIV, appeared on the streets. (He died in 1715.) Roper's regular postscripts were 'Printed for A. Roper near the Black Boy in Fleet-Street', but this sham one was 'Printed for A. Ropar at the Black Boy in Fleetstreet'; the type was different, and the two head-blocks were imitations of those used by the *Post-Boy*. The person responsible for putting out this particular postscript may have been a stockjobber hoping to promote a rise in the stocks. Detection of such men cannot have been easy, but on 13 March 1708 the *Flying Post* told its readers that the postscript published 'on Thursday last' was a sham, 'and the Author of it is taken up'. Postscripts remained a feature of the newspaper press so long as England was at war with France. When peace came, in 1713, there was no longer the same occasion for them, and in any case the news they had to offer was now being given in regular evening papers.

Until 1696 all London newspapers had come out in the morning, and it was a considerable innovation when the first evening paper appeared. Here the pioneer was Ichabod Dawks, whose *Dawks's News-Letter* was first published on 23 June. Doing nothing by halves, Dawks had a special script type cut to imitate the handwritten news-letter, and each issue began with a 'S^r', intended to copy and suggest the personal approach, and was set to the full measure. Like the news-letter again, this thrice-weekly paper was obtainable by a quarterly subscription, although, when it became better known, it was probably also available from the hawkers. This ingenious development of a poor man's news-letter might have been only a passing fad, but in fact Dawks's paper survived till 1716. It appeared between four and five o'clock in the afternoon, and plenty of space was left blank for the purchaser to add his own personal news for dispatch by the country posts. When, some months later, Edward Lloyd the coffee-man brought out his morning paper, *Lloyd's News*, he almost certainly had Dawks's style in mind, for his news also began with a 'S^r', was set to the full measure, and printed in a very handsome italic type. The only close imitator of Dawks was the short-lived *Jones's Evening News Letter* (1716), which lasted in its script type for about four weeks.

No other evening paper appeared after that of Dawks for over ten years, until an *Evening Post* came out for a brief run in 1706; but in 1709 E. Berrington started his *Evening Post*, which was to survive till 1740. Other short-lived evening papers followed, until in June 1715 there appeared *The St. James's Evening Post*, which was still running in 1757, *The Whitehall Evening-Post* (1718–39), and *The London Evening Post* (1727–1806). *The Evening Journal* (1727–8) was published daily for 62 numbers. All of those evening papers were openly parasitical, coming out on post nights and plundering their news from the morning papers, with the addition of anything important that had happened during the day. The usual time of publication was between five and six o'clock, so as to give purchasers time to write their own news on the blank provided, and their format of a half sheet folded so as to make four small pages facilitated transmission by the post. This provision of space to write personal messages was an attraction that the morning papers were normally unable to provide.

There can be little doubt that the evening papers damaged the sale of the morning ones, particularly with country readers. On 25 October 1709 the *Evening Post* issued a notice complaining about 'the common Hawkers who refuse to cry this Paper, which they say if Gentlemen encourage, will hinder them the Sale of 3 or 4 others of a Post-Night, and only this will be taken'. In an undated 'Proposal for Regulating the Newspapers' John Toland asserted that

the sale of the usual papers set up under King William of immortal memory, namely the Post-man, the Flying-post, the Post-boy, and more lately the Daily Courant, has been visibly diminish'd by these Evening Posts . . for whereas before people us'd to send all or most of the four papers aforesaid to their friends and correspondents in the country every post-night, now the sale of them is almost confin'd to this town. Nay the vent of them is much lessen'd here, many persons contenting themselves to read over the same evening posts, which they send to their friends at night; as containing the substance of all the rest, with some fresher passages, commonly made up of scandal and sedition.

Toland's remedy was to propose a new Act of Parliament, stipulating that 'all the said News-papers whatever . . . shall be publish'd in the morning at or before ten of the Clock, and not later . . . and none allow'd to come out in the afternoon, under any title or pretence whatsoever'.[42] No such action was taken by any English government, and the evening papers were left to thrive. So long as they remained free to pillage the morning papers, they had everything in their favour. In the reign of Queen Anne a newswriter could have read, digested and marked for the press all the morning papers in about an hour. The rest was up to the printer.

Although the thrice-weekly newspapers were a logical development from the thrice-weekly country posts, and in consequence held their own for many years, the first daily newspaper made its appearance on 11 March 1702. Written by Samuel Buckley, a good linguist and a fluent writer, *The Daily Courant* prospered, and was to survive for 33 years. In the preference it gave to foreign and port news, and (during its early years) in its fairly restrained political tone, it resembled the *Post Man*. Later it was to become much more a paper of Whig comment, and ended its days as a subsidised organ of the Whig government. It was to have no daily competitor until the foundation of *The Daily Post* (1719–46), and *The Daily Journal* (1721–37). When *The Post-Boy* became a daily in 1728, London had four papers appearing from Monday to Saturday. (There were to be no Sunday papers till 1780.) Two mainly advertising papers, *The Daily Advertiser* and *The London Daily Post and General Advertiser* followed in 1730 and 1734; and in 1735 the government of the day transferred its subsidised journalists to a new paper, *The Daily Gazetteer*. Those last three papers survived into the last decade of the eighteenth century.

Providing the public with a daily news service required additional capital, and there is some evidence that the dailies were financed by small joint-stock companies. Writing to Lord Godolphin in 1708 Defoe remarked that the *Daily Courant* was run by a club of 20 booksellers, 'whose aim is to gain of it'.[43] So, too, in 1719, Hugh Meere the printer testified that the author of the *Daily Post* was employed by several booksellers, and that he had heard 'some of the Play-house are concerned therein'.[44] In February 1728, when the masters of various coffee-houses objected to the *Daily Journal* raising its price, 'some of the proprietors' of that newspaper met them in the Devil Tavern and agreed to return to the price of 1½d.[45]

It would appear that by the third decade of the eighteenth century some at least of the thrice-weekly papers were finding the competition of the dailies too hard for them. On 31 January 1722 the *St. James's Post* complained that the success of the *Daily Journal* was having an adverse effect on its own circulation; and on 4 May 1728 the author of the *Post-Boy*, answering the charge that its news was not so good as it used to be, pointed out that the public were too ready to forget that some years ago the *Post-Boy* was the only paper to be at any expense to entertain them with home news, but 'since the Publication of two new Daily Papers, who daily employ men on purpose, it is impossible he should be so early in that sort of Intelligence, his Paper appearing but once in two days'. Five months later, the *Post-Boy* went over to daily publication. Of the daily papers appearing between 1702 and 1735 the one with the best news service, domestic and foreign, was undoubtedly the *Daily Journal*. Its rival, the *Daily Post*, was certainly a successful paper, but the proprietors, greedy for profit, tended to crowd out the news with advertisements, to such an extent that occasionally the news filled only the first column of the front page.

Since they had started up again in 1695, the newspapers had been able to maintain their circulation by publishing war news. Now, in 1712, the Tory government was determined to bring the war to an end, and the Whig press was making a political issue of it. Something must be done to muzzle the press, and the means now taken (though ultimately unsuccessful) was tactfully disguised as a tax to raise additional revenue. A bill had been drawn up to levy a tax on various commodities such as soap, paper, linen, silk and calico; and to those was now added a stamp duty, designed to hit the newspapers, of ½d. on every printed half sheet or less, and 1d. on every whole sheet, together with a duty of 1s. on every printed advertisement. The bill duly passed, and took effect on 1 August 1712.[46]

There were a few casualties, but the thrice-weekly papers, the *Daily Courant*, and the *Weekly Packet* (not yet three weeks old) all passed on the tax to their readers and survived. Almost at once, however, a loophole was found in the new Act that was to lead to important developments. In drafting the Act the government lawyers had taken account of the newspapers as they knew them to be, either in a whole or in a half sheet; they had not considered the possibility of a sheet and a half. But if they hadn't, others had. The first newspaper to take advantage of the strict letter of the law appears to have been the *British Mercury*, published three times a week by the Company of London Insurers. On 30 July, two days before the new duties came into force, it was a two-page half sheet, set in double columns. But on 2 August it came out in an entirely new format as a six-page paper, set in a larger type in full measure, and without the new stamp. In a long and not entirely ingenuous preamble the proprietors explained why the change had been made. The nation had been pestered with swarms of printed papers, among which the newspapers had been 'not the least criminal'. The writers, overcome with zeal for a party, were 'very often too apt to fill [their papers] with their own Notions or Reflections, rather than with real Facts, and such other Occurrences as are their proper Subject'. Nothing, therefore, 'could be more seasonable than the suppressing of so licentious a Practice'. The *British Mercury*, it would appear, was all in favour of the new duty being imposed. But not for itself, since the *Mercury* was 'only intended for and deliver'd to those Persons whose Goods or Houses are insur'd by the Sun-Fire-Office'. The Company of Insurers, however, must have realised that their claim to be publishing a private paper would not have absolved them from paying the new tax; for they went on to explain how they proposed to get round it.

One great Reason for altering its former Method is obvious, since it is notorious that the Charge of an Half-penny on every half Sheet would have lain too heavy upon the Undertakers, or have oblig'd them to raise the Price, which might not be acceptable to those concern'd, some hundreds of whom have desir'd it should be done after this Manner, looking upon it as the most agreeable, especially under the present Circumstances. Accordingly, that there may be no just Cause of Complaint, they have resolv'd to furnish the same in Quantity, that is, a Sheet and a half once a Week, instead of dividing it into three. This, as is hop'd, will be satisfactory to all concern'd.

The statement concludes with some observations on the advantage of having the whole week to digest the news. From now on, at any rate, the *British Mercury* came out once a week in a sheet and a half, and so avoided paying any duty. It was not for nothing that it was run by an insurance company.

As a historian of the English provincial press has pointed out, the country newspapers took similar steps to evade the Act almost as soon as it came into force.[47] The London papers on this occasion were more ready to comply with the law. Only one evening paper made a deliberate attempt to cheat the revenue. In the 'Proposal' of John Toland already cited, he mentions the *St. James's Evening Post* as a paper that evaded the duty by 'printing a running Title of half a sheet, which serves for all the year round, and a sheet of small paper every post-night, which they sell with it'. In 1715–16 there were two papers called *The St. James's Evening Post*. The first, printed by James Baker, ran from 22 June 1715 to 1755, and perhaps longer. It was a four-page quarto; it carried the stamp imposed in 1712, and sold for 1½d. The second ran from 20 December 1715 to 19 January 1716, and this was printed by J. Applebee. Its first number, unstamped, carried the title full out on page 1, namely, *The Saint James's Evening Post, Or Nightly Pacquet*; it had a short 'Address to the Reader' on page 2, and the news on pages 3–6. Since it avoided the stamp duty it was sold 'at the small price of One Penny each'. It must have been this short-lived paper that Toland had in mind.[48]

The main beneficiaries from evading the stamp duty were the new weekly journals that sprang up and multiplied in the second decade of the eighteenth century. Owing to the difficulty of tracing complete files of those early newspapers it was impossible until recently to determine which was first in the field. The claim rested between the weekly journals of Robert Mawson and J. Applebee; and since Mawson referred on 19 February 1715 to 'two Pirating Printers [who] have published each a Sham Weekly Journal, at the Price of a Penny, . . . a bare Collection from the other Papers', the word 'sham' appeared to indicate that Mawson was claiming to be the originator of the weekly journal. We now know that Mawson's *Weekly Journal* first appeared on 6 January 1714, and Applebee's nine months later, on 9 October.[49] Read's paper, *The Weekly Journal; Or, British Gazetteer*, first appeared on 5 February 1715, and was to survive to 1761. The other important paper of this early period, *The Weekly Journal; Or, Saturday's Post* of Nathaniel Mist, commenced publication on 15 December 1716, became *Mist's Weekly Journal* in 1725, and survived (with a change of title to *Fog's Weekly Journal*) until 1737.

Mawson's paper had a comparatively short life, not because of any journalistic shortcomings, for it was well edited and written with some distinction, but because it was pronouncedly Jacobite. On 23 April 1715 *The Weekly Packet* reported that

one Robert Mawson, a book-binder, and an Interloping Printer, who has lately taken upon [him] to print very scandalous Papers, was taken into the Custody of one of His Majesty's Messengers . . . He was discovered by Mr. Will Hurt, late Printer of the *Flying-Post*; and, when taken, said, That if the Messenger had come an Hour later than four in the Morning, he should have been gone towards Scotland.

(The Jacobite rebellion did not break out till some months later, but already a man with Mawson's political sympathies would have been much safer in Scotland than in England.) On 24 September the *Evening Post* announced that a warrant had been issued for the arrest of Mawson on account of seditious matter in his *Weekly Journal*. At some time in 1716 he was said to have absconded.

The emergence of the six-page unstamped papers, published on Saturdays, created a considerable revolution in eighteenth-century journalism. Between 1679 and 1682 several attempts had been made to bring out weekly newspapers, but all were short-lived, presumably because they published only news, and most of that was already stale. A *Monthly Recorder* published by Langley Curtiss had a run of five numbers in 1682. Two successful weekly periodicals, Henry Care's *Weekly Pacquet, Or Advice from Rome* (1678–83) and Edward Rawlins's *Heraclitus Ridens* (1681–82), were not, except incidentally, newspapers, but papers of political comment. The new weekly journals of the second decade of the eighteenth century remained primarily newspapers, taking most of their news from the thrice-weekly papers, but they could never have filled their six ample pages with the news then available, even allowing for advertisements. Mawson had partly solved his problem by frequently following a piece of news with a comment; but comment was always dangerous, and frequently led to serious trouble. (It is significant that when a new paper was started we often find the assurance that it will avoid all reflections on public transactions, and deal only in matters of fact.) In those circumstances the majority of the weekly journals had recourse to more harmless methods of entertaining their readers. They published essays, poems, biographical anecdotes, romantic tales, dialogues, discussions of new books or plays, trials, sermons, speeches, letters sent by correspondents or, as often as not, written by the 'author' of the paper to himself, and answered by himself. They filled up smaller amounts of unwanted space by pointing out mistakes made by rival papers, and by carrying on a dog-fight with political opponents (a traditional exercise that was already well-established in the seventeenth-century newspapers). In the 1720s Mist and Read took this sort of warfare about as far as it would go, and other journals joined in the scurrilous fun. As the years passed, the serialisation of recent prose fiction or plays or other books became more and more common, and took up a welcome amount of vacant space. In this way W. Heathcote serialised *Robinson Crusoe* in *The London Post; Or, The Tradesman's Intelligence*; and in the winter of 1734 James Read was enlivening his *Weekly Journal* with extracts from Bishop Burnet's *History of my own Time*.

The weekly journals, in fact, survived and flourished by approximating to magazines. It became common for their first item to be an essay addressed 'To the Author', and dealing with some topic of contemporary interest. For the *Weekly Packet*, and later for the *London Journal*, Thomas Gordon wrote a series of essays which he afterwards republished in book form as *The Humourist*. For the *London Journal* and the *British Journal*, after they had passed into government control, Matthew Concanen also wrote essays which he republished with the title of *The Speculatist*. To the eighteenth century reader the literary essay, with its humour and its free play of the mind, must have been a civilising influence in a world of angry political controversy.

It is difficult to find any good reason why successive governments failed to amend the Stamp Act of 1712, once the widespread evasion had become evident. Legally the six-page papers of a sheet and a half were treated as pamphlets, taxable in the 1712 Act at 3*s.* for the whole impression. How much evasion of even this small payment there was it is impossible to say. On 20 October 1715 the *Flying Post*, launching an attack on Mawson's *Weekly Journal* for so obviously taking sides with the Jacobites, claimed that his papers were

writ on Purpose to poison the Mob with Prejudices against the Government, and for that End are cramm'd with idle Stories and Seditious Reflections, and carefully dispers'd thro' Alehouses etc. in Town and Country, and sold cheap on Purpose to give them a Currency among the ignorant Rabble, for by printing them in a Sheet and a half they avoid the Duty of Stamps, which other Papers pay, to the great Advantage to the Government, whereas this Method is contriv'd on Purpose to lessen that Part of the Revenue.

'Tis hoped when Parliament meets, it will be consider'd whether they should not be oblig'd to pay a Half-penny for each Half sheet, as well as others, to prevent their being able to poison the People by the Cheapness of their Papers, and to defraud the Revenue at the same time.

Similar exhortations were offered to the government from time to time, but nothing was done until April 1725, when a new Act imposed ½*d.* on *every* half sheet. The effect of this on a six-page paper selling at 1½*d.* would be to double the price to 3*d.*

During the passage of the new Act, however, the newspaper proprietors had been doing some quick thinking, and had arrived at a method of minimising the effect of the increased duty. The six-page weeklies disappeared overnight, to be replaced by half-sheet papers in four quarto pages. Some loss of space was inevitable, but much less was lost than might have been expected. Sheets used by the printer were not of a uniform size, and some were very considerably larger than others. By ordering his paper in very large sheets and then cutting them in half, the printer could obtain a half sheet that approximated in size to a whole sheet of the paper he had previously been using. If the new Act had not been circumvented as completely as that of 1712, the government now collected only ½d. from the transformed weeklies instead of the 1½d. it must have been expecting. If this new practice has all the appearance of another fiddle, it was one of which the *Gloucester Journal* openly boasted, when it told its readers that it was changing its format from 'a Sheet and a half of small Paper to one half Sheet of very large Paper, without omitting anything that it now contains'.[50]

The London weekly journals, whose problem was formerly how to find enough matter to fill six pages, all went through a number of physical changes to make up for their loss of space. The elaborate headpiece, with its devices of various sorts, gave place to a severely simple heading of title and date of issue. The width of the columns was increased, with a corresponding shrinking of the margins. Space was occasionally saved by the use of a smaller type. In 1727 Read's *Weekly Journal* changed from two column to three, and was in due course followed by others. The ½ d. duty was passed on to the reader, and the normal price of the weekly journals was now 2 d.[51]

The daily and thrice-weekly papers continued, as before, to pay ½d. duty. When trouble broke out at the *Daily Journal*, it had less to do with the duty to be paid than with that paper's plethora of news. In 1728 it was selling at 1½d., and on 19 January it announced: 'We shall, whenever we are pressed for Room, print the same, as at present, on larger Paper, in four columns, without raising the Price to the Publick, notwithstanding the extraordinary Expence to ourselves.' For the rest of the month the paper varied between three and four columns. By 1 February, however, the proprietors must have had second thoughts, for on that day the paper changed to four quarto pages, and the price was raised to 2d. A statement made it clear that the four-column numbers were thought 'inconvenient' by many readers, and that the proprietors considered them to be too expensive. By changing to four pages there would be more room for news, and country readers would be able to send the paper in this more 'commodious' form through the post. But here the *Daily Journal* met with an objection from the coffee-house proprietors, who called a meeting to protest against the raising of the price. On 22 February the *Journal* justified the increase in price by referring to the high expenditure on its news service, far greater than that of any other paper:

We may venture to appeal to the Publick, whether a single Half-penny per Paper can be thought sufficient to support such extraordinary Charges: for as the Stamp Duty is one Half-penny, and the Profits to the Mercuries and Hawkers another, that single Half-penny per Paper (at three Half-pence) is all the proprietors have to defray the Paper and Print, and all other incidental Charges of Management, exclusive of the Profit by Advertisements, one Shilling upon each whereof, as every one knows, is paid for the Duty.

None the less, some of the proprietors attended the coffee-men's meeting next day at the Devil Tavern, and agreed that 'the said Paper shall from the first of March be continued at the usual Price of Three-Half-Pence'. In due course the *Daily Journal* returned to its folio form in three columns. If all this fuss over a halfpenny seems to be a storm in a teacup, one must allow for the enormous difference between the value of money in the 1720s and at the present day: a daily newspaper costing 2*d.* cost 1*s.* a week. As for the coffee-men, the provision of the day's newspapers constituted a considerable part of their expenses, and with a paper much in demand two or more copies might have to be ordered.[52] The very fact that they called a meeting to resist the increased price of the *Daily Journal* would seem to indicate that it was one of those for which more than one copy was required. By the same token, the fact that the proprietors of the *Daily Journal* felt compelled to give way to their protest about the charge of 2*d.* shows how important a good sale in the coffee-houses was to them.

The newspapers, then, had their financial troubles, but these were easier to cope with than the disaster that might strike if they became involved with politics. In the reign of George I one of the government's most damaging critics was Mist's *Weekly Journal*, and Nathaniel Mist suffered severely on several occasions for his temerity. In 1721, for publishing comments offensive to the government, he was fined £50, sentenced to stand in the pillory, and given three months' imprisonment. He remained in prison for some months longer because he could not, or would not, pay the fine. In 1723 he was again arrested for a similar offence, and freed on bail of £1,400, a very large sum for those days. When he came up for trial early in 1724 he was found guilty, fined £100, sentenced to a year's imprisonment and to find securities for his good behaviour during life, and had his recognisances of £1,400 estreated. In 1727 he was fined £500, and again securities were demanded for his good behaviour during life. Mist may have thought the last part of the sentence impossible to fulfill, for in January 1728 he took refuge in France.[53] During his various bouts of imprisonment the *Weekly Journal* was carried on for him by others. However much

Mist may have suffered from the indiscretions of his writers, the circulation of his paper undoubtedly benefited. Writing in 1740, the author of *An Historical View of the Principles, Characters, Persons, etc. of the Political Writers in Great Britain*, remarked that in England a man is taken to be a man of honour and sense 'if he opposes the Court', and this 'opens the way for him into the Affections of the People'. He went on to cite Mist as an example, and noted the success that political writers have had in England 'if they have had the good fortune to be prosecuted'.[54] According to a writer in the *Daily Gazetteer* of 31 July 1741, 'Mist's treasonable papers were sometimes sold for half a guinea'.

The government's policy of leaning heavily on publishers and printers was admittedly successful. By constantly issuing warrants of arrest, to be followed by long and intimidating examinations, it was possible to bring even a highly successful paper to a close. This method was used with the desired effect against the *Freeholder's Journal* in 1722–3, when both printer and publisher were arrested, and the printer, unable to raise the money for bail, remained in prison. The paper closed in May 1733. With newspapers run on a shoe-string the final blow came sometimes with the forfeiture of recognisances. In spite of some notable successes, however, the government became wary of initiating too many prosecutions: if those failed, it might be embarrassed by public rejoicing, and if they succeeded, it might be accused of persecution. On such occasions the government usually consulted the Attorney-General about whether to prosecute or not, and it is significant that the Attorney-General of the day several times advised against taking action when the *Craftsman*, one of the leading opposition journals, was concerned.[55] It was the normal policy of Walpole to let sleeping dogs lie, and the *Craftsman* was a dog with sharp teeth.

The government found other and more circuitous ways of controlling the opposition press. On 27 January 1728 the *Craftsman* published an account of how the paper had been stopped in the post. On 3 November 1733 the *London Evening Post* made a similar complaint:

The Clerks of the several Roads in the Post-Office have received Orders not to send any of the LONDON-EVENING-POST to their Customers in the Country. These Orders, we presume, are occasion'd by this Paper having so often inserted Letters and Paragraphs against the late Excise-Scheme . . . But as this Paper has receiv'd the Universal Approbation of the Publick, for constantly pursuing THE TRUE INTEREST OF OUR COUNTRY, and as the same Spirit will be continued, it is not doubted but Gentlemen will either have the said Paper sent them by their Friends, or some other Way convey'd to them, and not suffer a Court Paper to be Impos'd upon them.

On 17 November, in spite of the recent attempts to suppress it, the sale of the paper was said to be 'considerably encreased'. Sometimes restrictions were imposed, not directly by the government, but by local magistrates, perhaps acting under instruction. In his *Commentator* (No. 20, 1720) Defoe tells how he visited Rochester, called for the newspapers at his inn, and found that it had nothing to offer but the *Post Man* and the *St. James's Evening Post*. The landlord explained what had happened:

Why really, Sir, we had Mist's Journal here and Dormer's Letter; but they did so much Mischief among the Seamen and Tradesfolks, that our Magistrates and the Justices of the Peace have forbid the Publick-Houses taking them in, and have given me a particular Charge about it as Post-Master. But this Restraint would not do: For Mist had a Man came down on Horse-back every Saturday with two or three Hundred Journals; however he happen'd last Week to be laid by the Heels for it . . .

Since Defoe was writing for Mist in 1720 we may assume that this story was based on fact. In the same essay he asserted that men and horses were employed to convey Mist's *Weekly Journal* in large quantities to Oxford and Cambridge, 'where, senseless as it is, it is constantly read and applauded'. It was also 'cry'd about' in all towns where troops were quartered, and 'among the Seamen through all the Building-Towns [i.e. ship-building towns] on the River Thames, at Deptford, Greenwich, Woolwich; so on to Gravesend, Rochester and Chatham; and the like again at Portsmouth'.

In the State Papers of 1721 there is a sensible letter from an anonymous correspondent who suggests that it might be a good idea to start a government newspaper, to be sold at ½*d*. to undercut all the rest. This would be a better way of dealing with the opposition press than prosecuting printers and publishers:

I will venture to affirm that there never was a Mist taken up or tryed but double the number of papers were sold upon it, besides the irritating of the people from the false notion of persecution.[56]

The government itself may have begun to think along these lines, although it never stooped to a halfpenny paper. In the early 1720s Walpole began to make use of the periodical press for political purposes. One of its most persistent critics was not a Tory paper, but a Whig one, the *London Journal*. The columns of this widely-read paper had for some time carried damaging attacks on the South Sea project and projectors, and on 12 August 1721 these culminated in a lengthy disclosure of the 'Examination taken by the Committee of Secrecy, with an Account of what appeared to them thereupon'. This was preceded by an inflammatory introduction written (as later came to light) by Benjamin Norton Defoe, the journalist son of Daniel Defoe. Who leaked the Committee's proceedings is not known; but young Defoe, who was well aware that in publishing them 'we run a Risque . . . in our private Circumstances', did not mince his words: 'We hope every Englishman that's not a Villain, or a Friend of Villains, will be obliged to us for this Publication'. The government, however, was not obliged; warrants were issued for the arrest of the printer and publisher, and the further instalment of the Examination that had been promised did not appear in next week's issue. Those temporary measures were followed by a long-term solution of beautiful simplicity; Walpole bought the *London Journal* from its proprietor, and turned it into an instrument for Government propaganda.[57] John Trenchard and Thomas Gordon, its chief political essayists, who wrote for it the once famous 'Cato's Letters', responded by starting a new weekly paper, the *British Journal*; but Trenchard died in 1723, and Gordon, making his peace with Walpole, was rewarded by being appointed a Commissioner of the Wine Licenses. The *Daily Courant* had for some time been a tool of the government, which also subsidised the *Free Briton* and the *Corn-Cutter's Journal*. Large numbers of those papers were distributed post-free to all parts of the country.[58]

Finally, in 1735, the government decided to concentrate the talents of its various writers in a single paper, and founded the *Daily Gazetteer*. On 30 June the new paper duly appeared. As William Arnall wrote in the first number, its aim was 'to vindicate the Publick Authority from the rude Insults of base and abusive Pens; to refute the Calumnies, and the injurious Clamours, of factious dishonest Men; . . . to set the Proceedings of the Administration in a true and faithful Light', and 'to inculcate the most affectionate Zeal for the *Sacred Person* of the KING'. The lucrative contract for printing the new paper was given to Samuel Richardson, not yet a novelist, but already an excellent printer.

When Walpole fell from power in 1742, a Committee of Secrecy was appointed to look into his financial conduct as first minister. Among its findings was the fact that £50,077 18*s*. had been paid to authors and printers of various newspapers 'such as *Free Britons*, *Daily Courants*, *Corn-Cutter's Journals*, *Gazetteers*, and other political papers, between 10 February 1731 and 10 February 1741'.[59] The newspapers had indeed come a long way since 1660.

Walpole's 'pensioners' presented no great threat to the unsubsidised papers, and indeed tended to increase their circulation: attacking the government nearly always makes for more interesting reading than defending it. In the 1730s, however, the newspapers, and more especially the weekly journals, found themselves competing with a comparatively new form of journalism, the literary magazines, published once a month. As early as 1692 Peter Anthony Motteux had started something of the kind, *The Gentleman's Journal: Or, The Monthly Miscellany*, and had carried it on for nearly two years; but the reading public had to wait almost forty years for anything comparable to this literary miscellany. On 1 January 1731 they were given the *Gentleman's Magazine*, to be followed the next year by the *London Magazine*, and in due course by many others, some surviving for only a few issues, but some, like the *Monthly Magazine*, long-lived. The first number of the *Gentleman's Magazine* began with a short table of contents, so that the purchaser could see at once the varied delights that lay in store for him. These included 'A View of the Weekly Essays and Controversies', Poetry, Domestic Occurrences, a paper on 'Melancholy Effects of Credulity in Witchcraft', Prices of goods and stocks and a List of Bankrupts, a List of the Sheriffs for the current year, 'Remarkable Advertisements', Foreign Affairs, Books and Pamphlets published, Observations on Gardening, and a List of Fairs for the season. With suitable modifications of the contents from time to time, the *Gentleman's Magazine* survived till 1907.

The magazine became a menace to the weekly journals by doing what the weekly journals had for so long done to the daily and thrice-weekly papers: it stole their contents. The magazine provided a summary of the month's news, collected from various papers, but there was no ownership of news: if there had been, the weekly journals would have been out of business. The grievance of the weekly journals, however, was that the magazines also filched many of their literary features, such as essays, articles and poems, on which copy money had been paid to the authors. There was nothing the weekly journals could do about it. The Copyright Act of 1710, in so far as it was observed, protected books from piracy, but did not extend the same protection to periodical publications. Even books could be safely pirated, as they were by many weekly journals, if they were serialised, a portion appearing every week. None the less, the weekly journals looked with a sense of outrage on the invasion of their property by the magazines. In 1737 a spokesman for the *Grub-Street Journal* complained of articles that cost twenty guineas in copy money being looted from it and published again in the *Gentleman's Magazine*. This parasitic practice, he claimed, was helping to weaken the journals, and he estimated that there had been a drop of £200 a month in stamp duty owing to their decline. Worst of all, the government had not imposed the newspaper tax on the magazines, and so added to the unfairness of their competition.[60] Published at 6*d.*, unstamped, and giving their readers the pick of the month, the magazines did indeed pose a considerable threat to the weekly journals.

CHAPTER 2

London news

The space allotted in a seventeenth-century newspaper to domestic and to foreign news varied considerably from one paper to another. In the early years of the Restoration, Muddiman and L'Estrange published a good deal of foreign news, and the *Gazette* had often little else to offer. Later, when the unlicensed newspapers were appearing, foreign news might take up one, or even two, of the four columns available in such a paper as Smith's *Currant Intelligence*. On the other hand, Harris, Thompson and Benskin, all of whow had the words 'Domestick Intelligence: or, News both from City and Country' in their titles, showed comparatively little interest in what was happening abroad, either because their appeal was to less educated readers, or because their papers were appearing in years of political crisis, when foreign affairs were crowded out by more pressing issues at home. In the reigns of William and Anne, when England was at war with France, European affairs inevitably became more important for most readers, and papers such as the *Post Man* and the *Daily Courant* concentrated on the latest foreign news. When the six-page weeklies began to appear in the second decade of the eighteenth century, and the problem of how to fill so much extra space arose, it was partly answered by including a considerable section of foreign news, whether readers wanted it or not. On the whole, however, domestic news predominated, and London rather than country news, not necessarily because it was easier to collect, but rather because more of importance was happening in London, and in times of political crisis a great deal might be happening at once.

When Muddiman was running his two news-books, *Mercurius Publicus* and *The Kingdome's Intelligencer* in the first three years of the Restoration period, his London news included fairly extensive parliamentary reports and matters involving the King and Court, but he also found time to cover a number of important trials. In *Mercurius Publicus*, 17 April 1662, he had a report of the trial of Lord Buckhurst and several of his companions for the murder of one Hoppy, a tanner. In the same number it also fell to him to give an account of the trial of three regicides, Miles Corbet, Sir John Barkstead and Colonel John Okey, who had been arrested in Holland and conveyed to London; and on 24 April he was able to describe their execution and their behaviour on the scaffold. On 12 June he reported the trials of John Lambert and Sir Henry Vane the younger, and a week later the execution of Vane. Muddiman's London news had little or no space for trivialities.

In his two papers, *The Intelligencer* and *The Newes*, L'Estrange gave most of his space to foreign news, and his domestic intelligence came mostly from provincial towns. Since he remained in London during the Plague he might have given the nation a valuable account of its progress; but if he stayed prudently indoors, he can hardly be blamed. Even before the plague broke out, however, he seems to have made little provision for gathering London news.

When the *Gazette* published London news it was usually dated from Whitehall, and was normally concerned with government affairs: the activities of the King, ministerial resignations and appointments, visits from foreign sovereigns and princes, the creation of peers and Knights of the Garter, the admittance of new ambassadors from abroad to kiss the King's hand, the appointment of English envoys to foreign Courts, births and deaths in the royal family or the death of some prominent statesman. Now and again, however, some news item concerned one of the King's humbler subjects. On 11 December 1679 the *Gazette* reported that 'one Claypoole, who writes the *Domestique Intelligence*, was ordered to be taken into Custody'; and on 18 April 1681 it carried the news that Francis Smith, publisher of the *Protestant Intelligence*, had been committed to Newgate on a charge of high treason. Had the *Gazette* cared to report on every newswriter, printer and publisher arrested and charged between the years 1679 and 1682 it would never have been short of home news; but only a few were singled out as a salutary reminder that under a Stuart regime it did not pay to 'pluck justice by the nose'.

On a few occasions even the staid *Gazette* could not avoid publishing the sensational kind of story that was normally provided by the popular papers. In April 1680, John Arnold, a Justice of the Peace for the county of Monmouth, who had been active in hunting Jesuits, was found apparently seriously wounded in Bell Yard, near Temple Bar. The last thing the King and Council wanted was to have another Sir Edmund Berry Godfrey on their hands;* and on 19 April the *Gazette* published a long account of the incident, with a promise that His Majesty would pay a reward of £100 to any person who should discover or apprehend the three persons suspected. The newspapers were already making much of the story, *Mercurius Anglicus* giving it almost two of its four columns on 17 April, and in due course a further report appeared in

---

* For Sir Edmund Berry Godfrey, see pp. 49–50, 56–7, 196.

the *Gazette* of 26 April, with information on what had so far been done to trace the assailants. Arnold made a good recovery, and in time a culprit was produced. On 15 July the *Gazette* announced that one John Giles had been found guilty of 'barbarously Assaulting and desperately wounding John Arnold, Esq.', and on the following Saturday he was sentenced to stand three times in the pillory, pay a fine of £500, and find sureties for his good behaviour for the rest of his life. A little less than two years later the *Gazette* was forced to intervene again (and probably for similar reasons) when Tom Thynne, a rich and prominent Whig and a friend of the Duke of Monmouth, was fatally attacked in Pall Mall.* On this, as on the earlier occasion, the *Gazette* showed how good its reporting could be when it was put to it.

One must not suppose that a seventeenth-century newspaper had a posse of reporters ready to investigate any story that reached it. At best only one or two men could be so employed. If someone was sent out to find out the facts about an incident that had occurred in, say, Southwark, he had to set off on foot across London Bridge and tramp back again; as likely as not, since houses were not numbered, he might have difficulty in finding the right place, and by the time he found it there might be no one there to interview. A paragraph in Thompson's *Domestick Intelligence* of Tuesday, 28 October 1679 begins with: 'It is very credibly reported from Southwark that on Wednesday night last . . .', and goes on to recount how the tide flowed two yards above the high-water mark, and 'about the same time was seen in the Air the Effigies of a tall man standing upright, with a drawn Sword in his Hand, which in a short time vanished, and after that various confused shapes were seen.' It is just possible that Thompson sent one of his men to investigate this strange happening, but more probable that he simply accepted the story as and when it reached him.

On the same day as Thompson published his very credible report from Southwark, he recorded another sensational event that took place nearer at hand, and that should have been easier to check. On this occasion Harris had a different version of the same story, and the discrepancies between the two accounts give some indication of the primitive state of news reporting at this period. Harris writes:

There hath lately happened a very Sad and Lamentable Accident beyond Drury-lane, where a Person who kept a Publick House, coming home suddenly and unexpectedly, found three Gentlemen in Company with his Wife, and discovering [showing] some signs of Jeaolousie [suspicion] and Dissatisfaction, those Persons Immediately fell upon him, beating and wounding him very

---

* For the Thynne murder, see pp. 59–67.

severely, and afterwards two of them holding him, the third man most Barbarously and Villainously Murdered him by Cutting his Throat.

Harris ends his story by stating that the three men had been arrested and committed to prison.

Thompson's account gives a very different turn to the story:

A person living at the upper end of St. Martin's lane near Leicester Fields, being lately Marryed to a very handsom young Gentlewoman, was for some time a little possest with Jealousie. It happened that on Saturday night last, Two of her old Friends came to visit her; and offered some incivility to his Wife before his face. He in a great Passion suddenly took up a Knife, and cut his own Throat, upon which he immediately fell down. The two Gentlemen being presently secured. But we do not yet hear he is dead.

It is common ground that the incident took place a short distance west of Drury Lane, but Thompson's location of the house is more precise than that of Harris. It is also common ground that the incident was provoked by the husband's jealousy, but here the two accounts begin to drift apart. Harris gives us the impression that the husband's jealousy was only aroused when he came home unexpectedly to find three men entertaining or being entertained by his wife; whereas Thompson, who mentions only two men, tells us not only that the husband had been jealous for some time, but also gives us the reason: he had recently married a very handsome young woman. (We are not actually told that the husband was an elderly man, but that may be suggested by the statement that his wife was young.) In neither account is the victim's name given, he is just 'a person'; but Harris scores a point by informing us that he kept a public house. Whether what followed upon his unexpected return was murder or attempted suicide, and whether he arrived home to find three men with his wife or two, we shall never know.

When we meet with the words 'It is reported' in a seventeenth-century newspaper, they usually mean nothing more than someone had been heard to say it. The word 'reporter' was used for the shorthand writer employed to take down trials and other proceedings, but it was not until the middle of the nineteenth century that it was used for newspaper reporters, who were earlier referred to as news-gatherers. The standard of reporting in a seventeenth-century newspaper was often abysmally low. Much of what got into print had been picked up at second or third hand in a coffee-house or at the Exchange, and published without further verification. The desire to be the first with the news was responsible, then as now, for much misinformation. When, in January 1682, Langley Curtiss, who had been making his own contributions to the pool of false news in his *True Protestant Mer-*

cury, decided to bring out a monthly journal, he explained to the reader how his *Monthly Recorder* would give a far more accurate account of the news than was currently available:

The Weekly *Gazettes, Intelligences, Mercuries, Currants*, and other News-Books, for haste to be the first Publisher, to make their News sell, take many things in trust from the first Reporter, which they often publish for true News, and in the next, having better Intelligence, are fain to recant, or amend what before they had published; so that their News proves wholly false, or much otherwise than they had related, by which means many are so much disgusted, that they give little heed to all those News-Books, and few will buy them for their uncertainty. Besides, there being Factions among them, they often abuse one another with Sham Letters of News, on purpose to do one another injury, by causing one another to publish things that are false, that they may be able to contradict one another . . .

The deliberate planting of false news by one newspaper on another had been made easier by recent postal developments. In 1679 London had no internal letter post. If one wanted to send a letter to a London address, one normally entrusted it to a porter. On 27 March 1680, however, thanks to a remarkable example of private enterprise, William Dockwra and some others started a well-organised penny post, with seven sorting offices in London and Westminster and numerous offices all over London where letters could be collected. Deliveries were made hourly to places of 'quick negociation', and to more distant places five times a day. In summer the service continued from 6 a.m. to 9 p.m. Inevitably there were some who managed to persuade themselves that the new penny post was a papist scheme. On 27 March 1680 Smith's *Currant Intelligence* cited Titus Oates as saying it was 'a farther branch of the Popish Plot'.[1] On 1 March 1681 the author of *Heraclitus Ridens* added his own objections:

Well! certainly this penny-Post was the most happy invention of this fortunate Age: there was never any thing so favourable to the carrying on or managing Intrigue: that and the Press being unpadlockt are two incomparable twins of the Liberty of the Subject! one may Write, Print, publish and disperse ingenious Libels, either against particular persons of the Tory party, or the Government it self, and no body the wiser or the better for it.

Whatever the political effect of the penny post may have been, it was undoubtedly a great convenience to the citizens of London, and a boon to the newspapers. For the newswriters it had obvious advantages. In 1681 we are told that one of them, Jasper Hancock, was accustomed to 'belabour' his correspondents with queries by the penny post.[2]

Written reports could now reach a newspaper within a few hours of some important event, and through the penny post the circulation of newspapers and news-letters to London readers was greatly facilitated at little cost. Yet the risk of publishing false news was correspondingly increased. It was not uncommon for a newspaper to complain that it had been deceived by a penny-post letter (subscribed, perhaps, 'your true friend and well-wisher', and sent by some rival newswriter); but other items of false news might be due to known correspondents sending in reports that they had not troubled to verify.

If we turn now to what may be called the serious news of the period, we shall find that the journalists were not only forbidden to report parliamentary debates, but also severely discouraged from reporting important trials in the law courts. In his *Domestick Intelligence* of 13 February 1680 Nathaniel Thompson tells how a judge issued a stern warning to anyone presuming to take notes in his court. It had been brought to his notice that one Mr C., a barrister, 'being well acquainted with shorthand, took Notes of some passages in the Court, and afterwards dispersed them abroad, by which means not only the Court, but others, were often exposed to scandalous reflections'. Mr C. was called for, and could not be found; but the Lord Chief Justice took the opportunity of stating that 'if he knew of any Barrester that exposed things done in the Court to the world without the order of the Court, (or to that purpose) he would take a course with him'. Mr C. had presumably come to a financial arrangement with some newswriter to supply him with legal information. In publishing this item of news Thompson was himself exposing what had been done in court; but he may have felt that his interpolation of the words 'or to that purpose' safeguarded him from quoting the judge's actual words, and that in any case he was doing the judge a favour by broadcasting his warning. Again, in his *Loyal Protestant* of 10 February 1683 Thompson described how, when Sir Patience Ward, an ex-Lord Mayor, was being tried in a crowded court for perjury, the newswriter Jasper Hancock had 'planted himself in a window' ready to take notes of the proceedings, 'till an Officer espying him commanded him down, at which he was hissed out of the Hall before the Court sat. So that he was forced to sneak away without one tittle of news for his country customers.' In spite of such set-backs the newspapers succeeded in publishing some information about court proceedings, although in an important trial anything approaching a shorthand account would have led to immediate trouble.

Since 17 October 1678, when the body of the London magistrate, Sir

Edmund Berry Godfrey had been found on a piece of waste ground, with his sword sticking through his back, the situation of the King's Catholic subjects had become precarious. Over the following two years the Popish Plot hung like the mushroom cloud after a nuclear explosion. Titus Oates had come forward with news of various Catholic plots to kill the King, and his murder (Oates claimed) was to be followed by the murdering of Protestants, a French invasion, and the succession of the Catholic Duke of York to the throne. Within a few months, on the evidence offered by Oates and other perjured witnesses, a number of Catholics had been arrested, tried, sentenced to death and executed. Among these were Edward Coleman, who had been the Duke of York's secretary, and several Jesuit fathers. On equally flimsy evidence three men were accused of murdering Godfrey, and were duly found guilty and hanged.

One of the earliest victims of Oates, Bedloe and Dugdale was a Catholic lawyer, Richard Langhorn, who was sentenced to death by Lord Chief Justice Scroggs on 14 June 1679. The trial, like all those just mentioned, took place too early to be reported by Benjamin Harris, whose *Domestick Intelligence* had not yet begun to appear; but in his first number, on 7 July, he was able to state that although Langhorn was being urged to confess what he knew about the Popish Plot, he had maintained that he knew nothing whatever about any plot. 'Yet in hope he might come to a better mind, he hath obtained a Gracious Reprieve for 8 days longer.' Langhorn, however, had no information to offer that could have saved his life, and on 17 July Harris gave all but two lines of his front page to a detailed account of the execution, including the burning of the victim's bowels and the quartering of his body, and ending with the news that 'his Corps was by His Majesties most gracious Order delivered to his friends, who put it in a Hearse, with Escutcheons about it, and was afterwards interred in the Temple-Church, in which place he was once a Student of the Laws'. Harris was wrong about the place of burial: in his next number he published an advertisement sent to him by the clerk of the Temple Church, stating that Langhorn was buried in the churchyard of St Giles-in-the-Fields.

On 18 July, only four days after the execution of Langhorn, Scroggs was presiding over another trial for high treason, and listening again to the fabricated evidence of Oates, Bedloe and Dugdale. On this occasion the accused were the Queen's physician, Sir George Wakeman, and three Benedictine monks, who were all charged with conspiring to poison the King, or, in the legal jargon of the indictment, 'our Sovereign Lord the King, to Death and final Destruction to bring and put'. Since some of the evidence appeared to implicate the Queen, the atmosphere in court must have been tense; and when Oates had testified that while he was in an ante-room to the Queen's chamber he had heard her say that 'she would not endure these Violations of her bed any longer, and that she would assist Sir George Wakeman in the poisoning of the King', the trial reached its most sensational moment. Scroggs passed over in silence the Queen's alleged involvement, and for some reason he was not his old bullying self at this trial: it was soon being suggested that he had given way to Court pressure, or had been bribed by the Portuguese ambassador. As the trial progressed, he questioned the prosecution witnesses closely, and in his summing-up he left the jury in no doubt that he had found much of the evidence open to suspicion, more especially that of Oates. 'And so,' he concluded, quite uncharacteristically, 'I pray you weigh it well, let us not be so amazed and frighted with the noise of Plots, as to take away any man's Life without any reasonable Evidence.'[3] In the eyes of all good Whigs the ensuing verdict of not guilty transformed Scroggs overnight from the champion of Protestantism to a judicial apostate.

To Harris the unexpected acquittal of the four accused must have been a bitter disappointment: up till now Scroggs could have been counted upon to see that no Roman Catholic got a fair hearing. Yet however Harris may have felt, he gave the whole of his front page to the trial. His report included an episode that may have given him some consolation. A 'Tall proper gentleman' who was seen giving the doorkeeper something to obtain admittance was recognised by his former landlord as a priest who had lodged with him. He was at once seized and taken before a Justice of the Peace, but refused to give his name or say where he lived. When the trial was over he was taken for identification to Oates, who immediately recognised him as 'one Dormer, a popish priest or Jesuit', and had him committed to Newgate.[4] This could be John Dormer (1636–1700), a Jesuit 'whose real name was Huddleston, . . . son of Sir Robert Huddleston, knight' (DNB). In the reign of James II he was appointed one of the court preachers.

In October 1678 William Howard, Viscount Stafford, along with four other Catholic peers, had been sent to the Tower, and all five were subsequently impeached by the House of Commons. At length, on 30 November 1680, Stafford was brought out to be tried by his peers on a charge of high treason. The trial, which opened on Stafford's sixty-sixth birthday and was to last for a week, took place at Westminster Hall, in the presence of the King, the Lords and Commons, and (in the gallery) ambassadors and other persons of distinction. The ageing peer, who had to conduct his own defence, did his best; but he had some difficulty in hearing what was said owing to the noise and shouting outside the Hall, his own replies were often inaudible, and at one point he broke down and wept. He was found guilty by a large majority, and sentenced to death.

This protracted trial would have been a great occasion for the newspapers, but since the King's proclamation of 17 May suppressing the publication of unlicensed news-books, all newspapers except the *Gazette* had ceased to appear. (The *Gazette* gave 14 lines to the trial on 2 December, three lines on 6 December, and seven lines on 9 December to the closing stages and the sentence. The execution was dealt with in four lines on 30 December.) On 28 December, however, Harris resumed his old Tuesday-Friday publication of the *Domestick Intelligence*, and on the same day Langley Curtiss brought out the first number of his *True Protestant Mercury*. Too late for the trial, both men were just in time for the execution. Curtiss indeed anticipated it in his first number, with a brief statement about the scaffold erected on Tower Hill, and a longer account of four requests that Stafford had made to the sheriff who was to be in charge of his execution. He had asked that the scaffold might be large enough to allow several of his friends to be present; that it should be hung with mourning; that his body might be carried off with his own clothes on, and, finally, 'that the people might not be suffered to shout'. To the first two requests, if we may believe Curtiss, the answers were that the scaffold would be 12 feet square, and that if the prisoner or his friends were prepared to pay for the mourning, 'and Authority were pleas'd to permit it, he might have his desire'. To the third request the answer was that 'the dispute about his Cloaths might perhaps be more properly treated of and concluded with another person' (no doubt the executioner). To the pathetic appeal that the people should not be allowed to shout, the reply was sardonic, not to say brutal: 'he might expect all the Civility that became Men and Christians towards a Malefactor under his Circumstances: but it did not lye in the Sheriff's power to restrain the people from expressing their just detestation against Treason, for he had no Commission to cause any bodies breath to be stopped, but His.' The two sheriffs in office were Slingsby Bethel and Henry Cornish, and the news of the response given to Stafford's request must have come, either directly or at second hand, from one or other of them. No doubt Curtiss was retailing what had already become common talk in the City.

Stafford was beheaded on 29 December. On Friday 31 December, Harris gave two and a half of his four columns to an eyewitness account of the execution. The writer of this account (possibly, but not necessarily, Harris himself) seems to have kept in mind the four requests that Stafford had made to the sheriff. He must also have been close to the scaffold, for he gives us one or two short scraps of dialogue, and in one of those Stafford returns to the vexing question of his clothes.

Stafford. Have you received any Money for the Cloaths? Answer. No. Then his man took out a Purse of five Pounds, which the Hangman objected against, and W. S. gave him two Guineas more.

What lay behind this macabre exchange between the condemned peer and the man who was about to cut off his head was the traditional right of the executioner to the dead man's clothes. The payment made on the scaffold was therefore a recompense to the executioner for waiving his perquisite. The writer of the report appears to have Stafford's last request in mind when he records the behaviour of the crowd, estimated at about 10,000. When the executioner held up Stafford's severed head, 'they were satisfied, making no great shout nor reflection.' That Harris could bring himself to print this is some indication of the fairness and accuracy of his long report, for he would almost certainly have expected and preferred a different reaction from the spectators. Almost his only hostile comment comes at the end when 'many threw up Hankerchiefs to be dipt in W.S's blood, in which some were gratified, though several were wet with the blood of a Carman who cut his finger, and gave two pence more a piece for it'.

The *English Gazette* and the *True Protestant Mercury*, both appearing a day later, on Saturday, gave less than a column to the execution. Both accounts were hostile. The *English Gazette* reported that there were 'divers spectators', and that the scaffold was 'not hung with mourning as desired'. What particularly shocked it was the behaviour of 'divers of the Popish party' dipping their handkerchiefs in the dead man's blood, 'to be kept for holy relics, or other superstitious ends'. Worse still was the action of

a person in the habit of a Minister of the Church of England standing on the scaffold, who did not only officiously dip several Hankerchiefs in the blood of this Traytor, but also pulls out his own Hankerchief out of his pocket, and after he had dipped it in the blood of the executed Traytor, put it again in his own pocket, which was very ill resented by the people, that any man in his habit should be guilty of so much superstition and folly.

Both newspapers concentrated attention on Stafford's faltering delivery of his speech on the scaffold, one claiming that those who were nearest to him observed that he must have taken 'some liquors that had intoxicated his brain, which was given, as is judged, to bear up his spirits', and the other stating that he appeared 'as one dozed with spirits or opium'. It was a sore point with both that the speech had been 'given forth to print the day before his execution', and that, according to Curtiss, it was on sale in the streets two hours after his death. This seventeenth-century scoop was the work of Harris, who announced in his issue of 31 December that Stafford's speech in writing 'is printed for the Publisher of this Intelligence'. In those circumstances, Curtiss told his readers, 'we need not enlarge; for we would not nauseate the Reader this good time [i.e. Christmas] with cold Pye.' He did, however, give the reader one interesting piece of information that is not in the other two newspapers. In describing how Stafford read his speech, the *True Protestant Mercury* stated: 'And so little was the Prisoner acquainted or affected with the same that he could scarcely read it himself, and made mistakes, etc., and by the Character, 'tis believed, that the very Paper he read was a woman's handwriting.' In that case it may be possible to name the lady. When Edward Fitzharris was on trial for his life some six months later, Lord Chief Justice Pemberton permitted his wife to sit beside him in court and assist him. On the Solicitor-General objecting to this procedure, Mrs Fitzharris appealed to the Lord Chief Justice: 'My Lord, the Lady Marchioness of Winchester did assist in the case of my Lord Stafford, and took notes, and gave him what papers she pleased.'[5] The Marchioness of Winchester was the daughter of the unfortunate William Howard, Viscount Stafford. Her services to this weary old man may well have extended to writing out, perhaps even composing, his last speech.

On Wednesday 8 June 1681 the trial took place of Archbishop Oliver Plunket on a charge of high treason, to be followed next day by that of Edward Fitzharris. By this time Benjamin Harris's *Domestick Intelligence* had ceased to appear, but several new papers were now being published. Compared with other treason trials in the later seventeenth century, that of the Catholic archbishop was comparatively straightforward: a sufficient number of Irish witnesses had been paid enough to testify that he was involved in a plot to bring a French army into Ireland. Plunket was duly convicted, and sentenced to death one week later. The proceedings certainly aroused interest, but less perhaps than might have been expected; Plunket, after all, was just another Irish Catholic, the latest (if the most distinguished) of a long line of victims. Benskin, one of whose publication days was Thursday, was on this occasion the first with the news, and he gave it the first column on his front page. In the event this was better than might have been expected, since Benskin had just been arrested for publishing a pamphlet reflecting on the Earl of Danby, and had to find bail of £500 before he could be released.[6] It looks as if he must have had a reliable man in charge of his newspaper. The *Impartial Protestant Mercury*, appearing on Friday, gave both columns of its front page to the trial, concluding with evident satisfaction: 'In fine, Never was there a Trial more clearly proved than this . . . The Jury just laid their Heads together, and Sir William Roberts their Foreman pronounced him guilty.' Smith's *Currant Intelligence*, appearing on Saturday when the news was already stale, carried a short report of about 20 lines. Curtiss, whose *True Protestant Mercury* also appeared on Saturday, had no report at all; but, in accordance with his principle not to 'nauseate the reader with cold pie', he had already rushed out a two-page folio pamphlet, *An Account of Some Particulars in the Tryal of Mr. Ed. Fitzharris . . . Together with a Brief Realtion* [*sic*] *of the Tryal of Oliver Pluncket*. Only 15 lines were given to Plunket: the fate of Fitzharris was of much more interest to the general public.

The paper that might have been expected to give the Plunket trial the fullest coverage was the *Loyal Protestant* of Nathaniel Thompson, himself an Irishman and (in spite of the title of his paper) a Catholic. But he had no report, and in his issue of 11 June he explained why. It appears that Lord Chief Justice Pemberton, who had recently succeeded Scroggs, had issued an order 'that none (without his Lordship's Licence first obtained) presume to Print any of his words spoken in Court'. Ignoring this order Curtiss had, in Thompson's words, published an epitome of 'what passed at the Trial of *that Traytor in grain Fitz-Harris*', and the Lord Chief Justice had 'been pleased to issue out his warrant against him'.* Thompson himself, though he was sure he could give a more accurate account than Curtiss had given, was resolved 'in obedience to his Lordship's Order' to forbear. This uncharacteristic willingness to comply with authority invites explanation: Thompson had been in and out of prison several times for his journalistic indiscretions in the past two years, and on this occasion he may have felt a sudden twinge of caution.

At all events, the Lord Chief Justice had no power to prevent him describing the final scenes. The death sentence was carried out on 1 July, and Thompson gave the whole of his issue on Saturday 2 July to

---

* When the official version of the trial was published, along with that of Archbishop Plunket, it carried the warning: 'I do appoint Francis Tyton, and Thomas Basset, to Print the Tryals of Edward Fitz-Harris and Oliver Plunket; and that no other presume to Print the same. Fr. Pemberton.'

reporting the execution of Plunket, together with that of Fitzharris, which took place on the same day. The speech delivered by Plunket on the scaffold took up half the second column on the front page, and the whole of the back page in Thompson's smallest type. Better still, he had already had a copy of the speech selling on the day of the execution. According to the *Impartial Protestant Mercury* of 5 July, which gave less than one column to the two executions, it had been 'delivered out before . . . to decoy the People. For he was scarce Executed before a Copy thereof Printed was cryed about the Streets, Publish'd by Nathaniel Thompson'. This was a pamphlet of four pages, *The Last Speech of Mr. Oliver Plunket . . . Written by his own Hand.* No doubt Thompson had obtained a copy from one of his fellow Catholics. Curtiss and Smith, who also published on Saturday, were much less generous in their coverage: the first dealt with the two executions in one column, and Smith in eight lines. Curtiss, however, published *The Last Speeches and Confessions of Oliver Plunket . . . and also of Edward Fitz-Harris* as a two-page pamphlet.

If many Englishmen would have agreed with the *Impartial Protestant Mercury* that the guilt of Archbishop Plunket had been proved beyond any shadow of doubt, the case of Edward Fitzharris was bewildering in the extreme, and what this muddled man thought he was doing has never been satisfactorily explained. An impecunious Irish gentleman, he had hung about the Court for several years and had (he claimed) been employed by the King in various kinds of secret service. On 21 February 1681 he approached an old acquaintance, Edmond Everard, with the outline of a pamphlet that he wished him to write. When, betrayed by this accomplice, he was arrested by Sir William Waller, a highly seditious manuscript was found in his possession, with corrections in his own hand, calling on Englishmen to depose the King if he did not comply with parliament's demands for the exclusion of a Popish successor. The kindest interpretation of this is that Fitzharris may have been concocting another sham plot, and that the fatal pamphlet was written with the intention of planting copies on some of the leading Whigs, who would then be arrested and charged when the treasonable pamphlet was found in their possession.[7] On 10 March Fitzharris was visited in Newgate by the Recorder of London and Sir Robert Clayton, a former Lord Mayor. To those two firm Protestants he declared that he had been offered £10,000 by the envoy of the Duke of Modena (brother of the Duke of York's second wife) to kill the King, and that the Duke of York 'was privy to all those designs', and further that he had evidence to show that the murder of Sir Edmund Berry

Godfrey was 'consulted at Windsor'.[8] With Fitzharris talking like this
the King did what he should have done sooner, and had him removed
to the Tower. But the evidence of what he had said to the Recorder
and Clayton soon got around; and when parliament met at Oxford in
March, the Whig majority, convinced that they must get Fitzharris out
of the King's hands and into their own, impeached him and sent the
bill up to the House of Lords, where it was rejected.

When proceedings against Fitzharris opened in the King's Bench on
28 April, the next two weeks were taken up by a prolonged argument
between the crown counsel and those appearing for the House of Commons about the competence of the court, in view of the earlier impeachment, to try the case at all. During the learned wrangle that followed,
the proceedings of the court were summarised clearly and at some
length in several of the newspapers. On 7 May the *Impartial Protestant
Mercury* reported that 'this famous Case being to be debated, there
attended a vast Concourse of People, and many Peers of the Realm, as
the Duke of Monmouth, the Lord Shaftesbury, and divers others'. On
10 May the *Loyal Protestant* remarked: 'Fitzharris's Case is now the only Subject of all People's Discourse, both in City and Country, and all
are big with expectation to see the issue of the Cause'. Many people,
it added, were much less interested in the fate of Fitzharris than in what
he might have to reveal about the Popish Plot. In the end Lord Chief
Justice Pemberton ruled that the court was competent to try Fitzharris,
and fixed his trial for 9 June.

In a treason trial the accused could not be represented by counsel,
but had to conduct his own case. He was permitted to call witnesses
for his defence and to cross-examine those called by the crown; but the
effective examination of witnesses calls for practice, and a mind not
distracted by anxiety or numbed by the menacing atmosphere of a
court of law. Fitzharris failed to press hard enough upon the crown's
witnesses, and the most important of those he called in his defence
almost certainly avoided saying what they knew.[9] The Solicitor-
General had no difficulty in ridiculing the idea that the King 'should
be at great pains of employ Mr. Fitzharris to destroy himself and the
whole Nation', and after only a short deliberation the jury brought in
a verdict of guilty.

The trial had produced some startling evidence, true or false, but it
was too hot for the newspapers to handle. Although the *Impartial Protestant Mercury* gave it one column on 10 June, it had recourse to a
blurred and almost meaningless summary when dealing with some of
the more dangerous evidence. All that it ventured to tell its readers

about the startling revelations of Titus Oates was that 'Dr. Oates first appeared on behalf of the prisoner, and spake something, as that Everard should say he wrote the Libel himself'. A pamphlet on the trial published by Curtiss was so uncommunicative ('Dr. Oates accordingly appeared, and declared what he had to say') as to be worthless. It was left to Smith's *Currant Intelligence*, in its brief report of 11 June, to give the substance of what Oates told the court about the treasonable pamphlet: 'it was intended that the said Libel should be conveyed to several of His Majesties Subjects who were thereupon to be searched, seized, and prosecuted as Authors and Dispensers of the same.'

On the scaffold Fitzharris read a short speech, which was published in the *Loyal Protestant* of 5 July, and (in a slightly fuller form) in the *Impartial Protestant Mercury* of the same date. What else happened on the scaffold is variously reported in those two newspapers and in Curtiss's *True Protestant Mercury*. According to Curtiss, Fitzharris had delivered two separate papers to Dr Hawkins, the chaplain of the Tower (who had been frequently with him in his last days, exhorting him to confess, either for the salvation of his soul or for the benefit of the King). One of those papers was now handed to him by Hawkins, and Fitzharris proceeded to read it aloud as his last dying speech. Sheriff Bethel suggested to him the need for a fuller confession, more especially of what he had said on being interviewed in Newgate, when he had claimed to know 'more of the Popish Plot than any other'. His answer to this was that 'he had left his mind with Dr. Hawkins'; i.e. in the second of the two papers mentioned. The sheriff (or sheriffs) then demanded to see this other paper; but Dr Hawkins replied, 'they should have a copy of that Mr. Fitz-Harris read, and the other he should deliver to those whom it properly concerned.' The *Impartial Protestant Mercury* merely confirms that the sheriffs received a copy of Fitzharris's last speech from Hawkins. It was left to Thompson to throw this final scene into the form of dramatic dialogue. Benjamin Harris, it will be recalled, had interpolated a few fragments of dialogue into his account of Viscount Stafford's execution some months earlier, but on this later occasion Thompson gave his readers a fuller and more sustained exchange between the prisoner and those attending him on the scaffold. As soon as Fitzharris had ended his speech Sheriff Bethel said he must have a copy ('We must have it, it is our right'). To this Fitzharris replied, 'I desire the Paper under my own hand may be given to my Wife.' In the ensuing altercation 'Short-hand-writer' intervened with a suggestion, and Hawkins agreed that the Sheriff should have a copy.

Sheriff. Why should not we have the Original?
Fitz-Harris. Because I promised it to my Wife under my own hand.
Sheriff. Well, well, we'l leave that off now, but let's have a Copy.

The rights of a sheriff of the City of London had been safeguarded; and for Bethel, if not for Fitzharris, life could now go on. With that problem out of the way there was no need to keep the spectators waiting any longer. After offering up a short prayer, Fitzharris was 'turned off' by the hangman.

All the trials so far considered took place during the excitement generated by the Popish Plot, and could not fail to arouse the deepest interest. Yet, when circumstances were favourable, and even when there were no political implications, a trial for murder in the first degree could be just as profitable to the newspapers, and even had certain advantages. In a treason trial the public usually knew little or nothing about the accused until he appeared in court and the crown opened its case against him. But a murder case began with the death of the victim, the search for the assailant or assailants, their arrest and examination. In the next few days, or even weeks, fresh evidence might come to light and be reported in the newspapers, and then at last, after the public expectation had been thoroughly aroused, there came the trial and verdict.

On the evening of Sunday 12 February 1682, Thomas Thynne of Longleat, one of the richest commoners in England, was gunned down while passing along Pall Mall in his coach. Three men on horseback had stopped the coach, and one of them had shot him at short range where he sat. He died early next morning, after suffering great pain. Thynne's murderers were arrested remarkably quickly, and much of the credit must be given to Sir John Reresby, at that time one of the Justices of the Peace for Middlesex and Westminster. We are fortunate in having his own account of what happened, for it enables us to check the accuracy of the newspaper reports. Reresby happened to be at Court when news of the attack reached the King, who was much concerned about it, not indeed from any love of Thynne, but 'apprehending the ill constructions that the anti-Court party might make of it'.[10] His apprehensions were well founded. As a member of parliament for Wiltshire, an intimate friend of the Duke of Monmouth, and a follower of Shaftesbury, Thynne had given prominent support to the campaign for the exclusion of the Duke of York from the succession, and had inevitably incurred the enmity of the King. Although eventually it would be established that the murder had no political motive, the Whig newspapers were to make what they could of this possibility for several days.

The newsmen were quick to realise that they had a sensational story to tell. Apart from his wealth and his political prominence, Thynne had obtained widespread notoriety only a few months earlier by his marriage to a very rich young heiress aged 14, who had previously been married just after her twelfth birthday to the young Earl of Ogle and left a widow less than a year later. Her marriage to Thynne had not been consummated; for almost immediately after the ceremony she had fled to Holland. Until her third marriage less than four months after Thynne's death, when she became Duchess of Somerset, the newspapers regularly referred to her as Lady Ogle.

In considering how the five newspapers then appearing dealt with the murder, it must be remembered that the *London Gazette* and Benskin's *Domestick Intelligence* both appeared on Monday and Thursday, and that their Monday issue must have been already in print before the news broke. The *Impartial Protestant Mercury* came out on Tuesday and Friday, and Thompson's *Loyal Protestant* on Tuesday, Thursday and Saturday, so that their issues for Tuesday 14 February were the first to give the news. The *True Protestant Mercury* was published on Wednesday and Saturday.

It will be as well to begin with the long official account published in the *London Gazette* of Thursday 16 February, which carries the story from the attack on Sunday evening to the latest developments on Wednesday. From this we learn that the murder weapon was a musketoon (a short musket with a large bore), four bullets entering Thynne's body. When the King was informed of the attack, he gave immediate orders for 'stopping all Persons that could not give a good Account of themselves in the several Ports; and for making diligent search here in Town, in order to the discovering the Assasinates'. The three men who had been seen escaping from the scene of the attack were traced to their several lodgings and arrested. Their leader was a German, Captain Christopher Vratz, who had been accompanied on the fatal Sunday evening by his Polish servant, George Boroski, and by a Swedish lieutenant, John Stern. Vratz 'readily confessed the whole Fact'. He had been keeping company with Count Charles John Königsmark on his travels, and had recently come to England with him. His friendship with the Count 'had made him take very much to heart the Affronts which Mr. Thinn had put upon the Count by his Discourses and other ways; and [he] therefore resolved to take Satisfaction of him'. Learning on Sunday that Thynne was in his coach, he went on horseback with his servant and a friend to find him, the servant carrying the musketoon and his friend and himself armed with swords and pistols.

Meeting with the coach in Pall Mall, he bade the coachman stand, intending to challenge Thynne to a duel, but 'his Servant being a Polander, he not rightly apprehending what he said, discharged his musketoon upon Mr. Thynne, whereupon they made their escape.' All three were committed to Newgate for trial at the next sessions.

On Wednesday (the *Gazette* continues) several other persons were examined. In spite of the story Vratz had told 'to palliate so wicked an Action', it now appeared that there had been a barbarous and malicious plot to murder Thynne, 'suspected to have been contrived by the abovementioned Count Charles John Connigsmark, who has lain about a Fortnight concealed in Town, under a false Name, and left his Lodging in great haste last Monday morning'. There followed a short description of Königsmark, with a reward of £200 to anyone supplying information that should lead to his arrest. The *Gazette* had one other item of news arising out of Thynne's death: 'This day [15 February] Mr. Nathaniel Thompson was ordered to attend the Council, for the false and reflecting account he had published concerning this Matter.'

We can now return to the two papers that first reported the news. The account given by the *Impartial Protestant Mercury* is comparatively short, and not very well informed. It begins with a mention of Thynne's marriage to Lady Ogle, 'since retired from him into Holland, and touching whose Estate he had Suits at Law and Equity depending'. The attack on Thynne is said to have been made by 'several Ruffians on Horse-Back . . . one of them discharging (as 'tis believed) a Blunderbuss'. Five bullets were found in Thynne's body, and he died before morning. A 'diligent search' was made for the assailants, and several were discovered and arrested, 'being all Outlandish Men of several Nations'. No names are given. They were examined at Whitehall, where some confessed that what they had done was 'in respect of an Outlandish Count'. This is reporting of a hearsay kind, without focus or certainty. One fact, however, is given due significance: 'His Grace the Duke of Monmouth had just before been in the Coach with [Thynne], but was then newly gone out.' This circumstance was soon to acquire political significance.

Thompson's account of 14 February, which is considerably longer, is a mixture of fact and rumour, and bears all the marks of having been put together (and set up in type) as the news came in over some 24 hours. He knew that there were three assailants, that the attack took place at the Haymarket end of Pall Mall, and that one of the three men fired a musketoon into Thynne's coach. He knew that four or five bullets lodged in Thynne's body, and that for some hours before he died he kept crying, 'Oh, my belly!' This last information may have reached the *Loyal Protestant* after it had been repeated many times, but possibly it came from a witness at the coroner's inquest, which (Thompson's readers were told) took place about noon. Up to this point none of the three men had been named, except for several cryptic allusions to 'the Capt.'. When they were questioned by the King, 'the Capt. was not at all dismay'd, but said boldly that it was agreeable to their custom; that if any Gentleman receive a Challenge, and refuse to answer it, then to Pistol him the next opportunity'. At last, however, in a final paragraph dated 'Newgate, Feb. 13', in which Thompson reports that all three were committed to prison by Sir John Reresby and Sir William Bridgman, he gives their names in full. This information had clearly been obtained by a visit to Newgate.

So far the *Loyal Protestant* deserves credit for a reasonably accurate and detailed account of the facts. Unfortunately it also indulged in some speculation on the possible cause of 'this Horrid Murther':

Some say the Capt. came from beyond Sea on purpose to do this Bloudy Business, he being a Servant to Count Coningsmark, who (it seems) about 7 or 8 weeks ago, as he was travelling betwixt Strasburgh and Metz, was set upon by 5 Ruffians; whether they design'd to Murder, or only to Rifle the Count, is variously conjectured, for he had in his Coach 1500 French Pistoles in Gold: Two of the Ruffians were kill'd in the Attempt, but the rest got away: the Count receiv'd a Pistol-shot in the Back, whereof he is not yet recovered. The said Count after this Assault had some jealousie that Mr. Thyn might be an Abettor thereof (they being both Pretenders to a young Lady of Great Quality), [and] thereupon sent over this Capt. with a Challenge to Mr. Thyn, which he not accepting, the Capt. challenged him himself; which being also refused, these Villains in the Manner Barbarously murder'd the poor Gentleman.

Thynne had friends in high places, and it was no doubt some of them who were responsible for Thompson's appearing before the Privy Council to answer for his 'false and reflecting account', with its suggestion that Thynne had attempted to procure the assassination of Königsmark. (It was true that the Count had been a suitor of Lady Ogle, and Thompson was the first to relate that fact to the murder.) That his appearance before the Council was due to his slur on Thynne was quickly emphasised in the *Impartial Protestant Mercury* of 17 February, which dismissed his story of Königsmark's being attacked by five ruffians as 'Malicious Forgery and Falshood', and repudiated as 'altogether fictitious' the insinuation that Thynne 'had been the Abettor thereof, and that the Barbarous Murder might be committed in Retaliation thereof'. The following day another Whig newspaper, the

True Protestant Mercury, noted with satisfaction that Thompson, 'who so often rejoices at the misfortune of others, was sent for by the Council for misrepresenting the Relation of Mr. Thynne's most horrid Murder, which he slubbers over after his Tory manner . . .' On this occasion Thompson appears to have tried to save his own skin by divulging the source of his information, for on 28 February the *Impartial Protestant Mercury* reported that the Grand Jury had found an indict-ment against 'a certain person upon whom Thompson had shuffled the false Relation he gave of the Count Conningsmark's being wounded near Stratsburgh.' Meanwhile Thompson, who had by this time been questioned and no doubt rebuked by the Privy Council, made a public admission in the *Loyal Protestant* of 23 February that he had been misinformed in his first report, 'which related only as to the discourse that passed about the Town, upon that sad occasion (and not otherwise) as any may, if they please, satisfie themselves: it being far from our thoughts to make any unhandsome or false reflection upon the memory of that Worthy Person, who was so Barbarously and most Villanously murdered.'

The *True Protestant Mercury* of 15 February (one day before the long account given by the *Gazette*) reported the murder in eight lines, and then went on to add 'some particulars not yet published'. These included a circumstantial account of the rounding up of the assailants and of their examination by the Council, bearing a general resemblance to that given next day in the *Gazette*, but with two interesting pieces of addi-tional information. When the Pole testified that his master had ordered him to shoot, he was asked to give the precise words of the command, and replied: 'Be sure you fire into the coach I stop.' The other item not in the *Gazette* refers to 'the servant that was taken in Leicester Fields', who was said to have 'only served the Captain that day, and only watched the coach, and told them when the Duke of Monmouth went forth'. If this is true, it would indicate that Vratz had carefully refrained from taking any action until the Duke 'went forth', i.e. left the coach.

Benskin, whose first chance to tell his readers about the murder came on 16 February, gave only a few lines to the fatal attack, and obviously tried to find something new to say about Thynne. He had heard that orders had been given to embalm the body 'the which it is said will for some reason be kept unburied a considerable time'. (Thynne was buried in Westminster Abbey on the night of 9 March. If any explana-tion is required for the embalming and the long delay, it may be con-nected with 'the sumptuous monument' that Benskin told his readers on 6 March was being prepared for Thynne. This monument is something of a curiosity. Below the draped recumbent figure of Thynne, a delicately cut relief portrays the attack on his coach by three men on horseback.

For the next two weeks the newspapers were to report every turn in the Thynne case with more than usual detail. On 18 February Thompson had news of 'a flying report' that Königsmark had been taken 'in the habit of a page or footman', but added that it had proved false. In his next, however, he was able to confirm that the Count had been captured at Gravesend, and brought to London. Again Thompson gives us one of his eye-witness reports: Königsmark was 'very well Guarded by a File or Two of Musqueteers with light Matches, besides divers other Gentlemen, and was taken to a Celler in Whitehall'. So great was the excitement that the gates of Scotland Yard were shut 'to prevent the great recourse of the Mobile which ran thither upon hearing of the news'. On the same day (21 February) the *Impartial Protestant Mercury* gave about half a column to the Count's arrest and his committal to Newgate; and in its next issue noted that he had complained that Newgate was 'a Degradation to his Honour and Quality', and had petitioned the King to be removed to the Tower. The Council, however, let him know that 'there were very convenient rooms in Newgate', and that it was 'the legal Gaol for such Facts'. On 22 February the *True Protestant Mercury* carried only a short statement about the capture of the Count, referring the reader to 'our yesterday's narrative', where they would find the story given 'at large'. Rather than be a day behind two of his rivals, Curtiss had published the news in a broadside, *A True Account of the Apprehending and Taking of Count Koningsmark*. A note at the end reads: 'This Account is taken from Mr. Gibbins, who first seized the Count.'

So far, in spite of the gaffe that led to his appearing before the Council, Thompson had handled the Thynne story with considerable ability. But now he made another deplorable mistake. In his issue of 23 February he announced that the sessions had opened at Hicks's Hall, and that the first business concerned 'one Mr Cooper, one of the Coroners for the County of Middlesex, who was partly Indicted for refusing to view the murthered Body of Tho. Thyn Esq; and partly for extorting, demanding and receiving, at several times, several Sums of Money above his Fees . . .' There was clearly something wrong here; for the name of the coroner who conducted the inquest on Thynne was not Cooper, but White, and he not only 'viewed' the body, but (as he later testified at the trial of Vratz and his accomplices) was present when the surgeon removed the bullets.[11] There is no need to speculate about how Thompson came to make this serious mistake, since in his next issue (25 February) he saves us the trouble. Without a word of comment or explanation he now tells his readers: 'At Hicks's Hall a Bill was found against Mr. Cooper the Coroner, for not going to view the dead body of a poor man who was fallen into a Ditch, unless he was first paid his Fee; whereupon the poor man lies yet unburied, only cover'd over with a little Dirt, it being a fortnight since he was found.' But Thompson's tacit correction of his erroneous first report had come too late to save him from further trouble. On 28 February the *Impartial Protestant Mercury* told its readers that the Grand Jury had indicted Thompson 'for Inserting in his Intelligence a false Relation about the Coroner's refusing to attend the Corps of Thomas Thynn Esquire'. Thompson got much of his news from Benjamin Claypoole; but Claypoole was apt to be lazy and unreliable* and may have been so on this occasion. Since the murder of Thynne was still the great topic of conversation, a muddled or fuddled newswriter might easily have mixed up one Middlesex coroner with another.

The trial of Vratz, Stern and Boroski, together with Count Königsmark as an accessory, took place on Tuesday 28 February. The first three were found guilty of murder and sentenced to death, but Königsmark was acquitted. The case against Vratz and his two accomplices was straightforward; for although all three pleaded not guilty, they never denied being present at the scene of the murder. That against Count Königsmark was more involved, and took up the greater part of the court's time. In any case the trial was bound to proceed slowly, for with two Swedes, a German and a Pole in the dock, interpreters had to explain to each prisoner what he was being asked, and then to give the court his answer in English; and a further complication ensued when three of the accused asked that half the jury might be foreigners, and the court agreed. According to the official report of the trial it was 'late' when the jury at last retired; and when they returned with their verdict the judges withdrew, and left the Recorder to pronounce the sentence. The meagre reports of the trial that appeared in the newspapers cannot be unconnected with the baffling conditions under which it was carried on: even a trained reporter might have found it difficult to produce an intelligible summary.

If the trial had presented difficulties for the newspapers, the execution of the three condemned prisoners on Friday 10 March was the

* See p. 111.

kind of occasion to which they were well accustomed. At the trial Count Königsmark had been the centre of attention, but now Captain Vratz was the hero of the hour. In his issue of 11 March Thompson gave the best part of a column to describing the final scene. All the newspaper accounts were in agreement about the undaunted behaviour of Captain Vratz. Thompson reported that the other two appeared 'somewhat dejected', but to the *True Protestant Mercury* Boroski 'seemed unconcerned'. Benskin described Vratz as being 'resolute to the last', and 'having his Eye very often upon the Duke of Monmouth, who stood in a Balcony not far distant from the place of Execution'.

Normally, as we have seen, the newspapers were unwilling to print news that was already growing stale; but on this occasion the fullest and best account of the executions was not published till Tuesday 14 March in the *Impartial Protestant Mercury*, which had last appeared on the previous Friday some hours before the three men were executed. Most of the report is given to Vratz. He had dressed himself carefully for the occasion, and appeared in a black suit and embroidered slippers, 'a Scarlet Ribbon in his Crevat, and on his head a new fashioned Embroidered Feather'd Cap'. While he was paying two guineas to his coffin-maker, he asked 'if he had made it *long enough*, for he should *stretch a little*'. With the same unruffled composure he turned aside the exhortations of the divines that he should prepare his mind and repent. To Dr Burnet he replied that 'God had pardoned as great a sin, and he hoped he would do the same to him'; and to another 'who represented to him the danger of his Condition, he was so vain as to say, He was born and Bred a person of good fashion, and had acted as such, and therefore he hoped *God would have respect to him as a Gentleman*'. From the same account we also learn that when Boroski's body was cut down it was taken to Mile End Green, and hanged again in chains, no doubt as a salutary warning to incoming Germans, Poles and Swedes, who, arriving at Harwich, would normally reach London by that route.

It was some time before the last repercussions died away. Several papers recorded the return of Lady Ogle from Holland. According to the *Impartial Protestant Mercury* she had come home to avoid the renewed attentions of Königsmark, since he was unlikely to show his face again in England, being 'suspected to have been the original con-triver of the barbarous murder of Thomas Thynn, Esquire'.[12] If we are to believe the *Loyal Protestant* of 23 March, the rich young widow was under some suspicion herself. A lady, we are told, went shopping in the New Exchange, and spent a great deal of money. But while she was still making her purchases 'some persons (no doubt out of a good Design) gave out that it was the Lady O., whereupon the Mobile cry'd out that she was a Murderer etc. and what not; adding, *Let us pull her in pieces.*' The poor lady was forced to leave her goods behind her ('tho' paid for'), and steal away in a hackney coach. All in all, the murder of Thomas Thynne had been a windfall to the newspapers.

Trials of statesmen or persons of high rank were only the big events of the criminal year. When the courts were sitting, humbler malefactors of many kinds appeared at the Guildhall, Hicks's Hall, Westminster Hall and the Old Bailey, to be tried, and in all too many cases condemned to death. Considering the severity of the punishment meted out to so many of those wretches, their fate was recorded by the newspapers in what must seem to us a perfunctory fashion. Yet the very frequency with which the death sentence was pronounced must have made it seem almost a commonplace legal ritual, and therefore news of no special importance. In any event the newspapers, with only four columns available for all the happenings of two or three days, could not possibly cover in detail all the trials for capital offences. In his *Domestick Intelligence* of 2 March 1680, Harris published a characteristically brief report on the Old Bailey sessions:

Last Thursday the Sessions of Oyer and Terminer for London and Middlesex began in the Old Bailey, and ended upon Monday the first instant; 25 Condemned to dye, 18 Men and 7 Women, some for Felony and Burglary, others for Murther, 4 were burned in the hand, 5 ordered to be whipt, and 2 to be Transported.

No names were given. Harris, however, followed this bare statement with a further paragraph on two of the accused, 'James Baker, alias Haskins, and John Naylor, alias Carpenter', who had been 'indicted as Popish Priests'. He gave 18 lines to the two priests, ending with the news that Naylor was acquitted, and Baker sentenced to be hanged, drawn and quartered. They achieved this prominence in the *Domestick Intelligence* because Harris was the chief baiter of the Catholics among the newspaper men.

There was no consistent pattern in the reporting of run-of-the-mill trials. Proceedings at the Old Bailey were frequently summarised in about half a column, and on other occasions were not reported at all. On the other hand, Benskin gave almost two of his four columns on 20 October 1681 to the Old Bailey, and on 12 December only a little less. In his *Domestick Intelligence* of 24 October 1679 Thompson announced that of the 31 men and women condemned to death at the

Old Bailey, 18 had obtained reprieves, but he then went on to name those who were to be hanged and the crimes they had committed. Harris, who had given almost a column on 21 October to the same sessions, followed this up on 28 October with an account of the executions at Tyburn. After a rapid enumeration of the criminals and their crimes, he gave a considerably fuller report to 'the most deplorable object' of all, a woman found guilty of clipping the coinage, and sentenced to be burnt at the stake. It is only fair to Harris to say that he did not seek to sensationalise the occasion. Instead, he laid emphasis on her repentance, which was so apparent that 'some worthy Divines who were with her in her solitude were very well satisfied with her sober and relenting Carriage'; and when he had to describe the final scene at Smithfield he was content to say only that when a stake had been set up, 'she was bound thereto, and Faggots being kindled she was in a short time burnt to Ashes'.

For a criminal offence or an execution to be given more than perfunctory treatment in a seventeenth-century newspaper, it had to be in some way unusual: horrific, peculiar, or likely for some reason to evoke disapproval of the legal system. On 26 July 1681 the *Loyal Protestant* carried a summary report of the Surrey Assizes at Kingston, in which five were condemned to death, three to be transported, one to be burned in the hand, two to be whipped, and one fined: the charges included murder, manslaughter, clipping, felony and burglary, all of them common crimes. But one much milder offence that was given some prominence must have been reported on account of its oddity, and perhaps because it was calculated to make some readers reflect upon the state of contemporary society:

A Barber was Indicted upon the Statute of 35 Henry VIII for Bowling; that Statute forbidding any Handicrafts-man (under a severe Penalty) to use Bowling, or any other Game. The Bill was found, and the Barber was fined £25.

We shall never know why this case was brought; but the most likely explanation is that the bowling green was being used regularly by a number of local gentlemen, and that they resented the intrusion of a mere barber. One of them may have remembered the ancient statute (many seventeenth-century gentlemen were well versed in the law), or they may have consulted a lawyer who was able to tell them how to get rid of the unwelcome intruder.

In June 1682 the *Loyal Impartial Mercury* reported another peculiar piece of litigation involving the seventh Earl of Pembroke. This dissolute young nobleman had taken part in more than one fatal brawl, and in August 1680, on his way home from a drinking bout at Turnham Green, he had killed a constable called Smith or Smeeth. On 4 June 1681 John Smith's *Currant Intelligence* reported that the Earl had compounded with the dead man's kin and 'thereby hindred the bringing of an appeal', and that several persons of honour had obtained his pardon from the King. On 22 June 1681 he appeared in the court of King's Bench, pleaded the royal pardon, and was discharged. Smith, Thompson and Curtiss all reported this in their issues of 25 June. There the matter might have ended. But a year later, on 20 June 1682, the *Loyal Impartial Mercury* drew attention to an appeal that had been lodged in the King's Bench 'against the Right Honourable the Earl of Pembrook, by Mrs. Haire, Daughter to Mr. Smeeth'. The decision of the court was then summarised:

But it appearing that her Mother was deceased, and that she was Married, . . . the Court were of opinion that no Appeal in that case could be brought by any Female, unless by the Wife of the Deceased, nor by her neither, except during her Widdowhood; so that in fine, it was over-ruled, and the Appeal lay'd aside.

Who wrote the *Loyal Impartial Mercury* is not known, but it may have been Thomas Vile, who had been writing for the *Impartial Protestant Mercury*. Before that paper came to an abrupt end on 30 May he had begun to write a new paper, *The London Mercury*, on 6 April, but he may also have found time to start the *Loyal Impartial Mercury* on 6 June. One reason for connecting him with this second paper is the paragraph on Pembroke and Mrs Haire. When Vile was in trouble in 1679 he had sought the protection of the Earl, but although Pembroke claimed that Vile was his 'servant' the sheriff had refused to release him. The matter was then discussed in the House of Lords on 2 April 1679, but it was decided that Vile could not claim Pembroke's protection since he was a 'pewterer and Master of the Mercury [advertising] Office'. At all events Vile would have had some reason to repay Pembroke's intervention on his behalf, by giving publicity to the Earl's vindication in the court of King's Bench. Whether or not this accounts for the insertion in the *Loyal Impartial Mercury* (and in no other contemporary newspaper except for a brief reference in Vile's *London Mercury* for 23 June) of this minor legal decision, it had undoubted curiosity value.

From time to time, then, we find in the seventeenth-century newspapers, as in those of the present day, items of news that have no special importance, but that are calculated to amuse or surprise the reader. One further such event involving the law may be noted here: on 17 June 1681 the *Impartial Protestant Mercury* drew attention to the case of a man who had been cited by Doctor's Commons for burying his wife in unconsecrated ground. In replying to the charge this person had quoted a rubric in the Book of Common Prayer that 'no person that dies unbaptized is to be buried with the Solemnity of the Church, and so not in holy ground'. Nearly one third of a column was given by the newspaper to this macabre case, making it almost what would now be called a 'feature'.

To qualify for insertion in a newspaper the unusual or peculiar event did not, of course, need to be connected with the law. When Benskin told his readers on 20 August 1681 that a fire in the King's Bench prison had been caused 'by a certain Prisoner setting a Pan of Coals under his Bed, to kill Buggs as he pretended', he must have felt that the queerness of this procedure would attract the attention of his readers. It was probably for the same reason that on 13 October 1696 the *Flying Post* gave its readers the story of an accident with unforeseen consequences:

Yesterday Mr. Stephens the Messenger of the Press, assisted by Mr. Turner a Constable, burnt a Cart-load of debauch'd Pictures and Cards near the Gatehouse, Westminster, and the Flames of Paper flying out of the Chimney, did so much surprise the People that they burnt the last of 'em in an Oven.

If this had happened in the twentieth century it might have appeared in the scenario of a René Clair film.

Although brutality was all too common in Restoration London, few examples of it were recorded at any length by the newswriters. The explanation for this, however, is not to be found in their unwillingness to shock their readers, but once again in their chronic shortage of space. The traditional outlet for horrific news in the seventeenth century was the broadside, in which there was room enough to satisfy the reader with blood-curdling details. So we get *Barbarous and Bloody News from Bishops-gate* (1678), *Strange and Horrible Murther committed in Whitefryers* (1684), *Dreadful Account of the Horrid Murther of Mr. Tilly* (1694). The broadsides that have survived probably represent only a small proportion of those that were printed; but they are sufficiently numerous to suggest that, for all sorts of sensational news, they acted as a supplement to the necessarily briefer reports given in the newspapers. Some, indeed, were brought out by the publisher of a newspaper; for example, the first of the three broadsides cited above was printed for 'L.C.' (Langley Curtiss).

Occasionally, however, a newspaper found the space to report at some length the sort of ghastly murder that would normally have been published in a broadside. In the *True Protestant Mercury* of 18 January 1681, Curtiss gave almost a column to the trial and conviction of a woman for 'murdering a Child of about 12 or 14 years of Age, and in such a barbarous inhumane manner that the like has scarce been heard of'. He called this woman 'one Mrs. Wiggons'; Harris, who gave her two lines on 21 January, referred to her as 'Lattice Wiggin'. Her true name, as later emerged, was Letitia Wigington. The unhappy child, whose name is not given, was the daughter of 'a person that used the seas'. Since his wife was dead, and he was about to go on a long voyage, he had entrusted his daughter as an apprentice to Mrs Wigington, who was a schoolmistress 'teaching several works usually learned by the Female Sex, as Wax-work, Gum-work, etc.'. He had paid her £5 down, with the promise of a further £5 when he should return from his voyage. But the woman treated her apprentice very harshly; and having persuaded herself that the child had stolen two or three shillings from her, she was determined to punish her severely.

She caused a boisterous fellow one Sadler, a Baily's [bailiff's] Follower, that lodged in her House, to make a terrible Whip, which they called a Cat-with-nine tails, . . . and then stript the poor Child barbarously and immodestly stark naked, and the Prisoner held her and ram'd an Apron down her Throat, to prevent her crying out, and the foresaid Baily's Follower most inhumanely whipt her for 4 hours or more, with some short intervals of their Cruelty, and, having made her body raw, and all over bloody, sent for Salt, and salted her Wounds, to render their Tortures more greivous. Of which Savage usage she dyed next morning.

Sadler thereupon 'fled out of a window', but was later arrested and sentenced to death. Mrs Wigington, tried at the Old Bailey on 17 January, was found guilty of murder, but pleaded her belly and was reprieved. On 9 September, however, the postponed sentence was carried out, and she was duly hanged. The only newspaper to report the last scene at Tyburn was Benskin's *Domestick Intelligence* of 12 September 1681. Mrs Wigington was hanged along with another criminal, and both were extremely penitent.

They both bewaild their mispent time, and desired the Standers by that they would put up their Prayers to Almighty God, to Pardon their many great and grievous offences and at last have Mercy on their Souls, and so with Pious Exhortations, desiring all to take warning by their sad Ends, they left this Life.

For Curtiss, who had reported Mrs Wigington's trial so fully, the execution presumably came too late for his issue on the Saturday morning of 10 September; but he had not forgotten her. He published his own account in a broadside, *The Confession and Execution of Leticia Wigington*, which was probably selling on the streets by Saturday afternoon.

Among the minor, but recurring, causes of public disturbance were the activities of the bailiffs who went with a warrant to arrest some debtor, or to attach his goods and chattels. On such occasions the sympathies of the bystanders were usually engaged on the side of the victim, and from time to time the violence that was never far from the surface in Restoration London erupted in attacks on those men in the execution of their office. One such incident gained additional notoriety because of those who were involved in it. On 31 July 1679, Harris reported that 'a Bayliff having arrested a Person belonging to the King's Colledge at Westminster' was so violently beaten by 'some young persons thereabout' that his life was in danger. On 19 August Harris was able to give his readers a fuller account of what had happened, because in the interval the bailiff had died and a coroner's inquest had taken place. The bailiff, legally executing his warrant, had taken possession of a house and goods near Westminster Abbey, 'which it seems was Priviledg'd from Arrests by Ancient Custom'. A woman (Harris was not sure whether she was the woman of the house or a neighbour) went to Westminster Abbey, and informed the young scholars about the 'arrest' of the debtor's property; whereupon the scholars, 'inflamed with this Infringement', fell upon the bailiff with clubs, and beat him so severely that he died shortly afterwards. At the inquest two witnesses swore it was the scholars who had murdered him, and 'the Schoolmaster' (Dr Busby) was ordered to bring the whole school into the Abbey for identification. As a result, four scholars (one the son of a peer) were picked out from the rest and committed to the Gatehouse, although Dr Busby asserted that two of them had been with him at Chiswick on the day of the assault. With them went 'the Woman and some other that Instigated them thereunto'; and Harris concluded by telling his readers that the issue might be expected at the next sessions.

As often as not this would have been the last his readers heard of the case. On 21 October, however, Harris published about 20 lines on the trial. No fewer than eleven of the Westminster boys had been indicted; but 'to Eight of these Ladds, His Majesty upon Consideration of their Youth, and some other Circumstances, was graciously pleased to grant his Pardon before Tryall'. The evidence against the other three 'seemed positive'; but since Busby testified that one of them had been out of town with him that day, and there was no direct proof against the other two, all three were found not guilty. On the other hand, three adults, with no academic or social advantages, were less lucky. One was a man who had been very active in instigating the boys to the attack, another was the woman who had summoned them, and the third was a woman who had invited them to go through her house. All three were found guilty of the bailiff's death.

In September another bailiff lost his life in very similar circumstances. On this occasion a man named Green had gone with three other bailiffs to serve an execution on a widow living in the Savoy, a recognised sanctuary for debtors, and Green was so severely wounded that he died soon afterwards. On 26 September Harris published a short report on the fracas, but Thompson's account of the same date is fuller and more detailed:

The Woman looking out at the Window and crying for help, some Soldiers who were Drinking at an Alehouse hard by run to her assistance, and finding the Door Lockt, broke open part of it, and threw a Hatchet (through the Breach) at the Bailiffs, who stood with their Swords drawn in the house, threatning the first that entred with death. The Constable whom the Bailiffs had brought to their assistance, took up the Hatchet, telling the Soldiers that it should be shown to their Betters. The Soldiers thereupon, with a great deal of Rabble by this time that was gathered about the Door, thrusting altogether, broke in upon them, Wounded three of them, and the other Bailiff made his escape through a back way to Somerset-house. Green 'tis thought is mortally Wounded, and it's reported he has had three or four pieces of his Skull taken out by the Chirurgion; but he is not yet dead, as we hear.

This report has all the marks of someone seriously attempting to collect the facts. In his next issue Thompson was able to state that Green had died, that his death had been attributed by the coroner to wounds received from one of the rioters, and that 'a Victualler living in the Savoy is said to be the person, and is secured'. On 21 October Harris gave an account of the ensuing trial, which took place on the same day as that of the Westminster boys. Four men and the woman were indicted for the murder in the Savoy. The woman, we are told, gave the bailiffs 'good words' and promises to pay, but instead of that she called in the soldiers and 'other rude fellows', telling them that the constable wasn't a constable, and that he and the rest were 'rogues who were got into her house'. She was found guilty and condemned to death, along with two of the rude fellows who had attacked the bailiffs. On 28 October, however, Harris was able to report that all six persons sentenced to death for their share in the two attacks had been reprieved, although on what grounds he did not state.

On 7 July 1681 Benskin published an account in half a column about an over-loyal apprentice who, when some bailiffs were arresting his master, killed one of them with a pistol shot. It is pleasant to record a less lethal encounter that he described a few days earlier. On 27 June he told his readers how a poor woman of Clerkenwell, arriving home to learn that her husband had been arrested by bailiffs, took up a broomstick, caught up with them, and beat them so furiously that they had to let the man go — 'to the no small diversion of the Spectators, so that several Gentlemen that were there present gave the Woman money for her farther encouragement'.

Violence of one sort or another provided the newsmen with much of their copy, and on one occasion Nathaniel Thompson was himself the victim of the attack he related. On 17 November 1681, in the neighbourhood of Temple Bar, he was suddenly assaulted by a young man with a cane. 'God damn you,' the young man was shouting, 'my name is Charlton; and I am resolved to be revenged upon you, you Dog, you have abused my father.' Thompson took refuge in a shop; but while he was brushing his clothes, some of Charlton's companions burst in upon him, crying, 'Come, let us carry him to Smithfield, and burn him with the Pope'. Thompson eventually escaped upstairs. He gave about a quarter of his *Loyal Protestant* of 19 November to reporting this unexpected attack, which happened on the anniversary of Queen Elizabeth's accession, a day regularly celebrated by a Pope-burning procession. Francis Charlton, the father of the angry young man, was a well-to-do Shropshire gentleman, a Whig member of parliament and a close friend of the Earl of Shaftesbury. On 27 October Thompson had published a letter from a correspondent in Shrewsbury, describing how Charlton refused to meet a clergyman who had just preached 'a very Honest, Learned and Loyal Sermon before the Judges and Justices of the Assize'. Being asked why, he had replied that '*the breath of a Clergy-man stunk in his Nostrils*, for which he was reproved by the whole Company, they not believing it agreeable to the *Standard of Loyalty* in a true Salopian, which is not at all agreeable to that of his own'. The physical retribution that followed this open attack on a prominent Whig was perhaps no less than Thompson could expect. The only surprising feature is that it should have taken place at 11 a.m., in broad daylight.

The extent to which crimes of violence were reported varied from one newspaper to another. If a paper put politics first (as some of them did), or if it provided its readers with a regular account of news from abroad, it had necessarily less space to give to crimes being committed daily in the streets and alleys, the dwelling houses and taverns, of Restoration London. Among the newspapers that gave most prominence to criminal activities were those of Harris, Thompson and Benskin. Thompson even appears to have had a Newgate correspondent. In his *Domestick Intelligence* of 24 February 1680 he gives a detailed account of how five men escaped from Newgate prison; and in the *Loyal Protestant* of October 1681 he began publishing short accounts of the latest arrivals in Newgate and the crimes with which they were charged. It seems possible that the correspondent who sent him those reports of persons 'brought into our custody' was a friendly warder who had come to know Thompson when he was himself an inmate.

Public disturbances, offering sudden glimpses of a disordered society, had always considerable news value. From time to time the London apprentices would muster in strength and get out of hand; or the aristocratic 'sons of Belial, flown with insolence and wine', would demonstrate how thin a partition divided them from the humble apprentices. On 5 September 1682 the *Loyal Impartial Mercury* reported that 'on Saturday Last' eight hundred apprentices marched from Lincoln's Inn Fields to Whetstone's Park, a place of ill fame in the parish of St Giles-in-the-Fields, and 'fell upon the Leud Houses there'. They returned on Sunday night to complete their work, 'breaking down all the Doors and Windows, and cutting the Feather-beds and other Goods in pieces'. On 4 October 1681 the *Impartial Protestant Mercury* had an account of a debauch in the church of All Hallows in Mark Lane. An apothecary and a confectioner, who had obtained the keys of the church, collected a crowd of apprentices and rabble and set the bells ringing. Later they sent for wine, got drunk and became sick, and made a horrid noise; and although the churchwarden succeeded in stopping them, the disturbance started up again. For reporting this unusual debauch Richard Janeway the publisher and Thomas Vile the author of the statement were summoned to appear before the Privy Council, but were able to establish the truth of their account.

A potential source of unruly behaviour in the Restoration period was the two London theatres, where gentlemen who had dined too well sought further entertainment, and where the heated atmosphere of a crowded playhouse did nothing to alleviate their intoxication. On 7 February 1680, *Mercurius Anglicus* had related one such riotous evening:

On Munday night last happened a great disorder in the Duke's Play-house, some Gentlemen in their Cupps entring into the Pitt, flinging Links at the Actors, and using several speeches against the Dutchess of P[ortland] and other persons of Honour, which has occasioned a Prohibition from farther Acting, till his Majesties further pleasure.

But the night was still young, and the gentlemen had more to say:

Later they went in a coach to Lincoln's Inn Fields, where one of them ascended the Coach-box . . . and made an Oration to the Multitude against Popery and Arbitrary Government; which though [it] seemingly pleased the Rabble, yet the manner of Delivering it is condemned by the most moderate as tending to Sedition. At the same time a Person of Quality took the opportunity to set on the Tumult to batter the Fortress of a certain Lady of Pleasure, then residing in the Fields.

The paper that brings us closest to London life in the early 1680s is Benskin's *Domestick Intelligence*. Since Benskin does not appear to have had strong political convictions, and since his usual stance was one of uncritical loyalty to church and state, he was all the more free to provide an unbiased chronicle of what was going on in and around London. His news was not of a high intellectual standard, nor was it very well written; it was simply what was new, what had happened. Some of this news was concerned with accidents (e.g. a gentleman killed by a falling tile in Covent Garden); but the greater part of it originated in human depravity, and more especially in temporary loss of self-control. Benskin therefore tended to concentrate on violent or unusual incidents: tavern quarrels, street robberies, duels, rape, the attempted abduction of an heiress, the jilted lover who stabbed his rival, the suicide of another jilted lover, the attempted suicide of a young lady ('as some report, by reason her Father would not consent to her Marrying with his Butler'). There were acts of casual homicide (the gentleman who killed a coachman after an argument about the fare; the lifeguardsman in a tavern who grew tired of waiting for the barmaid to serve him and shot her dead); acts of more deliberate homicide (the new-born infant with its throat cut); scenes of domestic strife (the jealous wife in Whitechapel who stabbed her husband while he was asleep; the maid in Westminster who, being knocked down by a rolling pin that her exasperated mistress had thrown at her, caught up a knife, stabbed the woman in the breast, and fled). If we examine Benskin's first 36 issues between 3 May and 26 September 1681 (from which all the examples cited were taken), we shall find reports of varying length on seven suicides, four attempted suicides, four murders, four fatal quarrels, one rape (followed by the suicide of the victim), one attempted abduction, and several muggings, burglaries, and highway robberies.

From other information supplied by Benskin over the same three months it becomes clear that the summer of 1681 was unusually hot, with a long spell of drought. Here we may have a clue to the sudden and sometimes fatal eruptions of bad temper he records so frequently, and perhaps also to the abnormal number of suicides and suicide attempts. Whether this is so or not, Benskin has reports on no fewer than 12 persons drowned at various dates while bathing or swimming in the Thames. On 20 June, in a paragraph dated from Windsor, he announced: 'his Majesty will not Heal any more of the Evil till after the heat of the Weather is somewhat abated, nor any wise till after Midsummer.' At the best of times, touching for scrofula, however useful for the royal image, can never have been one of the King's favourite rituals; and there is no need to elaborate on the effects of close contact with his subjects in hot weather. Further evidence of what sort of summer England was having comes from two of Benskin's country correspondents, one of whom reported from Westchester on 3 June that a shoal of porpoises had been seen sporting in the sea for three days, while the other wrote three weeks later that several dolphins had been sighted 'Playing and Sporting in the Mouth of the River Severn, which is not a thing usual, neither in that River, nor in the Brittish Seas'. When there came a break in the drought towards the end of June, the same situation developed as Thomas Hardy was to describe in *The Mayor of Caster-bridge*. On 4 July Benskin published a letter from a correspondent in Wallingford:

Several Monopolisers of Corn, who in the dry time made it their business to ride up and down the Countrey to buy all they could light on, in hopes of a dearth, seeing how divine Providence has defeated their covetous expectations, by sending Rain in due season, have refused to stand to their contracts, and several of them have been arrested by such Farmers as they bargained with, and obliged to receive, and pay for as much as they bought.

Not all of the crimes reported by Benskin in those summer months of 1681 were of a violent character. In the popular literature of the Restoration period the so-called 'rogue histories' chronicled the confidence tricks, sharp practices and ingenious thefts of petty criminals; and Benskin entertained his readers by adding some fresh examples to the traditional stock. On 11 July he gave them an account of how a man and a woman had knocked at a door in the Strand, and told the maid that 'they came to speak with a Gentleman that Lodged there, who (as is supposed they knew was gone into the Citty) or at leastwise being given to understand it by the Maid'. They asked if they might stay for a while in case he should return 'in any convenient time', and the maid, who saw no harm in this, showed them into a room. A little later the woman 'slipped up stairs', picked the lock of the gentleman's trunk, and took from it £200 in gold and silver. When she had rejoined her accomplice, they told the maid they would come back again within an hour, and left the house. How Benskin's informant knew that it was the woman, and not the man, who slipped upstairs and picked the lock we are not told. In his next number we read of a gentleman who had a bag of money 'under his arm'. As he was walking near St Giles-in-the-Fields, a gang of three men closed in upon him, one of them snatching his money-bag, while another 'struck up his heels'. On the gentleman's crying 'Stop thief!' several people came running to the scene; whereupon the third member of the gang shouted, 'A Jesuit! A Jesuit!', and while the unfortunate gentlemen was explaining what had happened and denying that he was a Jesuit, the three robbers got away safely. Whether those two incidents really happened within a week in July 1681, or whether they were both old stories revamped to fill a blank space in Benskin's *Domestick Intelligence* it is impossible to say.

What is certain is that crime of one sort or another, then as now, was nearly always the most marketable section of the day's news. There was still room, however, for much other miscellaneous news. Fires, which were numerous, must have been especially welcome to the hard-pressed journalist, for they were easy to locate in the maze of London streets and lanes, a pillar of smoke by day and a glowing blaze by night. Once on the scene, he could question bystanders about the origin of the fire or the number of casualties, and compile his report from the greatest common measure of agreement. On 3 February 1680 Harris devoted one and a half columns to discussing a fire that had started at Mr Delanoy's house in Southwark, near London Bridge. A week later he announced that the attempt to burn the house down 'being further enquired into, it was judged to be a treacherous Contrivance of the Papists to make a second Conflagration of what was left unburnt by their former fire' (of 1666). In due course Mr Delanoy's maid confessed that she had started the fire on promise of a £2,000 reward, and that she had been put up to it by John Satterwait, a soldier in the Catholic Duke of York's guard. She was sentenced to death, and on 26 March Harris gave over a column to her story. When he had a fire to report he almost invariably tried to blame the Roman Catholic community. Thompson, himself a Catholic, did what little he could to allay this sort of hysteria. In his *Loyal Protestant* of 14 May 1681 he reported a fire in a confectioner's shop in Fetter Lane, which began three floors up in a room rented by a French chemist. As a Frenchman this man was naturally arrested upon suspicion of being another fire-raising Catholic, but he turned out to be a Calvinist. Thompson's comment is sardonic: 'We the rather publish this to prevent the belief of the report spread about Town, as if this was not accident, but done designedly, and a Branch of the Popish Plot.'

Although one might expect that a fire would be a simple matter to report, it is surprising how often such reports are vague or confused. But there are exceptions. In the *True Protestant Mercury* of 9 November 1681 there is a serious attempt to report a destructive fire that started between five and six o'clock in the morning 'in a Warehouse belonging to one Mr. Lewis, sailmaker (the same person in whose House the late great Fire in St. Katharine's began, his Servants being beating of Tarr over the fire in a Shed)'. On this second occasion six or seven persons were said to have perished in the flames, and fourteen dwelling-houses to have been destroyed.

Many men made their escape in their Shirts, and Women in their Shifts, with their Children in their Arms; two Men and a Boy were overwhelmed by the fall of a Wall; the Boy crept out much bruised, and was carried off, but the Men were crushed to Death, their Heads only appearing. About 10 o'Clock some were heard to cry amidst the Ruins, which the People are in search for, two Houses being blown up; but the Engines playing continually upon the Timber still on Fire, it is now so much under foot that we hope no further danger will ensue. The extraordinary care and Kindness of Collonel Friend upon the occasion is remarkable, who very freely gave away several Barrels of Beer, and some Brandy, to those who were industrious in endeavouring to quench this dreadful Fire.

This reads like the report of someone who had arrived on the scene while the fire was still blazing, and who was not relying on vague and contradictory tavern gossip, but giving, in part at least, an eyewitness account.

On Tuesday 18 January 1681, the same paper published a long report describing a double drowning accident on a frozen pond near Islington. Two boys venturing on the ice, it gave way under one of them, and a young gentleman went to the help of the boy who had fallen into the water,

endeavouring to throw the corner of his Cloak for him to take hold of, that thereby he might be pull'd out, but his kindness prompting him to venture too far upon the Ice, he became equally endanger'd, and fell in too, only he had the good luck to keep his head above water, and both his arms upon a strong flake of Ice, and in that condition continued a considerable time, none daring to hazard themselves to save him, till at last they got a Ladder from a house a field or two off, and laid it upon the Ice, and so with much difficulty they got him out . . .

In the mean time the first boy's father, who was in a field near by, heard the noise coming from the pond, and learning what had happened, went to the help of his son. But he too fell in, and father and son were both drowned. In a seventeenth-century report it is not often that we are told as exactly as this what actually happened. The accident occurred on a Sunday. Islington was probably beyond the area of 'quick negotiation' for which the penny post promised an hourly delivery of letters, but it would have been well within the range for which the post could guarantee five deliveries a day. There would therefore have been ample time for the report to be written, taken to the receiving station, carried from there to the sorting office, and delivered to Mr Langley Curtiss for publication on the following Tuesday.

It remains to consider certain other categories of news that gradually became established in the seventeenth-century newspapers. High on the list of topics that provided the papers with a constant trickle of news were appointments, resignations and dismissals among those holding important offices of state; for readers were clearly interested in 'who loses, and who wins, who's in, who's out'. All too often such reports proved to be false; no more than the product of idle rumour, or the result of ill-informed speculation. On 30 July 1681 Thompson's *Loyal Protestant* carried two such canards:

'Tis said the Lord Conway hath desired leave to go into Ireland to settle his Estate in that Kingdom; and 'tis thought Sir William Coventry will supply his place of Secretary of State; and it is discoursed that his Grace the Duke of Ormond will in a short time be re-called.

We hear that an Order of Council passed last Council day, prohibiting any payments to be made to the Lord Ranelagh or his Deputy as Treasurer of Ireland.

All the statements in those two short paragraphs were untrue. Lord Conway was not being replaced at this time as Secretary of State, nor was the Duke of Ormonde being recalled from Ireland, where he was Lord Lieutenant. Sir William Coventry had finally retired from public life in 1679, and had no intention of returning to it. Thompson was not in the habit of correcting his mistakes unless compelled to do so, and the humble apology to Lord Conway inserted in his issue of 2 August was almost certainly extorted from him. So far as Lord Ranelagh was concerned, a similar apology did not appear until Thompson's issue of 9 August, and the fact that he took so long to offer

80

it seems to indicate that he would willingly have left ill alone if he had not been threatened, either by the Council, or by Lord Ranelagh, or by someone acting on his behalf. On this occasion, however, Thompson appears to have been guilty of little more than an indiscretion: an order was in fact made in Council in August prohibiting further payments to Ranelagh on account of his arbitrary taxation of the Irish people.

As the years passed, the desire to know what was happening in 'the establishment' grew steadily. In the newspapers of 1695–1700, and still more in those of the next century, more and more appointments and promotions – political, ecclesiastical, legal, naval, military and civil, whether important or trivial – were briefly chronicled or anticipated, as were the conferments on fortunate placemen of lucrative sinecures.

From this it was an inevitable step to entertaining readers with intimate details about persons of quality; who had been married or was about to be married, who had got a son or a daughter, and who had died; what peer was travelling abroad, or visiting Bath or Tunbridge Wells in the summer, which peer had fought a duel with which gentleman, who had dined with the Lord Mayor or the sheriffs, or at one of the Inns of Court. To satisfy the thirst for personal gossip the *Loyal Protestant* announced on 29 December 1681 that the benchers of the Middle Temple had invited the Dukes of Albemarle and Grafton, Lords Halifax and Feversham, and 'Chiffinch Esq.' to dine with them on a suitable date. (The last mentioned guest was William Chiffinch, Keeper of the Closet to Charles II and frequently employed by the King to further his amours, and in other backstairs business.) Two days later the same paper stated that the Duke of Albemarle and the other guests were expected to dine at the Middle Temple 'tomorrow', and on 3 January it reported that 'most of the Lords mentioned in our last were pleased to honour the Gentlemen of the Inner-Temple [*sic*] with their Company to Dinner on Saturday'. This was the festive season; and on 5 January the *Loyal Protestant* was able to tell its readers that the Duke of Grafton (recently appointed Colonel of the Foot-Guards) had given a feast at Whitehall to his senior officers, and that those below the rank of captain had been simultaneously entertained 'at Locket's, the great Ordinary'. The social column was well on its way to being born.

The provision of such amiable gossip would seem to indicate that some at least of the readers of a seventeenth-century newspaper were persons of lesiure. Yet there must be some significance in the fact that at a time when the London theatre was flourishing not a single theatrical advertisement appeared in the *Loyal Protestant*, nor in any of its contemporaries. Advertisements are not usually placed where they are unlikely to be read, and it is improbable that Lord Rochester's regular reading included Thompson's *Loyal Protestant* or Harris's *Domestick Intelligence*. When theatrical advertisements do begin to appear regularly in the early eighteenth-century newspapers, the mainly upper-class audience that patronised Restoration drama was giving way to one that contained a considerable element of middle-class playgoers. At all events there is a good deal of evidence to suggest that the main body of newspaper readers in the late seventeenth century belonged to the trading and commercial class: merchants, shopkeepers, financiers, and goldsmiths concerned in the business of banking. Their interests were served not only by the shipping news that was a regular feature, but by the small, yet steadily increasing, section devoted to such matters as the movements of stocks and shares, the assize of bread (the weight and price at which different sizes of the common loaf were sold), the market price of corn, wheat, barley, oats, hay, and, more especially after the foundation of the Bank of England in 1694, the bank rate.

As far back as 1667 a dialogue paper called *The City and Country Mercury* had been published twice weekly 'for the help of Trade and Dealing both in Country and City'. 'Countryman' asks the questions, and 'Citizen' supplies the answers.

Countryman. But pray, how goes the Grocer's Trade on, for next to the Back, we are concern'd for the Belly?
Citizen. It is a hard matter to deal with a Grocer, but I will the best I can inform you. Coarse Barbado's Sugars, formerly sold for thirty five shillings, are now worth forty five shillings the Hundred. Malaga Raisons rarely to be had . . . Currans, formerly sold at about three pound, are now £3 10s. Brandy at about forty five pound the Tun . . .
Countryman. But I pray, how goes fish?
Citizen. Fish of all sorts are very dear . . .

This is domestic economy without tears, set forth in a lively and colloquial style for the unlearned. In 1679 an exchange broker called James Whiston was bringing out a more sophisticated weekly, *The Merchant's Remembrancer*, which survived until 1702 with some changes of title. This gave 'the most excellent Prizes [i.e. prices] of most sorts of Merchandizes, with an Account whether they are a Rising, Highest, Lowest, Standing or Falling . . .'. Such financial information, together with stockmarket prices and exchange rates, was at first rather scrappy in the general newspapers of 1679–82, but increased in those of the 1690s, and still more in those of the early eighteenth century. In 1713 the *British Mercury* was giving 'the Course of Exchange' in Amsterdam, Paris, Genoa, etc., and in 1716 we find the recently-founded *Evening General Post* courting readers by promising 'a more exact Account of the chief publick Stocks than has yet appeared in Print'.

Another regular feature in many of the newspapers was an abstract from the Weekly Bills of Mortality published by the Company of Parish Clerks for London and Westminster. These bills gave the number of persons dying each week in each parish, listing them under the various diseases or accidents by which they met their deaths. When the newspapers began to use this information their reports were usually confined to the total number of deaths. From December 1679 both Harris and Thompson were publishing the mortality figures. Thompson, who always liked to give an impressive reason for doing what he meant to do in any case, explained to his readers on 19 December that 'for the satisfaction of divers in the Countrey, and others to whom the weekly Bills of Mortality do not come', he intended to publish the total number of deaths 'to prevent false reports, which often happen at a distance, of this City's being infected with extraordinary Sickness'. On 5 December, Harris had a paragraph about 'the sad Effects of the late Foggy and Bad Weather, and the general Coughs and Colds that followed thereupon'; but he added that the deaths recorded in the Bills of Mortality had now decreased by 307 persons. References to the weather are rare in seventeenth-century newspapers, and the forecasting of weather was in its infancy; but a periodical called *The Monthly Weather-Paper* ran for a short time in 1711.

Sports news, which the newspaper reader today has come to expect, was hardly reported at all in the papers of the Restoration period. Apart from horse-racing, organised sport scarcely existed. There are fairly frequent references to racing at Newmarket and Windsor, and scattered references to race-meetings at such places as Winchester and Burford; but the main reason for reporting those meetings was that they took place in the presence of the King, or the Duke of York, or the Duke of Monmouth. For the entertainment of the King and his guests, wrestling and cudgel-playing occasionally took place at Windsor; and Benskin reported from Newmarket on 12 September 1681 that 'His Majesty was divertized with a Match of Cock-fighting', and had betted on it. Betting on horse-races was already well established, and gentlemen often rode their own horses. On 3 September 1681 the *Loyal Protestant* reported that the King had gone to Bansted Downs 'to divert himself with hawking', and returned (to Whitehall) the same evening 'very well pleased with his Sport'. The kinds of sport that the ordinary Londoner could see for himself were cock-fighting, bull and bear baiting, prize-fighting and the occasional foot-race; but those were very seldom reported in the newspapers. Football at this time was a free-for-all played in the streets by anyone who cared to join in the fun. Tennis was an indoor game played privately by gentlemen for their own amusement.

Among the advertisements most frequently appearing in Restoration newspapers are those of books. Yet any kind of literary discussion of new books, let alone reviewing, is almost non-existent, and with the restricted space then available, is hardly to be expected. There are, however, a few exceptions. In his *Domestick Intelligence* of 19 September 1679 Thompson gives a fairly extended account of work then in progress by Fellows of the Royal Society, and we learn that Robert Hooke 'goes on with his Philosophical Transactions' and that the Honourable Robert Boyle 'hath a profound Philosophical Treatise now in the Press at Oxford'. We are also told about what Nehemiah Grew and Robert Plot are doing: 'Learned and accurate Dr. Grew hath published six Philosophical Transactions full of considerable Curiosities and Rarities of Nature. . . . And worthy Dr. Plot is said to be now surveying Staffordshire for a Natural History, as he hath done Incomparably well for Oxfordshire, in a Fair and full Folio.' Thompson may have received those notes from a Fellow of the Royal Society; but whether this is so or not, they must be the first publicity that the Society ever received from a newspaper. Not long afterwards, on 31 October, Thompson published, under the heading of 'Domestic Improvements', a short account of John Evelyn's *Sylva* and *Pomona*, together with notes on a few other learned books. This unfamiliar material probably reached him from the same correspondent. Not only is the Evelyn notice an embryonic book review, but the fact that Thompson gave this section a heading was quite unusual, perhaps unprecedented. Headings and sub-headings crept very gradually into the editing of English newspapers, probably because the various items making up any issue were normally no more than a few lines in length, and because, in the two-page papers especially, space was precious.

It was lack of space again that prevented the appearance of 'Letters to the Editor' in the seventeenth-century papers. That such letters occasionally reached the newspapers may be seen from one signed H.T. that appeared in the *Impartial Protestant Mercury* on 17 June 1681. In the previous issue this paper had exposed the methods being used to secure signatures for a loyal address by the London apprentices, and H.T. had written a vituperative letter about the two authors of the paper, 'that Damn'd Rogue Vile' and 'that Damn'd Rogue Care'. As for the publisher, Richard Janeway, who was by profession a book-binder, he was advised: 'Thou hadst better follow thy Binding, and Bind thy self to better Manners than publish that Lying Tool for a Company of Damn'd Factious Dogs'. The *Impartial Protestant Mercury* explained that it was publishing this letter to show what kind of people were promoting the apprentices' address. It was not until the appearance of the six-page weeklies early in the next century, when the problem was not how to find room for letters but how to fill the ample space in each issue, that letters to a newspaper began to proliferate; but even then some (perhaps the majority) of them were demonstrably written by someone on the paper.

In conclusion, something must be said about the obituary notices that were published from time to time in the seventeenth-century newspapers, for they throw some light on the conditions under which the contemporary journalist had to work. Deaths of important people were for the most part reported very briefly; anything approaching a full obituary was quite unusual. We are given, more or less accurately, the bare facts of a death, but further details or comment are rarely to be found. The most distinguished Englishman to die between 1679 and 1682 was Thomas Hobbes, who expired peacefully on 4 December 1679 at Hardwick Hall, a seat of his old pupil and friend, the third Earl of Devonshire. He was in his ninety-second year. Three contemporary newspapers recorded the event. In Thompson's *Domestick Intelligence* of 12 December Hobbes gets a single sentence:

Mr. Hobbs of Malmesbury, sufficiently known by his Works, died last week at the Earl of Devonshire's in Derby-house, in the 92 year of his age.

Even in this brief announcement Thompson is wrong in one of his facts. There were at this time two stately buildings in London called Derby House, both built for an Earl of Derby, but neither used by the Earl of Devonshire. Thompson's newswriter, hearing or reading that Hobbes had died in the Earl of Devonshire's house in Derbyshire, had managed to muddle it up with Derby House in London.

On the same day Harris published his account of the philosopher's death:

Last week Mr. Thomas Hobbs of Malmesbury died at the House of the Earl of Devonshire in that County. It is reported that he died much of the same Humour wherein he Lived, some of his Last words being to this Purpose, *That he had long waited for the Carrier Death,* and that he had been *four score and Twelve years in looking for a hole to go out of the world, which he had now found;* he being Ninety-two years of Age.

Harris, it will be noted, located Hardwick Hall in Devonshire. (It would be niggling to point out that Hobbes was 91 when he died, not 92.) Harris almost certainly obtained the interesting information in the second sentence from a news-letter dated 11 December, of which a copy is preserved among the State Papers.[13]

The following day *Mercurius Anglicus* gave Hobbes an elegiac tribute so well written that it might almost have come from the pen of John Dryden, one of his great admirers:

The last week died that great and learned Man, Mr. Thomas Hobbes, late of Malmesbury, Fourscore years of age: A Person who was thought to have little Religion, though a great portion of Reason. However, they that were acquainted with him knew him to be a person of a most fair Morality, and punctually just in his Dealings, which how far they may carry a Man, let the Casuists determine. Among his other Writings, his *Leviathan* has made no small noise in the World, which was the reason that two Attempts were made to put a Hook in his Nostrils, but to little purpose. Let him go with this Elogy, That he was a Man much blam'd, but little understood.[14]

If this is short on facts, and sadly wrong about the philosopher's age, it is admirably civilised and quite untypical, in its literary distinction, of the homely style of the seventeenth-century newspapers in general.

Among the other well-known people who died about this time, 'the Old and Famous Mr. William Lilly, Student in Astrology', got only a brief mention in the *Impartial Protestant Mercury*: he receives eight columns from the *Dictionary of National Biography*. The King's printer, Thomas Newcombe, fared rather better in the *Loyal Protestant*, which gave him a handsome 16 lines. In August 1680, when the unlicensed papers had been stopped from publication, the Earl of Ossory, the gallant son of the Duke of Ormonde, was accorded a tribute of 12 lines by the *London Gazette*. When Israel Tonge, the fabricator with Titus Oates of the Popish Plot, died in December 1680, Langly Curtiss gave him, for purely party reasons, 24 lines in the first number of his *True Protestant Mercury*. One must allow, as always, for the shortage of space available, but space was often allotted more generously to trivialities. No marked change took place in the early eighteenth-century papers. Although the Whig *Flying Post* gave the Whig Marquis of Wharton 37 lines in April 1715, and he got 22 lines of a different character from the Tory *Post-Boy*, he had only four lines from the *Post Man*. In April 1716 a greater Whig statesman, Lord Somers, was given a reasonably well-informed obituary in the *Weekly General Post*, which had more space to fill than the thrice-weekly papers, but he had only four and a half lines from the *Weekly Packet*. Again party considerations were uppermost.

The death of a king or a queen might be expected to call for an extended obituary, but this was not always so. When William III died in March 1702, the Whig *Flying Post* gave the whole of its front page to an account of his last illness and death, followed by a biographical tribute; but most of the press reported his death more briefly. On 10 June 1714 the same paper had a well-written obituary of the Electress of Hanover in over fifty lines. But when Queen Anne died on the morning of Sunday 1 August 1714, the press was unprepared for the news. The Queen had been ill, but she had been ill before, and on 31 July the *Evening Post* had been able to announce in a postscript that though she had suffered another fit she had recovered from it, and at three o'clock was much better. When the news of her death broke, the papers due to appear on Monday or Tuesday had already begun to set their first page. Accordingly the *Post-Boy* of 3 August opened with news items from Paris, the Hague, Dublin, Yarmouth and Deal, and only then, at the bottom of the first column, went on to a brief notice of the Queen's illness and death. No attempt was made by the use of a larger or heavier type to distinguish this important announcement from the Deal shipping news immediately above. The *Evening Post* of the same date began with the foreign mails, and then dealt with the Queen's last illness and death in 12 lines, followed by a biography of 15 lines. The six-page *British Mercury*, which was running a serial story called 'The Rover' began with that, went on to the foreign news on pages 4–5, and only then gave the news in three and a half lines that Queen Anne was dead, continuing with the proclamation of George I, a biography in 10 lines of the new King (giving the bare facts about his birth, marriage and children), and concluding with the names of the Lords Regent. The *London Gazette* dealt with the Queen's death in 12 lines.[15] All eyes were on the future. One can understand how the response 'Queen Anne is dead' became an equivalent for 'There *is* no news'.

So far as an adequate obituary is concerned Queen Anne fared no worse than most of her subjects. Many distinguished men died in the reigns of William III, Anne, George I and George II, but their deaths were rarely recorded in more than a single sentence, and even so the Christian name of the deceased is often a blank (e.g. '— Shute, Esq.'). The *Flying Post* was doing something new in December 1717 when it gave a list of the remarkable persons who had died in that year, and repeated this feature for several years ensuing. The fact that it was able to do this suggests the existence of some primitive practice of filing by the *Flying Post*, but there appear to have been no biographical files of the living kept in readiness for immediate use when they died. How hard put to it the newswriters were to produce an adequate obituary may been seen from a flagrant instance of theft by the *Flying Post*. On 2 February 1714 John Sharp, Archbishop of York, died at Bath, and four days later was accorded a well-informed obituary in the Tory *Post-Boy*. On 14 December 1715 Thomas Tenison, Archbishop of Canterbury, died in Lambeth Palace, and three days later was given an obituary in the Whig *Flying Post*. On 27 December the *Post-Boy* reprinted in parallel columns and without comment the obituary it had given Sharp in 1714 and that now given to Tenison in the *Flying Post*. Allowing for a few necessary alterations the two obituaries were identical. The two men had almost nothing in common: Sharp was politically a Tory, and Tenison was a Whig who had been active in securing the Hanoverian succession, and who would therefore be a proper person for a laudatory tribute in the *Flying Post*. One can only surmise that the printer, instructed to insert an obituary of Tenison, stumbled upon the old obituary of Sharp, and reproduced it with a few minimal changes. After all, they were both archbishops.

Some explanation is required, however, for the scanty and unsatisfactory obituaries found in those early newspapers. Allowance must be made for the lack of space available in two-page papers, but when the six-page weeklies began to appear there was no noticeable increase in the length or accuracy of obituary notices. The explanation is to be found in the absence of nearly all the facilities easily available to a modern newspaper. In particular there was an almost complete want of reference books to provide the facts that a journalist might require in a hurry. It is true that some progress had been made in supplying the newswriter with the tools he required to do his work properly: in the late seventeenth century Laurence Echard published a useful work that ran through many editions, *The Gazetteer's or Newsman's Interpreter*, which provided a geographical index to all the considerable cities, etc. in Europe, and must have assisted the newsman commenting on foreign affairs, more especially battles, sieges, and the movements of armies. In 1669 Edward Chamberlayne had begun to publish his *Angliae Notitia: Or the Present State of England*, and his son had continued it as *Magnae Britanniae Notitia*, with the addition of Scotland. By the 1720s this had become a bulky work of reference, including complete lists of peers and baronets, members of parliament, all those holding government offices or employed in the King's household, the chief army and navy officers, bishops and deans, Fellows of the Royal Society, and many other office holders down to the various placemen in the excise and elsewhere. Unfortunately the only biographical information included was the salary attached to each office, where it was thought appropriate to give such information. For biography, there was no contemporary *Who's Who*: such biographical compilations as existed dealt with the dead rather than the living. In 1720, however, Giles Jacob published *The Poetical Register*, dealing with the lives of the English dramatic poets, and followed it with *An Historical Account of the Lives and Writings of the most Eminent English Poets* (second edition 1733), both of which included a considerable number of those still living. This was the sort of publication that would have been useful to a newswriter when a contemporary poet or dramatist died; but there were no corresponding books for living statesmen, soldiers or sailors, ecclesiastics or lawyers.

When we do come upon an obituary of some length in a newspaper of the period, it was almost certainly written from personal knowledge by some friend of the deceased. In Mawson's *Weekly Journal* of 1 January 1715 there is a long obituary of Dr Basil Kennett, younger brother of the more famous Bishop White Kennett, but not himself especially distinguished. It is tempting to suppose that this was written by Mawson himself, and that the notice was a tribute to their friendship. Similarly, when the *Flying Post* published on 24 May 1716 a long obituary notice on the Reverend Robert Fleming, Minister of the Scots congregation at Founders Hall in Lothbury, the most likely person to have written it, less than three days after his death, was his fellow Scot, George Ridpath, 'author' of the *Flying Post*. When the most famous journalist of the whole period died in 1731, he had apparently no such friend to commemorate his remarkable career. *The Universal Spectator* of 1 May (edited by his son-in-law) had nothing to say but this: 'A few days ago died Daniel Defoe, Sen., a person well known for his numerous writings.' According to the standards of the day a routine job had been performed satisfactorily.

If obituaries were difficult to compile, funerals could be reported at length, for (like executions) they had only to be described by an eyewitness. In this way the *Loyal Protestant* of 27 August 1681 gave a detailed account of the funeral of an ex-Lord Mayor, Sir Joseph Sheldon, particularising the 18 categories of mourners, from 54 'ancient poor men in Mourning Gowns' to the Bishop of London and Sir Leoline Jenkins, the principal Secretary of State. Three days later

Smith's *Currant Intelligence* gave the whole of its front page to a description of the funeral of the Duke of Rothes in Edinburgh, sumptuous even for those days of ostentatious mourning. But the funeral of Queen Anne made as little impact on the newspapers as her death. The *Flying Post* reported with dismissive brevity that it had taken place 'with the usual Ceremony' in Westminster Abbey. Those papers that had least reason to welcome the Hanoverian succession were rather more generous in their coverage: Berrington's *Evening Post* gave it a 13-line notice in small type on 26 August, but was able to find room for a full account in 40 lines two days later.

Looking back in 1720 at the years of his adolescence, Defoe recalled the old primitive days when the *Gazette* was the only newspaper available:

Such was the Innocence and Simplicity of former Times, that even in this great *Metropolis* People contented themselves with the *sober Intelligence* of the *London Gazette*, which was left at every honest Shopkeeper's for the Perusal of the Family, and the Account of it kept in Chalk behind the Door, as regularly as the Milk-Score.[16]

How different it all is now, was the inference. Yet if the two-page, two-column, unlicensed papers that began to appear in 1679 were able to give their readers much more of the sort of news that interested them than the *Gazette* could provide, they must still seem, by modern standards, deplorably meagre. It is unlikely that they seemed so to the seventeenth-century reader looking forward twice a week to buying the paper of his choice, whether it was the *Domestick Intelligence* of Harris, Thompson or Benskin, the *True Protestant Mercury* of Langley Curtiss or John Smith's *Currant Intelligence*. What we have come to expect we learn to want; and what the seventeenth-century reader got from his newspaper was the bare news, with little or no comment. When news was presented in this way and taken neat by the reader, there was room for a surprising variety of news items. If this meant passing abruptly from one short piece of news to another, that was no disadvantage; for, as an eighteenth-century essayist remarked, 'It has been often observ'd, that a News-Paper is commonly read with more Delight and Attention than a regular Narrative.'[17]

CHAPTER 3

Country news

If what was happening in the capital city and its suburbs was the most important source of home news for a London newspaper, news items from other parts of England, and from Scotland and Ireland, were also provided in varying measure. When Harris and Thompson were both producing a *Domestick Intelligence* in 1679, and when Benskin started his *Domestick Intelligence* in 1681, all three papers carried in their sub-title the words, 'News both from City and Country'. The word 'City' referred to London, and the word 'Country' to the rest of the United Kingdom and Ireland. Country news came in from villages, from provincial towns and cities, such as Leicester or Tewkesbury, York or Bristol, but also from the two capital cities of Edinburgh and Dublin. It therefore varied considerably in kind and importance; but it has seemed best to deal with it in this chapter under the heading then accepted of 'Country News'.

News from the country districts would normally reach a London newspaper by way of the letter post. The incoming mail arrived at the London letter office three days a week, on Monday, Wednesday and Friday, with as much regularity as the weather, the state of the roads and unforeseen accidents permitted. The only exceptions were the Dover Road, and (from the late 1670s) the Colchester Road, both of which had a daily service, Sundays excepted. A regulation dated 1654 required the post-boys to cover seven miles an hour from April to September, and five miles an hour for the rest of the year.[1] By the 1680s there may have been some small improvement in the roads, if not in the weather. Yet, writing in 1681, Thomas Delaune claimed no more than that 'every 24 hours the Post goes 120 Miles'.[2] If he had in mind a second post-boy ready to set off as soon as the first arrived, the two between them were averaging only five miles an hour. (To achieve 120 miles at seven miles an hour a single post-boy would have had to be on the road for over 17 hours.) Thomas Gardiner, a seventeenth-century Controller of the Inland Office, reckoned in 1682 that a letter posted in London would reach Plymouth (about 210 miles away) in three days, and one for Edinburgh (370 miles), within five days. To be ready to deal with the incoming mail all the clerks had to be on duty at the London office at 4 a.m. from April to September, and at 5 a.m. from October to March. As often as not letters were not pre-paid, but were accounted for by the recipient. The rates for inland mail were 2*d.* for the first 80 miles, 3*d.* for any distance in England and Wales beyond that, 4*d.* for Scotland, and 6*d.* for Ireland.[3] Allowing for the rate of wages and incomes in the seventeenth century, those postal charges were sufficiently high to make frequent and nation-wide correspondence impracticable for newspapers with the small circulation of those days.

For Henry Muddiman, with his grant of free postage, this consideration did not apply. His news of 'the affairs now in agitation in England, Scotland and Ireland' was extensive, reliable, and reasonably varied. As a semi-official newswriter, he had inevitably to publish a number of royal proclamations and other government and ecclesiastical ordinances, but he still had plenty of room in his sixteen-page news-books for ordinary domestic news, and he had at his disposal a news service not to be equalled for many decades. Those two news-books were in effect one; for each gave the news of a whole week from Monday to Monday or from Thursday to Thursday, so that *Mercurius Publicus*, published on Thursday, repeated verbatim the latest news that had appeared in the *Kingdomes Intelligencer* of the previous Monday, and vice versa.

That Muddiman usually printed his correspondents' letters without much alteration becomes clear from the wording of the reports. From Gloucester, for example, he has a news item, dated 25 August 1662, which begins: 'I purposely deferred my writing till the Subscription of the Ministers of this Diocese was past, and now I can assure you that there is scarce a man that hath not subscribed, the whole Ministry as one chearfully Conforming to the Act of Parliament.'[4] The Act of Uniformity, to which all ministers had to subscribe on pain of being deprived of their benefices, had received the royal assent on 19 May 1662, but the last day for conforming had been fixed for St Bartholomew's Day, Sunday 24 August. For some weeks after the Act had come into force, Muddiman kept publishing reports from his correspondents about the loyal way in which the ministers were conforming; but since it has been estimated that about one fifth of them refused to subscribe and were deprived, it looks as if he must have been publishing only those reports that gave the most favourable figures. That he had been prodding some of his correspondents to send him news of how the new Act was working is indicated by a report dated from Lincoln, which he published on 11 September, and which begins,

'In order to your desires, I thought it necessary to trouble you with a short account of affairs in these parts . . .'[5]

Since the re-establishment of the Church of England was very much a key issue in the early years of the Restoration, Muddiman gave a good deal of his space to ecclesiastical affairs: reports from Dover, Cockermouth, and Bothel in Cumberland about the baptism into the Church of unchristened children (at Dover, 'some four, some five, some eight years of age'); the appointment of bishops, and their visitations; repairs at Canterbury Cathedral 'at the great cost of the Dean and prebendaries', and to Durham Castle and Cathedral by the Bishop. There were reports, too, of action taken against nonconformists, of ministers not using the Book of Common Prayer, and of itinerant ejected ministers teaching sedition and rebellion in private houses. His Hereford correspondent, who had nothing better to write about in February than 'a violent storme of raine mixt with Lightning', was able in April to send Muddiman a sensational story about a certain Lieutenant Thomas, said to be 'a most violent Quaker' and formerly active in the rebellion against Charles I. This man went to an apothecary and bought two pennyworth of arsenic, which he said he needed for poisoning rats; but instead of giving it to the rats he took it himself, and died 'with hideous ravings'. At the end of May the same correspondent was fortunate enough to have a second poisoning case to report, and was clearly determined that it should lose nothing in the telling. 'It may seem strange,' he wrote,

that this County in so few weeks should afford two such notorious examples of the Quakers' most desperate practices. Lieut. Thomas (as we formerly acquainted you) as falsely imagining himself above the injury of Poyson as the wholesom Discipline of the Church, tooke himself a Preparatory for greater heat and scorchings. What he so wickedly acted on himself another of that gang of Pretenders, one Elizabeth Powle, Widow, at Lower-Hide, in the Parish of Leominster,attempted on her Brother-in-law Hugh Powle, and his eldest son . . .

She prepared some milk 'in which she had put a great quantity of Ratsbane', and when her victims had drunk most of it and were feeling the effects, she herself 'to cover her horrid fact, took a little of what remained in the bottom, and feigned herself to be in the same condition'. The brother-in-law survived, but the boy died; and Elizabeth Powle, who confessed after persistent questioning what she had done, was sent to prison to await her trial.[6]

Most of Muddiman's news is less sensational than this, dealing rather with public events in a reassuring manner. Inevitably his correspondents varied in quality, and often they had nothing much to report. In April his Edinburgh correspondent was content to write: 'The news here is the same that I sent you last, that is, all things are very peaceable.' Faced with the same pressure to make bricks without straw, the Cirencester correspondent did rather better:

Here is no news but is equally in all parts of this Kingdome. I mean such a Trade of Horse-stealing, that the Owners are forced to hire Men to watch their Horses. . . .

Important news was usually given in a consciously heightened style, but even so, humanity kept breaking in. Towards the end of May 1662 word arrived from Portsmouth that Charles II's bride, Catherine of Braganza, had come ashore safely from Lisbon. A little earlier in the same month Muddiman's Southampton correspondent had reported that 'some few dayes since a Sturgeon came into this River, which was presented to our Mayor'; that 'this day [8 May] another Sturgeon is come in', and that this second 'royal fish' was sent by the Mayor to Portsmouth in expectation of the future Queen's happy arrival. The story ends with a pleasant coda: 'The good people of this place observe that these two Sturgeons (male and female) came into this River in purpose to meet the King and Queen's Majesty.'[7]

It is clear that Muddiman was able to draw upon a very considerable list of country correspondents, some of whom were probably the local postmasters. From Edinburgh and Dublin he received reports almost every week. In England, if we take the four months of July to October 1662, we find his correspondents sending in one or more reports from the following places: Bishop Auckland, Bedford (3), Bristol (3), Bury St Edmunds, Chester (4), Chippenham, Chipping Ongar (Essex), Colchester, Coventry, Dorchester, Durham (3), Exeter, Gloucester, Henley upon Thames, the Isle of Wight (3), Leicester, Lichfield, Lincoln, Northampton, Norwich (2), Oxford, Plymouth, Pontefract, Southampton, Taunton, Totnes (2) and Yarmouth. This list, of course, does not tell us how many reports he may have received, but only those he used. The other towns from which he received news in 1662 include Canterbury, Cirencester, Dover, Hereford, Ludlow and Tiverton. No other newswriter in the seventeenth century came anywhere near Muddiman's full and efficient coverage of provincial news, or presented it with such a happy blend of the formal and informal. Because many of his correspondents knew him personally, they wrote to him with an easy and familiar freedom. It was a sad day for English journalism when the monopoly of printed news was transferred to Roger L'Estrange, and Muddiman's two news-books came to an end.

When L'Estrange began to publish his *Intelligencer* and *Newes* in the autumn of 1663, he was without previous experience of conducting a news-book, and he appears to have plunged into the business without any clear idea of the difficulties involved. Taking his readers into his confidence in the first number of the *Intelligencer*, he told them that, so far as he could see, 'once a week may do the business . . . Yet if I still find when my hand is in, and after the planting and securing of my correspondence, that the matter will fairly furnish more without either uncertainty, repetition or impertinence, I shall keep myself free to double at pleasure'. L'Estrange's statement has the unenthusiastic and off-hand tone suitable to a Restoration gentleman undertaking the 'mechanic' task of providing the public with the current news; but we need not take too seriously the implication that he had started to publish his news-book without first 'planting and securing' his correspondence. He had, as we saw,* come to an understanding with Henry Muddiman, and while it lasted he was no doubt able to obtain and print reports from some at least of Muddiman's numerous country correspondents.

Fortunately for L'Estrange, the months of September and October 1663 were especially favourable for the sort of news he liked to release. On 26 August the King and Queen had set out on a royal progress to Bath. In his *Intelligencer* of 7 September L'Estrange was able to give a full account of their movements through Maidenhead, Reading and Newbury to their reception at Bath, with the address of welcome from the Bath Recorder; and in the *Newes* of 1 October he published another lengthy account of their visit to Oxford on the return journey. Most of L'Estrange's news was coloured with royalist propaganda, and he never failed to note the rapturous acclamation of the citizens, and the pleasure given by the King's gracious presence among his loyal people. It is not easy to determine whether those reports reached him from local correspondents along the route, or whether they came from someone attached to the royal party; but from later issues of his two news-books it becomes clear that he was receiving information from many parts of the country.

It was a good thing for him that he was so well supplied, for by the middle of October he had his first experience of that recurring nightmare of all early journalists – a complete dearth of foreign news owing to a prolonged spell of stormy weather. On 12 October he told readers of the *Intelligencer*, 'We have no Pacquets this Bout from

---

* See p. 9.

France, or Flanders.' He therefore substituted scraps of home news: a paragraph, dated 'Epping, Oct. 7', about the mustering of the local militia, one from Leominster giving an account of a storm there, and one from Ipswich ('The Phanatiques hereabouts are observ'd of late to be very busy with Prodigies, and Prophesyes . . . I have directed certain enformations be sent you'). The *Intelligencer* for 19 October carried accounts sent from Stamford, Norwich, Lancaster, Preston, Richmond and Chester, mostly about a threatened rising of the 'fanatics', the so-called Northern Plot, which the government soon succeeded in snuffing out. On 22 October he was forced to tell his readers that 'the wind lyes still in a crosse Corner for the French and Flemish Pacquets, so that we must have Patience for Intelligence from Those Quarters'. But again he was able to provide news about the Plot from Nottingham, Lincoln, York, Hull and other towns; and when at last it was possible to publish foreign news again he still kept reverting to the troubled situation at home. L'Estrange was particularly well supplied with information about the Plot from a correspondent in York, whose report in the *Newes* of 29 October begins, 'Since my last . . .', and who writes again in the *Intelligencer* of 2 November, 'I have been stay'd here beyond my Purpose, by reason of some Other Prisoners taken since my Last.' It looks as if the reports from York may have emanated from an agent sent there from the Secretary's office to keep the government informed, and then passed on to L'Estrange for publication. On the other hand, the account he gave in the *Newes* of 12 November 'from a sure hand in York' about the suicide of one Blackburn, accused of treason, may have come from Muddiman's York correspondent.

Whoever his correspondents may have been, they were clearly loyal to the Restoration settlement, and L'Estrange continued to publish frequent accounts of the exercises of the citizens' military trainbands, the raiding of Quaker meetings and the suppression of other religious conventicles, and to record such agreeable occasions as the Duke of York dining at Rufford with Sir George Savile (later Marquis of Halifax). As war with the Dutch drew nearer in the winter of 1664, he published more extensive reports from seaport towns about the movements of ships. Realising that if war broke out he would need all the information he could get about naval affairs, L'Estrange attempted several times to make the acquaintance of Samuel Pepys, and at last, on 17 December 1664, the two men met. 'It is to get now and then some news of me,' Pepys wrote in his Diary, 'which I shall as I see cause give him.' Some months later Pepys saw good cause to set L'Estrange right on a matter of some personal importance to himself. When, on 3 June 1665, the

English and Dutch fleets fought the stubborn engagement known as the Battle of Lowestoft, L'Estrange's account in the *Intelligencer* of 12 June was based on information released to him by the government, and Pepys was disturbed to find that the very considerable part played by his cousin and patron, the Earl of Sandwich, had been almost completely ignored. He saw to it that a letter from Captain Ferrers relating how Sandwich 'was with his ship in all the heat of the day, and did most worthily' was passed on to L'Estrange, and in the *Newes* of 15 June Sandwich was given due credit for his heroic part in the day's fighting.[8]

Although the greater part of L'Estrange's news was politically slanted, he occasionally condescended to gratify his readers with a purely sensational story. The opening paragraph in the *Newes* of 20 June 1664, dated from Addington, Kent, related how, as the Lady Clark was on her way to church with her two daughters, one of them was shot by a man who escaped to London. In the *Newes* of 13 July 1665, L'Estrange published an account, sent by a correspondent in Norwich, of a violent storm in which the parish church at Erpingham was struck while the parson was preaching on a Sunday afternoon. 'There descended the appearance of a great grey Ball, which as was supposed did beat down the Southwest Corner of the Steeple . . . It left a great smoak and stinck behind it.' In the *Intelligencer* of 17 July the same correspondent was able to amplify his statement about 'the dreadful Tempest I told you of', and friends of the author of *Religio Medici* and *Hydriotaphia* were able to learn that he was one of those who suffered from the storm. 'A Ball of fire fell upon Dr. Browne's house, and did him some little damage, brake some of the Glass-windows in his Court-yard . . .'

As a political pamphleteer L'Estrange was pre-eminent, but as a newspaper man his heart was never really in the business. He had made that abundantly clear in the first number of the *Intelligencer*:

I do declare myself (as I hope I may in a matter left so absolutely indifferent whether any or more) that supposing the Press in order, the people in their right wits and news or no news to be the question, a Public mercury should never have my vote, because I think it makes the multitude too familiar with the actions and counsels of their superiors, too pragmatical and censorious, and gives them not only an itch but a kind of colourable right and license to be meddling with the Government, all which (supposing as before supposed) does not yet hinder but that in this juncture a paper of that quality may be both safe and expedient; truly if I should say necessary perhaps the case would bear it, for certainly there is not anything which at this instant more imports his Majesty's service and the public, than to redeem the public from their former mistakes and deliver and protect them from the like for the time to come.

L'Estrange saw his two news-books as a means of keeping the people from having the wrong ideas, and of inculcating in them the right ones. As Surveyor of the Press his task was to expose libels and to trace and arrest their authors; and as writer of the *Intelligencer* and the *Newes* his aim was to support the government by selecting such items to print as showed the King and his ministers in a favourable light, and to denigrate, ridicule and point a finger of scorn at their enemies. Yet if propaganda was his primary concern, and he never allowed himself to forget that it was his duty 'to detect and disappoint the malice of those scandalous and false reports which are daily continued and bruited against the Government', a certain amount of harmless news could be released, and he was prepared to admit that a news-book was 'none of the worst ways of address to the genius and business of the common people'. But it was too much to believe that one whose main function was censorship should produce 'a public mercury' that would satisfy the vulgar desire of the common people for the latest news, and from first to last L'Estrange gave them little enough. Yet what he did give he gave in an informal, even familiar manner; and in the arid years that were to follow from 1665 to 1679, when the only newspaper available was the meagre and impersonal *Gazette*,[9] many honest Englishmen may have looked back on the days of his *Intelligencer* and *Newes* as belonging almost to a golden age.

When Benjamin Harris and his contemporaries started their newspapers in 1679–80 they gave their readers plenty of country news, but it was mainly of a kind very different from that normally provided by Muddiman. What the country supplied in abundance was a long list of casualties, often of a sensational sort: storms, floods and fires; men and women struck dead by lightning, others drowned or burnt to death; murders and suicides. Many of those stories introduce a supernatural element: Harris and Thompson have several accounts of strange and elaborate celestial apparitions; and ghosts, sometimes groaning horribly, appear in various parts of the countryside. A woman milking her cow in the parish of Stoke Edith in Herefordshire observes something like drops of blood falling on the grass, and finds that the milk in her pail is discoloured.[10] Much of this is similar to the popular narratives that appear in the broadsides of the period, with a crude woodcut and a cruder moral.

To illustrate the variety of this popular news from the remote and credulous country districts no better source can be found than Benskin's *Domestick Intelligence*. What follows is drawn from his first 50 issues. There are reports from Lewes, Newcastle, Nantwich and Carmarthen of women having monstrous births, and from Reigate of a foal born with six legs. From Stamford comes news of a ghost that appeared to a gentleman in bed, 'a dreadful Apparition or Spectrum, with burning eyes and Vissage horrible'. From different parts of the country come four accounts of sea-monsters, one with a head like a horse, and another like a crocodile. A great flock of vultures is seen near Berwick, 'a sight very rare in those parts'; and a few miles from Nottingham 'great Flocks of voracious Foul or Birds of Prey . . . met upon the Wing, and fought in the Air', so that it was filled with 'the deplumation, which the Wind dispersed over the Fields'. In a ruined building at Holyhead workmen came upon a snake four or five yards long.

Violent storms strike the country, one at Wallingford with hailstones 'three inches about', one at York that was followed by melodious voices in the air. At Monmouth a storm of rain, hail and lightning was accompanied by strange shapes of horses, elephants and camels in a bright cloud. We might be reading in John Aubrey's *Miscellanies*. Men fall dead from their horses; one is found hanging in a wood, and a young man falls to his death from the battlements at Dover. There are cases of fratricide, matricide, suicide and rape. A widow in the Isle of Wight hangs herself and her children. Near Lancaster a man who wished that he might be burnt alive if he had wronged his neighbour in any way is found next day at his fireside burnt almost to ashes. Of more normal happenings in Benskin's 50 issues, there are no fewer then 30 cases of robbery by highwaymen and footpads. Of numerous fires recorded, the most serious was one reported from Windsor, which burnt for five or six hours, 'with such force and vehemence that the like has not been seen (as most report) since the late dreadful Conflagration of London'. Benskin's correspondent was obviously carried away by the spectacle, but the blaze was extensive enough to destroy two inns with their stables and barns, and reduce twenty or thirty houses to ashes.[11] Oddly enough, there was no report in the *Gazette*, nor in Thompson's *Loyal Protestant* and Smith's *Currant Intelligence*; but short reports appeared in the *True Protestant Mercury* of 20 July 1681, and in the *Impartial Protestant Mercury* of 22 July, which noted that the suddenness and fierceness of the fire put 'the whole Court into no little Consternation'.

The reliability of much of the news reaching London from the country is often questionable. We know that on several occasions Harris was deceived by false accounts sent to him. On 16 March 1680 he had the misfortune to publish a sensational story from Deal about 'a strange battle between two prodigious great Whales several hours together which made the sea bloody for some miles'. Many boats put out to sea to watch this unusual spectacle, but the whales sank five of them with the loss of fifteen men, and chased many others to the shore. On 20 March a correspondent of the *Currant Intelligence* ridiculed the whole story, 'in which there is not one syllable of truth; neither was there the least ground for any such report'. This drew a feeble retraction from Harris: he now realised that the letter he had received from Deal, which 'was pretended to be from a friend', was 'an abuse put upon us, on purpose to scandalise and discredit any other News'.[12]

A year later Harris was guilty of a more serious distortion of the truth, and on this occasion he was the victim of a man he had previously employed, a freelance newswriter. On 8 March 1681, naming his source as a letter from Wigan, he published a long incriminating account of 'one Jolly' who had been surprised while saying mass to a secret gathering of some thirty papists, of whom three were killed on the spot while resisting arrest, and the rest sent under a strong guard to Lancaster jail, where several confessed that Jolly had supplied them with money and arms and told them to be ready when occasion should serve. Apparently not one word of this was true. In his *Loyal Protestant* of 19 March Thompson claimed that Harris had been duped, and was able to name the man who had given him the letter as one William Beckett. According to Thompson, this man told Harris that he had received the letter from his brother, but later, fearing that his brother would be prosecuted by Jolly, had confessed that

he forged the Letter himself, and gave it to be put into this kind of Protestant Intelligence . . . Thus we see how these Factious Scribling Hirelings are in a great measure the chief cause of our present Distractions; who to keep themselves from starving, study night and day how to invent Factious Stories to frighten the people out of their wits.[13]

When we find two newspapers publishing almost identically-worded reports on the same day, we may be sure that they were taken from a written source, and reasonably sure that the source was a news-letter. On 9 September 1679 Harris has a story beginning 'We are informed', and going on to relate how Samuel Pepys turned up 'last week' at Windsor, hoping that he might kiss the King's hand; but meeting with a person of honour he was told that 'it was strange he should presume to come to Court, since he stood charged with Treason'. After addressing himself to some other persons, however, Pepys succeeded in gaining admittance to His Majesty's presence, 'but however could not be admitted to the honour he desired'. The same story is related by

Thompson, but ends on a more dramatic note: 'his Majesty frowned angerly upon him and turned from him'. The upshot of all this was that Pepys compelled Harris to publish a complete retraction, stating that 'all and every part of the relation . . . is as to the matter, and every particular Circumstance therein mentioned, altogether False and Scandalous; there having no such passage happened, nor any thing that might give Occasion for the Report'.[14] The notice was repeated by Harris on 23 September. On this occasion Thompson came off scot-free. Since his rival newspaper had been appearing for only two weeks, it looks as if Pepys did not know of its existence.

On 21 October 1679 Harris and Thompson shared another piece of news. In Thompson this reads:

Letters from Scotland say, that the people about Hamilton have got a Distemper much like the Plague, the cause of which is imputed to the Stench of the dead Bodies that were slain thereabouts in the late Rebellion. Many of those miserable Wretches being wounded, crept into the Corn, where, when it was reap'd, they were found lying in a very nauseous condition . . .

Harris, who gives his own lightly edited version, begins with the curiously obfuscating and awkward introduction, 'There is an Account in Town, that there are letters from Edinburgh . . .', which suggests that he is deliberately covering up his source. That it was a written source is clear from the repetition of the same phrases in both versions, and again the source is almost certainly a news-letter. As to the truth of this story, the Battle of Bothwell Bridge was fought on 22 June, when the corn in Scotland would not normally be high enough to offer wounded men much cover. Nor would one have expected the local farmers to be so incurious about the progress of their crops that they never went to have a look at them.

As a final example suggesting that much of what appeared in the newspapers had been silently lifted from news-letters, we have three almost identical stories in the issues of Harris and Thompson for 5 March 1680. The first concerns two gentlemen found dead near Putney, one thrust through with a sword, the other with his brains dashed out, and money in the pockets of both. The second ('We hear from Edinburgh in Scotland') tells how there had recently been so many storms of thunder and lightning that 'the Bells were ordered to be rung backward, that everyone might thereby be alarm'd and in a readiness to extinguish the fire if any should happen'. The third (a piece of London news) relates how a thief snatched a gentleman's sword out of its scabbard, and made off with it at a leisurely pace before taking to his heels. Harris's account of what happened when the man was caught is reasonably polite: he was brought to the Temple and pumped, 'and afterward used . . . so scurvily, that his Villany was easy to be smelt out.' Thompson, or his author, spells this out for the reader: 'they first Pump'd him, and then pickl'd him in the House of Office, that every one might smell him for a rogue.' Otherwise the two versions are almost identical.

It is clear, then, that a good number of the news stories published by Harris and Thompson did not come from their own correspondents. Anything happening within a few miles of London might be picked up orally. No doubt a considerable amount of country news could be obtained from coachmen, post-boys or carriers, or from talkative gentlemen arriving in London on horseback with something to tell. The first item in Harris's first number is concerned with a man found hanging by the arms in a wood between Woolwich and Greenwich, with his head and hands cut off and his bowels pulled out. By a paper found in his pocket he was identified as 'a Purser belonging to one of His Majesties New Built Frigats'. It was a good story with which to start a newspaper, the first of many startling events that Harris was to record. He introduces it with 'We have an Account from Greenwich', but it need not have reached him directly from that place. Since Greenwich and Woolwich are only a few miles down river from London, it would not have been long before this gruesome news was circulating in the City taverns and coffee-houses, and there is no need to suppose that it reached Harris from a correspondent. A good deal of his news came from villages and small towns such as West Ham, Deptford, Uxbridge, Barnet, Putney, Brentford and Ilford, which are now part of greater London. On 22 August 1679 he published an account of a gentleman at Dullidg (Dulwich) who surprised some deer-poachers in his park, and on 2 December he had a report of a Wimbledon farmer who had been robbed. Such news, usually prefaced by 'We hear', 'We have an account', 'It is credibly reported', probably reached him as often as not by oral transmission. On 5 September 1679, when he published what he called 'a very credible account' of how the Cirencester carrier, coming with five passengers towards London, saw a remarkable celestial apparition near Abingdon, the news could have been obtained when the carrier and his passengers arrived in London and started to talk. In that way, certainly, the *True Protestant Mercury* of 15 June 1681 was able to give its readers news of an extensive fire:

By a Gentleman lately come to London who was an Eye-Witness thereof, we have an Account, that the farthest part of Windsor Forrest hath been on fire several days.

This gentleman had been told that 1000 acres were destroyed, and that the fire was now within three miles of Bagshot Heath.

How much of the country news appearing in the papers was acquired in this casual way it is impossible to say. Yet from the first some of the news printed came from correspondents of one sort or another. When Harris has a written source for his news he usually makes that clear to his readers. In his second issue he has a paragraph which begins: 'Essex, By Letters from a place called Much Waltham in this County, we have this strange but true Relation . . .'. He goes on to tell of a violent storm on 30 June, of 'Rain, intermixed with great flakes of Ice the bignes (as the Relator speaks) of an half-penny loaf cut in sunder', which 'cut off whole fields of Corn as if they had been Reaped', and 'rent and shivered several Trees to pieces'. If, like L'Estrange, Harris had gone about 'planting and securing' a correspondence, we might have expected him to choose more important centres of information than Much Waltham. Perhaps the letter had been passed on to him by some friend or acquaintance who had relatives there. At all events, he had further news from Much Waltham on 17 July, confirming and amplifying his first news of the hailstorm, and then nothing further.

From the first Harris was receiving reports from Lincolnshire. On 24 October 1679 he published an account of severe flooding there, resulting in a stage-coach being overwhelmed, and six passengers drowned along with the horses. A month later he gave his readers a long and sensational story of fratricide in Stamford. What might have remained an unsolved crime was put beyond all doubt for the seventeenth-century reader by 'the shape or spirit' of the murdered man appearing on horseback, pointing to his wounds and naming his brother as the murderer: the guilty brother then confessed, and was said to be 'now' in prison.[15] From Fosdekstow, on 18 January 1681, came another grim story of a man who had murdered his mother. Fosdekstow, which I take to be the modern Fosdyke, is about 22 miles north-east of Spalding. Another report in the same issue is dated from Pinchbeck, about ten miles from Fosdyke, and less than three miles from Spalding. This is worth quoting in full, for it was apparently set by the printer exactly as it reached him, and it provides a typical example of a seventeenth-century country correspondent dealing with local news:

Near this Town on the 1st of this Instant was a Robbery committed by six highway-men upon a Gentleman's Coach, from him they took 200 pounds in money, and from his Lady several Rings and Jewels of great value: This Robbery was committed in the day time, whereupon the Thieves were pursued, and 'tis said two of them were taken at a by-house about ten miles from this place:

we have a strong report here, that a strange and monstrous Fish has been seen to play in the Ocean, for several days past near Spalding, and that several boats have put out to take it, but it is so swift that they cannot come near it, it is said to be 30 foot long, with a head like a Lyon, of which upon further confirmation, I shall give you a more particular account: the Snow having fallen Incessantly in these parts, so that 'tis confirmed from all hands, several small Cattel were covered in one night, and are not as yet found, and that several great Cattel perished in the Fens.

This has the marks of a conscientious country correspondent doing his best to collect the news in his area. Harris's last news from Lincolnshire concerned a disastrous fire in the little town of Caistor.[16] There is at least a possibility that all these Lincolnshire reports came from the same correspondent.

In September 1679 Harris had news from four Hampshire towns: Eastleigh, Southampton, Winchester and Stockbridge. The long election report from Winchester that he published on 5 September was in the first person and printed verbatim. All four Hampshire reports could have come from someone based in Winchester: Eastleigh is seven miles away, Southampton twelve, and Stockbridge nine.

Leaving aside those tentative speculations about the ground that may have been covered by any one of Harris's correspondents, it will prove more useful to list briefly the places from which he received his least infrequent reports. From York he had seven; from Stafford six, mainly about papists and the assizes; from Windsor five. From Nottingham, Portsmouth and Lewes he had four reports. Those reaching him from Lewes were all of considerable length, including the 1679 celebration of Guy Fawkes day (with the ghost of Sir Edmund Berry Godfrey as a topical feature),[17] a fatal poisoning case, and yet another ghost story. From only two English cities, Bristol and Oxford, did the reports published by Harris reach double figures. The eleven items dated from Bristol included sinister activities of the papists, and four reports on the election of 1681. Oxford supplied two reports in November 1679 about the brutal murder of a Balliol student, and in February 1680 an account, with some apocryphal details, of the annual service on St Scholastica's day at the University church of St Mary's, commemorating the occasion when some medieval students had been killed by the enraged citizens after one of them had 'offered some abuse to their Mayor's daughter'.[18] Early in 1681, when the King decided to hold his new parliament in Oxford, it became temporarily a place of the first importance. Harris's first political news from Oxford appeared on 25 January, and from then on his correspondent kept him well supplied with news, mainly, but not entirely, political. It is impossible to give a precise figure for the number of reports Harris received from Oxford between 1679 and 1681, for during the short life of the 1681 parliament accounts of its proceedings are scattered through several numbers of his *Domestick Intelligence*. If we make allowance for this, the tally from Oxford comes to seventeen. On 17 March, a few days before the opening of parliament, the King went to the little town of Burford (twenty miles from Oxford) to watch some horse-racing, and it was probably Harris's Oxford correspondent who sent him the engaging account he published on 22 March. The royal visit was marked by a special gift from the town, highly renowned for its saddlery; and the King, a master of public relations, responded splendidly to the occasion. He was met by the bailiff and the capital burgesses in their robes of office, and the bailiff then addressed the King:

'May it please Your Majesty, We the Baylyff and Burgesses of this poor Burrough of Burford, do now come to Welcome Your Majesty to this Town . . . And we do humbly beseech Your Majesty, that you will be Graciously pleased to Accept of this small Present, viz. this Saddle . . .'

His Majesty Graciously Accepted of the Saddle, which was a Rich one, and was pleased three times very Courteously to say (putting off his Cap), *I thank you very kindly*.

During the run of his newspaper Harris was fortunate in having two general elections to report, in the summer of 1679 and in the early months of 1681. The 1679 election came upon him soon after he had started his newspaper and he was clearly unprepared for it. The returns he printed for the first few weeks were probably picked up by him, or by one of his men, at the Exchange or a coffee-house, or in some other casual way. In introducing those results he used such terms as 'The best account of those chosen since our last is as followeth . . .', or 'The Election for Members . . . are according to our best information as followeth . . .'. Inevitably he made mistakes, and on 16 September he had to apologise for giving false returns from Rye and several other places.[19] Yet some at least of his election news was reaching him from correspondents on the spot, as may be seen from the letter already cited giving him the results from Winchester. By the time the 1681 election was held, he had either organised a better correspondence, or Shaftesbury and his friends had seen to it that he should be well supplied with reliable political returns. On 25 February he gave the return of the county members for Essex and Surrey, taking up the greater part of his front page, and similar reports followed from Bridgwater and Nottingham. Early in March it was the turn of Bristol, where his correspondent reported that the Whig candidates were expected to carry it, only to have to admit a few days later that they had lost.[20]

In marked contrast with the scattered and often unreliable and trivial reports most newspapers received from the English countryside were those reaching them from Scotland. Edinburgh was a capital city, with its own parliament and law-courts; and when the Duke of York arrived there in November 1679 as High Commissioner, Holyrood Palace had all the activities and attributes of a lesser royal court. A few weeks before Harris started his newspaper the Duke of Monmouth, the 'Protestant Duke', had defeated the Covenanters at the Battle of Bothwell Bridge. From the first, therefore, Harris's Edinburgh correspondent was at no loss for news, much of which must have been of absorbing interest to readers of the *Domestick Intelligence*. In his first issue Harris was able to report that the rebellion was over, and that Monmouth had been 'received and entertained with all the splendour imaginable by the Magistrates of Edinburgh'. On 10 July he gave the number of the rebels killed as 'about 900'; and on 14 July he published a long account from his correspondent about the many prisoners taken, including some of the murderers of Archbishop Sharp, and about their approaching trial:

It is thought they will be booted and then hanged, which booting is an Iron Instrument, into which they put their Leggs, which by degres crushes them to pieces, and is generally used to procure confession from the Partie tormented therewith.

The Edinburgh correspondent who wrote this may have been an Englishman passing on to his fellow countrymen in London information he had just obtained, but, in view of some of his later reports, he was almost certainly a Scot carefully explaining for the English reader an old Scottish custom. With Monmouth's return to England, reports from Edinburgh become much less frequent, but with the arrival of the Duke of York in November they pick up again, and take on a decidedly anti-Catholic tone. References in January 1681 to 'our nobility and gentry' and to 'the opinion of your Parliament' suggest again that the Edinburgh correspondent was a Scot.[21]

Harris had only two news items dated from Dublin, one of which was promptly exposed as false by Thompson, and ten others that were dated from Ireland. On the whole it seems likely that he had no regular Irish correspondent, but picked up his Irish news from various sources. In his *Domestick Intelligence* Thompson had six reports dated from Dublin, and another fourteen dated from Ireland. (In comparing the two newspapers it must be remembered that while Harris's *Domestick*

Intelligence lasted for 114 numbers, Thompson's had a run of only 76, from the end of August 1679 to the middle of May 1680.) Whether Thompson had his own Irish correspondents it is hard to say. The same applies to his Scottish news, where seven items are dated from Edinburgh, and nine from Scotland. Few of them have the personal note of a correspondent addressing the proprietor of a newspaper.

On the whole Thompson was less well supplied with English country news than Harris, and what he published was no more reliable. One of the surest marks of the country correspondent is his interest in unusual weather. On 24 October 1679 both Thompson and Harris published apparently separate accounts from Welshpool of the torrential floods following upon a thunderstorm there. On 16 March 1680, when Thompson next had news from those remote parts, it came from Montgomery, eight miles from Welshpool, where a jilted lover was said to have taken revenge on his bride-to-be by stabbing her to the heart. Unfortunately for Thompson, Smith's *Currant Intelligence* checked this report with its Montgomery correspondent, and on 27 March published his reply:

I have according to your desire made very strict enquiry concerning the murther, which the never true Domestick Intelligence of the 16. instant affirmes was committed by one Richard Morgan upon his sweet-heart near this town, and can assure you that it is a most Notorious untruth, there not having been any such thing acted in these parts.

Thompson left it at that. On 16 April he published his second piece of news from Welshpool, and again it was of a kind that strained credulity. This time it was the story of another rejected lover, but one who reacted quite differently: he castrated himself. Whether all three items of news from Montgomery and Welshpool came from one correspondent, or from news-letters, it is perhaps useless to enquire. But as was suggested with Harris, one man might be responsible for collecting the news of a single area. In this way the single reports that Thompson published from Leominster, Ludlow, Worcester and Hereford may be by the same correspondent, whether true or false.

Thompson had seven news items dated from Deal, four from Bristol, Newcastle, York and Oxford, and two from a few other places. But in one important respect he was better informed than Harris. As a loyal supporter of the royal family he saw it as his duty to keep his readers supplied with news from the Court. The King spent much of the year at Whitehall, but he also stayed at Hampton Court and (mainly in the summer) at Windsor, and he was fond of visiting Newmarket for several weeks at a time. When Charles was recovering at Windsor from a serious illness, Thompson gave a fairly detailed account (2 September 1679) of his medical treatment, which included the use of 'Jesuit's powder' (quinine); and he followed this in his next number with the assurance that 'His Majesty (to the great joy of all people) is in a very hopeful way of Recovery, his Fits having quite left him . . .'. On 9 September he was able to announce that 'His Majesty (God be praised) is wholly Recovered of his Indisposition.' Later in the same number he confirmed this report, adding that he was repeating the good news 'because it was Reported about Town that His Majesty was Relapsed'. Whoever was sending those reports, his interests may not have been restricted to the Court; for it was probably the same correspondent who sent Thompson the Windsor election results that he published on 2 September, and news of a tapster who had been committed to Reading jail for speaking treasonable words when the poll was in progress. In all, Thompson published nine reports from Windsor during the run of his *Domestick Intelligence*.

He published the same number from Newmarket. That he had an informant at Court is suggested by his announcement on 26 September that the King intended to go 'this day' to Newmarket 'against the advice of his physicians'. On this visit Charles made only a short stay, and Thompson published only two reports from Newmarket, the second saying that he intended to return to London because he had not met with 'that Diversion he expected'. When, however, the King again visited Newmarket in the following March, Thompson gave half a column to a list of the horse-races to be run, and he had further news of the royal visit on 12, 16 and 19 March (when his correspondent sent him five paragraphs), and again on 30 March.

That Thompson sometimes suffered from a dearth of news and had to fill his paper with anything that came to hand may be seen from his issue of 16 September 1679. Among the few items that could fairly be called current news were accounts of a fatal quarrel in a Southwark tavern, and of the warm welcome given to the King on his return to Whitehall after his illness at Windsor. The rest of Thompson's news in this number looks as if it had been kept in a drawer in readiness for use when he had nothing else to give his readers. One such story begins: 'In the last lightning two Gentlemen were travelling into Hampshire . . .'. It goes on to relate how one of them was telling a story that the other 'seemed not to give credit to'. The first gentleman, however, persisted with his story, and 'wished the lightning might consume him if his Story was not true; and presently [immediately] after his Horse fell with him, and he never spoke word more'. Whether or not this ever happened 'in the last lightning' (whenever that was), this cautionary tale seems to belong to the popular literature of tempting providence, and might still be met with in a modern religious tract.

Equally suspect is a long story located in Newcastle upon Tyne in Thompson's *Domestick Intelligence* of 28 March 1680. A young gentlewoman who had been 'got with child by a Neighbour Gentleman' decided 'to conceal her fault and prevent her shame'. To this end, 'as it is generally believed', she

murthered her Child; and her Guilt making her unsecure in her thoughts, she concluded the City of London might not only be a security for her person, but also that by the variety of the company, she might stifle the stings of Conscience . . .

She hired a neighbour and his horse to take her to London. But the horse refused to go forward, however much it was whipped, and she was twice thrown to the ground. She tried another horse, and it refused to budge. She hired a coach, and again the horses refused to proceed, but kicked out and at last overturned the coach. At this point she 'betook herself to her feet', and reached the port of Shields, where she agreed for a passage to London.

But though all the other Ships went out with a fair Gale, the Ship she was in making severall essays to do the like the Wind would not permit them. At last Hue and Cry overtook her, and [she] was sent to Prison; after which the Ship sailed away.

Several objections may be made to this story as a piece of news. No date is given for a series of events that must have lasted some days: ordinarily such a narrative would begin with 'Last week' or 'Some time ago'. We are not told if anyone ever saw the child that the gentlewoman was suspected of murdering. On the other hand, we are told so much about her thoughts and feelings, and what prompted her to undertake the proposed journey to London, that readers with an enquiring turn of mind might well wonder how the narrator could possibly know all this. We seem, indeed, to be reading another cautionary tale, suitably tinged with the supernatural. The very shapeliness of the story, with its repeated frustrations culminating in the final impasse at Shields, only confirms the impression that Thompson is not here giving us the latest news, but a piece of timeless folklore.

In his issue for 30 December 1679 Thompson has a well-written story that reads like the fantasy of a literary alcoholic; and again it is one that seems to hover uncertainly between fact and fiction:

Very near a little Village (being a Fisher-Town) in Yorkshire, between Scarborough and Burlington [Bridlington], a French Vessel of considerable Burthen, laden with French Wines, Brandies, Prunes and Sugar, struck upon a Rock with such force, that she lay upon the point of the Rock as it were equally poised, it having struck through the middle of her Keel, so that she lay unmovable by the Waves when the Tide was out. The Fisher-men with their Cobles and five-men Boats fetched off the Men, and unladed the Vessel, which so filled that little Town with Hogsheads, an Horse could not pass in the Town, nor Men, without getting over them. The poor People surfeited so with Wine and Brandy, that near halfe the Town, Men, Women and Children lay drunk upon the Sands, of which excess several of them have since died.

Next day, the Countrey people adjacent hearing of the Wreck, came down in multitudes to participate of the Spoil, where every one might drink what he would; for partly through the Seamen's gratitude for the preserving of their lives, and what the People got by force and theft, there was no lett to any person, so that the plenty was great, and the company that flocked to the Town increasing hourly, that they burnt Brandy in their Brewing-Kettles, stewed Prunes in their Coppers, and threw in Sugar with Shovels; so that 'tis believed more people are already killed, and will die, than would have been lost if the Sea had swallowed all the men in the Ship. A poor Child that in all probability never tasted Brandy before, drinking a full draught of it as if it had been Beer, was immediately stifled, and never spoke word more. Two men, Father and Son, slept about 16 hours, as if they had been dead, and when they were with much difficulty awak'd, the Father died some few hours later; the Son recovered, but continues as it were distracted, and 'tis thought will never be in his senses again. The Ship could not possibly be gotten off, but most of the Rigging and what was most material was saved; the Vessel being broken by the following Tides.

If this seventeenth-century version of *Whisky Galore* was a genuine news item, Thompson had scooped the other newspapers appearing in December 1679, none of which makes any mention of the wrecked vessel and the ensuing debauch. It is only fair to add that on 27 October the *London Gazette* reported from Bridlington: 'We have of late had very bad weather in these parts, though, God be thanked, we hear not of any Ships Lost.' On the face of it, Thompson's story is plausible. One might perhaps have expected to be given the name of the little 'fisher-town', but there are certainly several villages scattered along the coast between Scarborough and Bridlington. A search in local records might reveal that a ship carrying the cargo described actually broke up somewhere along that stormy coast in the winter of 1679. But Thompson's account gives no date for the shipwreck, not even a hint that it happened 'lately', and no indication, such as 'We hear from Bridlington', how the news reached him. Yet such events did happen: on 7 February 1680, Smith's *Currant Intelligence* reported that 'a French

Fly-Boat laden with Brandy and Salt' had been cast away at 'Burl-ingate' (i.e. Burling Gap?). On such occasions, if the cargo came ashore, some sort of orgy might well follow. Remembering some such occasion, did someone, drawing largely on his imagination, supply Thompson with the story about a shipwreck on the coast of Yorkshire? If there were such a person he could have been Benjamin Claypoole, the writer of news-letters who gave Thompson some assistance in compiling his *Domestick Intelligence*. He was described in 1683 by another newswriter, William Cotton, as a man who 'generally depends on others for his news, for he will not take any pains, but will word things well if not in drink'. The story of the dionysiac revels on the Yorkshire coast is certainly well worded, and its theme is one that would have brought out the best in Claypoole's writing.

When, after a gap of ten months, Thompson started his second newspaper, *The Loyal Protestant*, he was in time to give the late election results for the Oxford parliament, and to report the main events of its brief session. An analysis of the first hundred issues hardly suggests any marked development of his English country news network. As before, he was well supplied with reports from Windsor (14) and Newmarket (11). On 28 June 1681 he published half a column from his Windsor correspondent about a sporting contest between twelve of the King's men in red waistcoats and twelve of the Duke of Albemarle's in blue. The elegant style of such reports suggests that Thompson's Windsor correspondent was a person of some refinement. The same may be said of the nine reports that he dated from Hampton Court, possibly by the same person. That Thompson had his own man at Newmarket is clear from the fact that he often gave the news in the correspondent's own words, as in the sarcastic message of 17 September: 'If you are curious after News from hence, let me recommend you to Mr. Benskin, for he can tell you things we have never before heard of . . .'[22]. Reports from Newmarket remained a regular feature of the *Loyal Protestant*; and in Thompson's final issue (No. 247, 20 March 1683) half the front page was given over to an account of the recreations of the royal family and townspeople.

In the ten months covered by the first hundred issues, Thompson published 15 reports from Oxford, but most of those were accounted for by two occasions: the meeting of parliament there in March 1681, and the second trial of Stephen College, the 'Protestant Joiner', when the Crown succeeded in obtaining at Oxford the verdict of guilty it had failed to get at the Old Bailey in July. On 20 August Thompson gave almost the whole of his front page to a report of this trial, and on 3

September he carried half a column on College's execution at Oxford.

He published ten items of news from Sarum and New Sarum (Salisbury). One, dated 25 June 1681, describes the havoc caused in the district by a wind of hurricane force: 'Trees [were] torn up by the Roots: so great was its force that the humility of the Shrubs was not a Protection for them, some of them being driven into the Air.' The 'humility of the shrubs' reads like the phraseology of a local clergyman. On 7 January 1682 this Salisbury correspondent showed his Church of England leanings by reporting that the Mayor had successfully tracked down a Presbyterian meeting-house, but when he arrived at the place the birds had flown and he had to be content with spoiling their nest. Whoever this correspondent was, he felt it his duty in July 1681 to report a case of bestiality, involving a woman and a dog, which most modern editors would regard as unprintable, but which Thompson duly printed. This was followed in his next issue by a fuller account of 'the Unnatural Slut' and what the two witnesses had observed. Finally, on 26 July, after the case had come up at the assizes, Thompson was able to tell his readers that 'the Wench who was accused about the Dog' had been acquitted. If his correspondent reported the judgement accurately, the acquittal turned somewhat surprisingly on the legal admissibility of the evidence: the two witnesses 'both looking through one crevis, and at several times, they were adjudged but as one Witness.'

In its news from Ireland and Scotland the *Loyal Protestant* shows a considerable improvement on Thompson's earlier paper. It is clear from his first number that he had taken steps to secure a Dublin correspondent, and in his first 100 issues he gave his readers 19 reports from Dublin, and a few more from other parts of Ireland. By the autumn of 1681 a revulsion of feeling had come about, and many Englishmen were beginning to look back with distaste, and even shame, on those first hectic months of the Popish Plot, when one victim after another had been condemned to death on evidence supplied by perjured witnesses. On 15 October Thompson published a report from his Dublin correspondent that the three O'Neals who had given evidence against Archbishop Plunket were 'now in jail for thieving'. To this the correspondent added a significant comment: 'We begin daily to discover the *Whiggish Intrigue* to be the same as is represented in England.' With the general turning of the political tide such observations could now be openly made and printed. Of all the unsavoury characters thrown up by the Popish Plot one of the very worst was the 'suborner', the man who remained in the background and bribed others to give false evidence. But even here the Dublin correspondent was able to provide a little light relief with a typically Irish story: on 13 August Thompson published his account of a play performed in Dublin that had as one of its characters a suborner, and how one of the audience recognised himself as the character being satirised and went to complain to the Lord Lieutenant. From first to last Thompson's newspapers provided more amusement than those of Harris, who was an inflexible bigot with a one-track mind. Thompson himself had considerable humour, and may have had some influence on the style of his correspondents. Not long after Shaftesbury was sent to the Tower, Thompson received and published a sardonic letter from Cranborne:

A Gentlewoman at Cramburn in Wilts was so zealous for the Cause that hearing of the Earl of Shaftesbury's Commitment to the Tower, [she] Cryed out, *Now no Bodie's Life is safe*; and immediately went up into her Chamber, and Hang'd her self.[23]

For his Scottish news Thompson appears to have secured a reliable man, who not only wrote frequently, but sent him, like his Irish correspondent, the sort of news he liked to print. Much of it was concerned with the Duke of York, whose activities as High Commissioner were duly chronicled, but also such recreations as a voyage to the Bass Rock to see the solan geese. In December 1681 the news from Edinburgh is mainly concerned with the impeachment of the Earl of Argyle, the preparations for his trial, and his escape from the castle in woman's clothes; but it also gives an account of how the Duchess of York, 'upon a hand-gallop', had a dangerous fall from her horse:

But by God's great Mercy his Bruitish heels missed her Royal Body: howbeit, she was taken up for Dead for some small time.[24]

On 7 January 1682 Thompson was able to reassure his readers with the news that she had made a good recovery. In that one month of December 1681 he published nine reports from Scotland, and in his first 100 issues no fewer than 41, of which 28 were dated from Edinburgh.

Among the other papers then appearing, Benskin's *Domestick Intelligence* was well supplied with Scottish news. In his first 50 issues he printed 23 reports from Edinburgh, and about the same number from other parts of Scotland. His Irish news was less extensive, and it is doubtful if he had a regular correspondent. Like Thompson, he published a good deal of news from the Court; 17 reports from Windsor and 11 from Newmarket. Other places from which he had five or more reports were Oxford, Deal, Dover, Lyme, Plymouth, Yarmouth and Newcastle. Curtiss's *True Protestant Mercury* had mostly single reports from various scattered places, chiefly of election results and the usual accounts of fires, storms, apparitions, fatal quarrels, and his own exclusive story of a mad dog that bit a mare that then bit a man. Such country news as appeared in Francis Smith's *Protestant Intelligence* and in the *Impartial Protestant Mercury* was predominantly political: both papers were carrying on a serious campaign against the government.

There remains John Smith's *Currant Intelligence*, which ran for 24 issues in 1680, and then, when he revived it in 1681, for 70 more. This was in a class by itself. Narcissus Luttrell, who noted that it was 'an intelligence well esteem'd of',[25] must have been impressed by the extent and quality of its news, which was distinctly superior to that of its contemporaries. From the first, Smith published much more reliable and detailed shipping news than the other papers. In his third issue he announced: 'There will be a List published in this Intelligence of all the Merchant Ships that either come or go out of any Port of the West of England'; and on 2 March 1680 he explained that the shipping intelligence was intended 'for the accomodation of Merchants and others'. In his first run of 24 issues, he had 22 reports from Plymouth and Deal, 15 from Falmouth, ten from Weymouth, eight from Portsmouth, five from King's Lynn, four from Harwich, three from Berwick, two from Holyhead and Bridgwater, and a single item of news from about a dozen other ports. So copious was his shipping news that in several numbers a much smaller type had to be used. That this news came from private correspondents is evident both from the style and content of the reports. On 6 March, for example, the Deal correspondent notes that 'the Hoyes laden with Oates for the French King's service set sail on Tuesday last . . . and are bound for Roan [Rouen]'. To this he added a postscript: 'Since my writing of this, they are coming back into the Downs, so that the seldom or never true *Domestick* [Thompson's *True Domestick Intelligence*] was mightily mistaken when he said that the said Hoyes were come into Falmouth.'

It would be wrong, however, to think of the *Currant Intelligence* as being only, or primarily, a trade paper. The port correspondents frequently enclosed local news of more general interest, and had probably been asked to do so. On 28 February, for example, the Bridgwater correspondent related how the citizens, hoping that the next assizes would be held there, had bought a great quantity of wood to build a hall, only to find that a gentleman had used his influence to have the assizes held as usual at Taunton. The report ends with a satirical couplet, and a joke at the expense of the Bridgwater men made by the Taunton men.

Apart from his port correspondence, Smith printed news from some of the more important provincial towns, such as Aylesbury, Colchester, Warrington, York, Exeter, Norwich, Oxford and Cambridge. In several issues he published short accounts of the assizes at Thetford and Chelmsford; and on 10 April 1680 he had a report from Bury St Edmunds about a local libertine who did penance in a white sheet on which a paper was pinned with the words, 'For Fornication', in capital letters. Smith published eight reports from Newmarket, mainly about the horse-racing there;[26] and, like other London newspaper men, he had correspondents in the capital cities of Edinburgh and Dublin.

When he revived his paper in 1681 it fully confirmed the favourable impression already made. In its 70 numbers there were 38 reports from Falmouth, 36 from Portsmouth, 30 from Deal, 27 from Plymouth, and 22 from Weymouth, to name only those ports where his correspondents were most active. The greatest development came in the reports from Edinburgh, which now amounted to 50, and those from Dublin, which totalled 28. Most of the news forwarded from both cities was of serious interest, and when nothing much was happening the correspondents still wrote, if only to say so. On 20 September the Dublin correspondent reported: 'We want the Company of the Court with us, and Gentry, so that we have nothing stirring here'; and on 15 October the Edinburgh correspondent had a similar story to tell: 'His Royal Highness is now at Glescoe, and with him a great many of the Nobility, so that we have little news here.' At other times the news from Edinburgh was concerned with the activities of the Duke of York, the opening and sitting of the Scottish parliament, the trial and execution of various Covenanters, the death of the Duke of Rothes, and other matters of moment. The Dublin correspondent had in general less of importance to write about, and he must have been grateful for being able to forward the sad story that appeared in the *Currant Intelligence* of 2 July, and which he spun out at some length:

On Friday morning about three of the Clock a fire broke forth in the Elephant's Booth, which being made of deal boards, and those exceeding dry, it was burnt down with the Elephant, and the Boy that usually rode on him, before any help could come to prevent it, tho a £1000 (as 'tis said) was offered for to save the Elephant . . . The flesh of the Elephant is taken off, and will be boyled for the fat of it, and the Skelliton is preparing to be showed . . .

We have already seen how the *Currant Intelligence* was able to send queries to various parts of the country asking for the news published by Harris or Thompson to be checked, and how the queries were promptly and firmly answered. Henry Muddiman, it will be recalled, had been granted free postage, and had used this concession to build up an extensive correspondence. Smith had no such privilege, but he appears to have hit upon a way of organising a private correspondence and avoiding the expense of having to pay for it. It is unlikely that we should know how Smith was obtaining his news, but for a bad-tempered outburst by Nathaniel Thompson, when, on 9 August 1681, he retaliated sharply on the *Currant Intelligence* for pointing out one of his many mistakes:

Mr. Currant Intelligencer of the 2d. of August is pleased to give himself the trouble of putting me in mind of a mistake of the 30th past; To which I answer, That Mr. Smith knows nothing of the News he prints, whether true or false: And Mr. S---r of the Post-House would do well to mind his own business, and not abuse so good a Master as he undeservedly has the Honour to serve, and let scribbling alone; The practice of which, by himself and others, if it were well looked into, 'twere an easie matter to make it out how many thousands somebody has been damnified by such Under-Hand-Traders, and what some Persons in Authority may suffer, themselves in time may consider.

The clerks of the Post Office were not well paid. In a Treasury minute of 5 April 1688 it was noted that 'they lie under very great temptation of being prevailed upon to do things very prejudicial to the revenue, and though divers of them have been turned out for the same, yet it is no terror to their successors, they not being able to live upon their employments'.[27] Business correspondence between the clerks and the postmasters all over the country went free, and the clerks had also been given the perquisite of franking copies of the *London Gazette* to postmasters. But this free postage was open to abuse, and was being dishonestly extended to cover mail on which postage should have been paid.

In 1679 Thomas Gardiner, who was controller of the Inland Office, sent a detailed account of the Post Office to the Duke of York. He admitted that one opening for malpractice was the difficulty of checking 'the clarkes books outward, being the same that giveth a charge upon the respective Postmasters for the unpaid letters sent out at post nights'. In making up the outgoing mail for his road, it was the duty of each of the six clerks to enter a note of all the letters and newspapers on which postage had still to be paid, and this amount had then to be collected by the individual postmasters when the post-bags reached them. Gardiner was aware that one had to trust the clerks not to fiddle their returns and pass mail free on which postage was due; but the alternative was to employ 'double the number of hands' to check the outgoing bags, and this would lead to intolerable delays at an hour 'when dispatch is the chiefest requisite'. Gardiner then refers to the clerks' privilege of sending copies of the *Gazette* post free to the postmasters, and notes that this works to the advantage of the postmasters 'in their common trade of selling drink'. (The postmasters were generally innkeepers, and a copy of the *Gazette* available in the taproom was an added attraction for customers.) But this concession, he continued, was being abused by extending it to all sorts of other pamphlets – chiefly, no doubt, newspapers. Gardiner finally passes to the most serious charge of all:

But that which is wholly new, detrimentall and scandalous, must not be omitted; and that is several partners and distinct interests, that farm newes of their own (like those in authority under the Secretaries of State) spreading the same to all sorts of Chapmen [dealers]. This doth but justifie the common reproach upon the office of opening letters; and in deed, men of that facultie lye under the necessity of very close inquiry.[28]

Whether the letters in question were in the outgoing or incoming mail Gardiner does not say. To this may be added the testimony of the already-mentioned William Cotton, the owner of a news-letter service. When examined in October 1683, he gave a detailed account of his rivals in the business, and ended by asserting that 'some others belonging to the Post Office strike greater strokes in this business than any of these. Sautell is one of them and Leeson another . . . Several others in that office, whose names I have not, drive, I am informed, the same trade.'[29]

In asserting that John Smith obtained the news he printed from 'Mr. S---r of the Post-House', Thompson was almost certainly pointing at one of the six clerks of the Letter Office. This person was presumably abusing his position in one or all of the ways outlined by Thomas Gardiner. In return for receiving the *Currant Intelligence* post free twice a week, various postmasters were reporting to him anything worthy of note that happened in their neighbourhood. The good master whom Mr S---r undeservedly had the honour to serve was not Mr Smith, but the Duke of York, who had been granted the profits of the Post Office in 1663, and who was losing some of his revenue through the dishonest practices of one of the Post Office employees. There was no one working at the Post Office in 1681 who can be identified with Mr S---r; but if, as is possible, S---r was a misprint for S--l, we have a very likely candidate, Edmund Sawtell, the clerk of the Yarmouth road, who, as already noted, was mentioned by William Cotton as one of those in the Post Office who supplied information for the compilers of news-letters. Another possible candidate might be William Searle, who was one of the 'window men' receiving outgoing letters for the post, but he was not in so favourable a position to deal direct with country post-masters.[30] How many other impecunious officials working in the Post Office were involved in selling news, we cannot tell; but we cannot overlook the possibility that some of the news emanating from the Post Office may have been sold direct to men like Harris, Thompson and Benskin, as well as to the writers of news-letters. Smith's *Currant Intelligence*, on the other hand, was receiving its news regularly from an employee of the Post Office who was so intimately connected with the paper as to be in effect what was then called the 'author'. In such circumstances there was every reason for its being 'an intelligence well esteemed of'.

The newspapers of the 1690s show little sign of having a well-organised service of country news, and as long as the war with France lasted they had little space available for trivial news from the provinces. Shipping reports, however, continued to appear more or less regularly, and they provide the clearest and most widespread evidence of established country correspondents in the seventeenth-century newspaper. When the foreign mails failed to arrive on the expected day, port news was often extended considerably to fill the vacant space. This in itself indicates that on many other occasions a paper was unable to find room for all the shipping reports it was receiving. (Apart from advertisements, the *Daily Courant* of 31 January 1712 was made up entirely of port news from Limerick, Kinsale, Cork, Waterford, Aberdeen, Greenock, Shields, Falmouth, Holyhead, Plymouth, Yarmouth, Bristol, Portsmouth, Harwich and Deal. Most of those ports lay in the west, and ships arriving from them would have been able to run before the westerly gale that was holding up the packet boats from the Low Countries.)

News from other parts of the country is much less frequent, let alone regular, and what there is of it may have been volunteered by some 'well-wisher' to the paper in which it appears. In this category it may be fair to place the *Protestant Mercury*'s report of 'a Whale that came ashore in Aberdeenshire, about 50 foot long'. On the whole, however, the country news published by the newspapers of 1695–1700 was of a more serious nature than most of that appearing in those of 1679–82. On 29 September 1696 the *Post-Boy* announced that the Bishop of Chichester had met with an accident, and was 'on the point of Death, but not dead'. On the same day the *Flying Post* was able to state that he had died. On 30 September the *Protestant Mercury* gave more details: the Bishop's coach had overturned on Monday 21 September, and on Wednesday his leg was amputated; but on Friday he had died, and he was buried next day in the cathedral. On 3 October the *Flying Post* had a further account 'concerning the unfortunate death of the Bishop', running to 16 lines. This may have come from the paper's regular correspondent in Chichester, or it may have been the result of an enquiry sent to someone in that town. On 8 October the same paper published an account of the King's arrival from abroad by way of Margate and Sittingbourne (where he had dinner), and so on to London, where he arrived at 11 p.m. On 19 October the *Protestant Mercury* had further news of the King:

We have an account from Peterborough, that upon News of the King's safe arrival [from abroad], they made great Rejoycings in that City, by Ringing of Bells, and Illuminations; and some, who either out of Covetousness or otherwise, neglected to put Candles in their Windows, had them sufficiently broken, which was no great Grief to the Glaziers.

Such introductory phrases as 'We have an account from Peterborough' or 'They write from Norwich' hardly suggest that what follows came from the paper's own correspondent; indeed, they are rather an indication that the news item has been appropriated from some other source, a news-letter for example. The surest sign that a news item has come from a paper's own correspondent is the direct quotation of his words, as in the following paragraph of news from Norwich (*Lloyd's News*, 24 September 1696):

We have already about £20,000 of Money and Plate brought in to be Coin'd, and we are in expectation of 2 or £30,000 more. We have already begun to coin.

(An Act had been passed in January 1696 for re-coinage of the silver money, and in June the Treasury arranged for setting up mints in the main provincial towns.)

In the early eighteenth century, news from country towns continued to be sparse. For country news to be considered interesting enough to print, something of far-reaching importance had to have happened. One such event was the Great Storm of 1703, which blew with hurricane force for many hours, leaving a trail of havoc and death in the southern half of England. Among the victims were the Bishop of Wells and his lady, who were killed when two chimney stacks crashed through the roof of their bedchamber. The *London Post* of 29 November gave the storm generous coverage, and on the following day the *Post Man* had news from Bristol, Deal, Portsmouth and Harwich of the damage caused to shipping and buildings, with further reports on 7 and 9 December. Nothing, however, gave the country districts more importance than a general election for parliament, when the results could be spread over several weeks as the counties and boroughs arrived at their own polling day. In general those contests, with their frequent intimidation and sharp practices, were more fully reported than those in the reign of Charles II.

Edinburgh and Dublin retained their prestige as cities likely to provide important news. In the months leading up to the Union of 1707, evidence of progress and lack of progress in the very difficult negotiations came from Edinburgh and was recorded in the press. The successful outcome, leading to the termination of a separate Scottish parliament, and a little later to the dissolution of the Scottish Privy Council, robbed Edinburgh of some of its importance and one of the main elements in its pageantry, but left it with its church, its law courts, and a good deal else. In 1715, when the Jacobite rebellion broke out, most of the reports going south still went through Edinburgh, although some might occasionally reach London by another route. Some papers still continued to publish reports from their own correspondents in Edinburgh and Dublin, but by the 1720s it was no longer so essential to maintain a private correspondent in those cities. On 4 May 1728 the readers of Mist's *Weekly Journal* were told: 'Our Edinburgh Papers this Week bring us but one material Piece of News . . .' In 1728 Mist could obtain Edinburgh news from the *Edinburgh Courant* or from the *Caledonian Mercury*. For his Dublin news he could draw upon *Faulkner's Dublin Post Boy* and the *Dublin Journal*.

How much of the news coming from other parts of Scotland and Ireland, and from important towns in England, reached the newspapers from their own correspondents, must remain largely a matter for speculation. From a satirical advertisement in Mist's *Weekly Journal* (20 July 1718) it appears that John Oldmixon, then living at Bridgwater as collector of the customs, was in the habit of sending items of local news to the *Flying Post*. When the *Daily Journal* was started in January 1721, its readers were told that care was being taken to settle a good correspondence 'not only Abroad, but also within his Majesty's Dominions, and especially at Edinburgh and Dublin'. There is some evidence that it was as good as its word. On 10 February it published a letter with news from Reading, the writer explaining that this was 'the first that has offer'd since your Request was Exhibited . . . and if Occasion and Opportunity offer any Thing worthy, I may give you more'. The statement that a request had been 'exhibited' appears to indicate that the *Daily Journal* has sent printed bills to Reading to be stuck up in places of public resort (such as coffee-houses) inviting anyone interested to become a correspondent for the paper. Some days earlier, on 28 January, the writer of another letter volunteered to supply the paper with news from Oxford:

I'll take care that you shan't want a Correspondent here, and you may assure your Readers that nothing Remarkable will happen in Oxford, but what they shall immediately be acquainted with.

It looks as if a copy of the same bill had been exhibited in Oxford. Whether those two gentlemen were to be paid anything for their pains is not mentioned in either letter; but as the Oxford correspondent ends by saying, 'In return for this Kindness, I hope you will answer me, as soon as possible, a Question or two . . .', it would appear that money did not enter into the transaction. There is, however, another possibility. So far back as 1692, when John Houghton was trying to settle a large country correspondence for his weekly *Collection for the Improvement of Husbandry and Trade*, he announced in his second number, 'Whoever are willing, from their Markets to send me Prices, in good time, I'll return them in lieu one of my Collections.' This method of rewarding country correspondents may well have become common; it is, or was, still in use in the present century.

With regular country correspondents sending in such news as they considered to be 'worthy' and 'sufficiently remarkable', there was less chance of the papers being full of trivialities. Some country news, it is true, was still trifling and inane, as an acid critic in 1729 sought to establish by ridicule:

The Athenians are recorded a People who *spend all their Time in hearing and telling some new Thing*; but what were they in Comparison with our Countrymen? who are so intelligent that if an old Woman does but sprain her Ancle going over a Stile in Yorkshire, in two or three Days you have the whole Account of the dismal Disaster in our News-Papers.[31]

In one direction, however, there was some quiet but perceptible progress. Drawing on his memories of early manhood (*Tatler*, 21 May 1709), Addison remarks that 'everyone remembers the shifts they were driven to in the reign of King Charles the Second, when they could not furnish out a single Paper of News, without lighting up a Comet in Germany, or a fire in Moscow'. (One of the comets thus lit up was that now known as Halley's comet, which the *True Protestant Mercury* of 2 September 1682 reported as having been observed at Turin, Vienna, Strasbourg, Paris and Brussels.) Addison goes on to recall that John Dyer in his news-letter was 'particularly famous for dealing in Whales' and Ichabod Dawks for dwelling on plagues and famines. He returns to this theme in the *Freeholder* of 23 March 1716:

It is an old observation that a time of peace is always a time of prodigies; for as our news-writers must adorn their papers with that which criticks call 'the

Marvellous', they are forced in a dead calm of affairs to ransack every element for proper amusements, and either to astonish their readers from time to time with a strange and wonderful sight, or be content to lose their custom. The sea is generally filled with monsters when there are no fleets upon it . . . The air has likewise contributed its quota of prodigies.

Addison then refers to 'a civil war in the clouds', alluding to a recent display of aurora borealis 'where our sharp-sighted male-contents discovered many objects invisible to an eye that is dimmed by Whig principles'. In 1716, Addison is saying, we are at peace again, and once more the enemies of the government are finding an ominous significance in celestial phenomena. But, though he would have been too modest to say so, the essays of Addison and Steele had done much to laugh such superstitious beliefs out of fashion. The rich vein of monstrous births, sea monsters, armies in the clouds, ghosts, voices in the air, witches and what not, that had been worked so assiduously by men like Harris and Benskin (and by Harris certainly for political purposes) was now all but worked out. (The last conviction for witchcraft in England happened in 1712, and the offender was reprieved.[32]) Whatever explanations may be offered – a general advance in education, the more particular influence of the Royal Society, the changes that took place when the Stuart monarchy was replaced by the Hanoverian, etc. – the intellectual climate was slowly becoming more stable. From time to time the more popular papers would show a willingness to revive the old shudders with some supernatural anecdote; but the age was gradually growing more rational, and even the remote country districts were no longer the dedicated and fertile breeding ground for the marvellous and the occult, the two-headed calf and the spectre 'with burning eyes and visage horrible'.

CHAPTER 4

Foreign news

In considering the supply of foreign news in the seventeenth and eighteenth centuries, it is necessary to distinguish between those few papers (notably the *London Gazette*) that had access to information provided by the government of the day, and all the others that were left to fend for themselves.* When, in 1655, Cromwell suppressed all unlicensed newspapers and Marchamont Nedham was given the monopoly of providing the nation with news, he was also given controlled access to the foreign intelligence organised by John Thurloe, who had his own agents abroad, and was able to draw upon the reports sent in from English embassies in the various European capitals. Nedham's foreign news was therefore both ample and reliable.

After the Restoration, when Henry Muddiman's two news-books were both published 'by order', he too obtained most of his foreign news from the reports communicated by English ambassadors and their secretaries. Under the methodical supervision of Lord Arlington's secretary, Joseph Williamson, the organisation of foreign intelligence reached a similar peak of efficiency to that attained during the Protectorate under Thurloe. When the *Gazette* was founded in 1665, this excellent service of foreign news became available to the Gazetteer. Ideally, ambassadors wrote a weekly letter in cipher, containing such news as they considered it important for the government to have, while the secretaries sent home the ordinary news. If a secretary was carrying out his duties competently, he would transmit to London the printed newspapers and the news-letters, together with any information supplied by his own correspondents. Further information was obtained from the numerous consuls stationed in important towns, not only in Europe but in more distant countries. In Madrid the secretary himself collected news from the consuls in the Iberian peninsula and compiled his own report. In supplying news for the *Gazette* the consuls were an

---

* In this chapter it has been found necessary to make more reference than usual to the early eighteenth century, mainly to establish beyond doubt the existence of regular foreign correspondents.

important link in the chain. They were stationed in such places as Elsinore, Hamburg, Ostend, Bordeaux and Marseilles, Bilbao, Seville, Alicante and Barcelona, Turin, Genoa, Leghorn, Naples and Venice. Outside Europe they were to be found at Smyrna, Aleppo, Tripoli, Alexandria, Algiers and elsewhere. Their reports kept Whitehall in touch with the arrival and departure of English and foreign shipping, the movement of armed forces, the latest political developments, and so on. What ultimately found its way into the *Gazette* would almost always be reliable information, and not idle rumour or speculation. Even if the Gazetteer had room for only a small fraction of the news at his disposal, the very fact that he was receiving such reliable reports would make it unnecessary for him to publish less trustworthy or tendentious news from a foreign newspaper or news-letter. His main problem was one of selection and compression.[1]

From time to time ambassadors had to be reminded of their duties. On 15 March 1666 Charles had exhorted them to send frequent accounts 'to Us, our Chancellors and Secretaries, of your negotiations and actings, and also of such matters as shall come to your knowledge, which may be of concernment to Us and our Kingdoms'.[2] What seems most often to have been overlooked was the sort of news that could be used in the *Gazette*. When Steele became Gazetteer in 1707, he drew up a memorial for Lord Sunderland, then Secretary of State for the Southern Department, proposing several steps that should be taken 'for the advancement of the credit and income of the *Gazette*'. That his first suggestion was for 'an instruction to all the Ministers in each province to send a circular letter every post of what passes in their respective stations, directed to the Gazetteer'[3] would indicate that this practice was not being generally observed. Early in the reign of George I, Lord Polwarth, then a plenipotentiary at the Court of Denmark, received an appeal from an under-secretary to order 'a circular newspaper to be sent every post for the use of the *Gazette*', since that official paper ought 'to be supported and fed by the fullest and best intelligence of historical occurrences'. A similar request reached him from Lord Carteret in 1723. He was 'to transmit constantly . . . particular accounts of such occurrences and transactions as do from time to time become the subject of news at the place where you reside, together with any printed news or other papers that your excellency shall judge may afford proper matter for the *Gazette*'.[4] No doubt Lord Polwarth found this part of his ambassadorial duties something of a chore, and he was not the only one to do so.

If the foreign news published in the *Gazette* was generally accurate, mistakes were sometimes made, either by the ambassador's secretary or one of his subordinates, or by the Gazetteer or one of his clerks in preparing it for the press. When, in 1705, De Fonvive was invited by Sir Charles Hedges, one of the Secretaries of State, to become a clerk in his office so that he could compile the *Gazette* and 'write now and then copies of letters', he turned the offer down without hesitation. Writing to Robert Harley, he gave his reasons:

The writing of the *Gazette*, though judged trifling by such who never tried the difficulties thereof, requires more learning than some imagine, and a great deal of care to avoid blunders and contradictions; and as it must take up a man's whole time ought to have a suitable encouragement, and I dare say that the committing the writing of it to a young clerk, and the revising to the four under-secretaries, which was done upon pretence of saving copy money, has been one of the chief causes of the decay of the *Gazette*; and the Secretaries of State would have got more money . . . had they given £500 to a gentleman of parts who had made it his sole business to secure that place to himself for his life.[5]

One of the *Gazette's* more persistent critics was Defoe, who exposed its muddled reports of military actions on the Continent, and the incompetent way in which it was sometimes written. As the years passed, the *Gazette* had to compete with better written and far livelier papers, and it became a natural target for ridicule and fault finding. When Steele took over in 1707 he began with high hopes (and at £300 a year); but before long he found the need to obtain authority for everything he wrote thoroughly frustrating, and he occasionally made mistakes by going to the wrong authority. Early in his career on the *Gazette* he offended Queen Anne's consort, who was also Lord High Admiral, by publishing an account (for which he had got clearance from Addison, at that time one of Lord Sunderland's under-secretaries) of the arrival of a fleet at Ostend.[6] Steele wanted the *Gazette* to be readable; but looking back on his years as Gazetteer, he reflected sadly that he had 'worked faithfully according to Order, without ever erring against the Rule observed by all Ministries to keep that Paper very innocent and very insipid'.[7]

For the unlicensed newspapers that came out between 1679 and 1682, the procedure was very different. All of them relied for the greater part of their foreign news on the Dutch and French newspapers reaching London, if weather conditions were favourable, twice a week. But although they had only a few other, and minor, sources of information, they seldom took their readers into their confidence about their indebtedness to the foreign newspapers. Instead, they went out of their way to conceal the source of their news, with such expressions as 'They write from Vienna', 'We have advice from Turin', and 'It is reported from Frankfurt'. Even when they are more specific, and introduce a piece of news with such words as 'Our Flanders Letters of the 14th. advise' or 'By our Letters from Moscow', we may be almost sure that the information did not come to them directly from a correspondent, but by way of such papers as the *Haarlem Courant* or the *Gazette de Paris*. It was only when a newspaper ran into trouble over some piece of foreign news it had printed that it willingly admitted its source to be a foreign paper. When Richard Janeway was examined in May 1682 about a paragraph of news in the *Impartial Protestant Mercury*, he explained that for foreign news was taken from the Latin *Cologne News*, the *Haarlem Courant* and the *Brussels Gazette*.[8]

The first newsman to take the public into his confidence about how he obtained his foreign news was Samuel Buckley in 1702. In his *Daily Courant* of 22 October he gave his readers the facts:

It will be found by the Foreign Prints which, as Occasion shall offer, will be mention'd in this *Courant*, that the Author has taken care to be duly furnish'd with all that come from Abroad. And for an Assurance that he will not impose any *Feign'd Additions*, he will always quote the *Papers* from whence he makes his *Extracts*, and represent *Foreign Affairs* just as he finds them in the *Foreign Prints*; that the Publick seeing from what *Place* a piece of *News* comes, with the *Allowance* of the *Government* of that *Country*, may be the better able to judge of the *Credibility* and *Fairness* of the *Relation*.

Buckley's practice of naming the foreign prints from which he took the bulk of his news spread in time to some of the more reputable papers of the early eighteenth century as readers grew more sophisticated, but it was by no means universal.

The main difficulty with foreign news arose from the uncertain arrival of the packet boats from the Low Countries and (when the country was not at war with France) from the French ports. In winter especially, all the packet boats might be laid up in harbour unable to venture out to sea. On 14 January 1680 *Mercurius Anglicus* had to tell its readers: 'The Letters from the Downs make but bad Relations of the violent Storms . . . And besides the Winds have sate so contrary for some days past that they have hindered the coming of three Males [*sic*] from Holland, and as many from Flanders, so that little Foreign News can be expected.' On 10 March the situation was even worse: 'We are now wanting thirteen foreign Males, seven from Flanders, three from France, and three from Holland, which has been occasioned by the late high Winds.' In such circumstances a seventeenth-century newspaper did its best to fill the empty spaces with additional home news, of which at that time there was usually plenty.

Gales continued to blow as hard as ever in the eighteenth century, and in the days of sailing ships wrought havoc with the delivery of the foreign news that the English papers were eagerly expecting. Even in stormy weather the odd packet boat from Ireland might arrive, or a stray vessel from Spain or Portugal might make port with torn sails and a mast missing; but nearly all news from abroad (the main section in papers like the *Post Man* and the *Daily Courant*) was cut off. In such circumstances something could be done by using a larger type face, lowering the heading of the paper, increasing the number of advertisements, and extending the section given to port news, even if it was only to enumerate recent arrivals and the ships that were unable to put to sea. (Merchants, who must have been among the more regular readers of newspapers, would have been the most avid devotees of port news.) But such shifts were insufficient to fill two empty pages, and the occurrence of stormy weather drove the newsmen to find substitutes for the missing foreign news.

At the beginning of 1704 atrocious weather completely disorganised the mail service for about two weeks: the packet boats were all bottled up at Harwich, and although two of them managed to put to sea on 3 January, they were driven back the following day. In this extremity the various newswriters were compelled to rely on their own resources. On 6 January the *Flying Post* told its readers that 'in the want of Foreign Mails, we shall give an Account of the Predictions of the Milan Almanack, for the Satisfaction of the Curious, and of those who lay any stress upon such Things'; and accordingly the whole of the front page and a few lines of the back page were given up to the *Milan Almanac*, along with a few items of port news and a paragraph dated 'London'. The next two issues gave further extracts from the *Almanac*; but at last, on 12 January, four Dutch mails arrived simultaneously, and the author of the *Flying Post* was able to return to his proper business. His was a wretched stopgap, but it was typical of the hasty steps taken to deal with an interruption of the foreign news.

During another long period of bad weather in early November 1711, the *British Mercury* published extracts from Symon's 'Dissertation on Presages'; the *Supplement* had an account of the life of Marshal de Boufflers taken from the *Mercure Galant*; the *Evening Post* produced a list of the Danish fleet off the coast of Pomerania and of the Danish troops before Stralsund; and the *Protestant Postboy* printed extracts from Dr Charles Davenant's *Essay upon the Right of Making War, Peace and Alliances*. On 8 November the *Flying Post* gave the whole of its front page to 'An Information about the Rabbling of a Minister of the Church of Scotland, as by Law Establish'd, at Kilmuir Wester, on the Lord's Day, September 23, 1711'; and the *Post-Boy* filled up with a long account of the setting up of a Church of England congregation at Aberdeen, and port news from Cork, Kinsale, Belfast, Dublin and other places. The *London Gazette* of the same date managed to complete its front page by resorting to large type for its last two paragraphs of news, and filled the back page with announcements and advertisements. The stormy weather continuing, the *Evening Post* relied mainly on stale news, and the *British Mercury* regaled its readers with 'Funeral Ceremonies in France'. The *Post-Boy* of 10 November, more up to date, came out with a leading article against the war and in favour of the proposed peace, and this was answered by the *Flying Post* three days later. Only these last two items showed any real attempt to cope relevantly with the temporary dearth of foreign news. In a facetious newspaper of 1709, carried on by 'Novel' and 'Scandal', there occurs a dialogue in which Novel says that he has no idea 'what we should do to fill up our Paper for Monday, for, Faith, I don't think of any thing at present'. Scandal has the answer ready:

Have you never an Old *Ordonnance, Memorial, Abstract*, never a *Sham Letter* from Geneva, nor nothing of that kind? If you were acquainted with any of the News-Writers, they'd furnish you presently: they have always Abundance of this sort of *Trumpery* by 'em, to serve 'em upon such Occasions.[9]

A few conscientious newswriters such as De Fonvive of the *Post Man*, were unwilling to demean themselves by printing irrelevant stuff when they were without news from abroad. During the stormy weather of 1704 already mentioned, he made a serious attempt to conduct his paper on intelligent lines by offering his readers some general remarks on Switzerland. In the following issue he extended his remarks to Germany, and explained why he was doing so: he did not think it reasonable to entertain a reader 'with vain and tedious repetitions' of what was contained in the former issue.

Therefore we shall pursue the method mentioned in our last, and make some observations which may be of use to some People; whereas the repeating of insignificant Stories is equally irksome and useless. This agrees likewise very well with the Title of this Paper [*The Post Man, and the Historical Account*], which admits of everything that may render our Accounts of the publick Transactions more intelligible.[10]

When Berrington started his *Evening Post* in 1709, he intended it to be a daily paper, but after about two weeks he went over to thrice-weekly publication. On 16 September, before he had made the change, he announced that on post-nights his paper would contain the substance of all the other papers, and 'on other Nights (instead of stuffing it with Prayers, Projects for Peace, Canting against Immorality and Profaneness, Irish Votes at large, etc.)' he would give 'the Geographical Description of those Places relating to the Seat of War, in order to a perfect Understanding of the Transactions'. He therefore began with a description of towns in Flanders; but when his paper started coming out only on post-nights there was no need or room for this sensible feature. But the old trouble of stormy weather continued to disrupt the newspapers. On 3 August 1722 the *Daily Post* found its own respectable substitute for the foreign news that had failed to reach it:

We News-Writers, like Stage-Coaches, must go our Stages, even tho' we have no Passengers; but with this Disadvantage on our Side, that they may go empty, we not. Therefore, while the Wind prevents the Arrival of Foreign Mails, 'tis hoped our Readers will not be offended, if, rather than new-vamp an old, perhaps exploded, Story, ornamenting it with turn'd Commas to intimate to our Proprietors that extraordinary Postage must be allow'd for it, we fill up this Paper with the following short Account of Malta.

By this time, no doubt, a well-run newspaper had learnt to anticipate an absence of foreign news by keeping a file of sensible substitutes, which could be drawn upon as the need arose without making the newswriter feel foolish.

The extent to which eighteenth-century newswriters had come to depend upon the foreign papers for their information from abroad may be seen by their occasionally taking from a foreign paper a piece of news that had originally appeared in an English one. On 7 August 1728 the *Daily Journal* drew attention to this having happened with two pieces of news it had earlier printed from its own correspondents:

We think ourselves obliged, in Justice and due Acknowledgment to divers of our worthy Correspondents, who favour us frequently with early Intelligence, to take Notice that the King of Portugal's Decree which Yesterday's *Post-Boy* gives us, with Justice, as a most remarkable Piece, together with two others which he promises, are all inserted in our Paper of the 22d. of July last; and in all Likelihood translated from us into the Foreign Prints, and so re-translated back again as a New Piece.

To give this charge more precise documentation, the *Daily Journal* then offered a second example, in which its news had taken an even longer route, naming the foreign newspaper that had first reprinted it before it was reprinted by an English paper:

As also, that in the *Daily Courant* of the same Day the Relation there inserted of the Massacre of some English Gentlemen at Jiddah, together with the Bashaw's Letter on that Occasion, were published in ours of the 30th. of March last, and transcribed by the *Boston Gazette*, and now brought back, and published as a New Piece of Intelligence.

Samuel Buckley, who had prided himself on his reliable handling of foreign news in 1702, ought to have blushed for this editorial gaffe. In 1717, however, he had been made Gazetteer for life and had less time to look after his old paper.[11]

Although the foreign newspapers were to remain for many years the chief source of news from abroad, there were always a few other ways of acquiring information. Letters received from merchants living abroad were frequently passed on to the proprietor of a newspaper or his newswriter, and printed in whole, or more usually in part. In this way the *Weekly General-Post* of 12 May 1716 was able to publish in extract 'a Letter received last Post by a Merchant of London from his Correspondent at Avignon', giving news of the Pretender, who was staying there, and of his Jacobite retinue. On 11 September 1716 the *Evening Post* made use of a letter sent to a London merchant from Marseilles; and on 20 May 1720, the *London Journal* gave more than a column to the substance of a letter from Carolina 'by a Planter and Merchant there to his Brother and Correspondent in England'. Enclosed with this letter, we are told, was another dated from 'Moon Castle, Havana', and several others from the same place. Much of the news reaching London from the New World came in this way, and most of it was probably reliable. On one occasion, it is true, some news published by Harris on 16 December 1679 met with a rebuke from the *Gazette*. Harris had heard 'by Letters from Port Royal in Jamaica' that the English settlers were dreading an attack from the French fleet commanded by Monsieur D'Estrée. This produced an indignant denial from the *Gazette*, which explained ('as we reported two months ago') that D'Estrée and his fleet had returned to Brest on 10 October, and added for good measure: 'The World . . . is every day most grossly imposed upon by those Pamphlets.'[12] Harris, however, was not to be browbeaten by the *Gazette*, and in his next issue he put the record straight, or at least managed to save face: 'The News in our last, of the posture of Affairs in Jamaica, came by many Merchants' Letters, and if D'Estrée be returned to Brest, they wish that the next Letters from Jamaica may assure them that he left no Fleet to endanger that Plantation, of which they are under great Fears.'

Other letters from abroad are simply described as 'private': 'by private Letters from Tangier', 'by a private advice from a Gentleman

130

in Paris to a Friend in London', and so on. As a source of news, private letters were only as reliable as the writer. In stating his policy for the *Daily Courant*, Buckley had shown a proper caution in the use of them: 'As for the News that he inserts from private Letters, he will take care not to be impos'd on, and will leave it to the Publick to give such Credit to those Letters as they shall be found to deserve.'[13]

No more reliable, but often relied upon by the newspapers, was a frequently cited source of information: ship news. When ships docked at the port of London, a news-gatherer could interview the captain or crew, and write down what he could remember. The value of news obtained in this way obviously depended on the credibility of the narrator, and the competence of the man who listened to his story. Defoe took a poor view of ship news; he found it uncertain, and 'an Intelligence we have been often deceiv'd by'.[14] At all events, ship news sometimes produced strange reading. 'By a Ship lately arrived from Genoa', Harris had news of an English Catholic gentleman who had been murdered by priests and buried under the high altar.[15] (It is only fair to point out that for the Catholic-baiting Harris such an episode would seem entirely credible.) 'By a ship called the *Olive* . . . lately arrived from Maryland', Smith's *Currant Intelligence* of 20 March 1680 had word of a Popish plot there. Since Smith's was one of the most reliable of the seventeenth-century papers, this news, however improbable it may seem, cannot be dismissed out of hand. Reports of this kind must indeed be given such credit 'as they shall be found to deserve'. Certainly the *Currant Intelligence, Lloyd's News*, the *Post Man*, the *Daily Courant* and the other papers that were receiving port news by every post, were in a position to publish not just the arrival and departure of merchant vessels (as was still common practice in the first half of the twentieth century), but sometimes stories of adventurous voyages and of English ships beating off or sinking Algerian, French or Spanish pirates and privateers. On 3 October 1695 the *Flying Post* gave its readers a long account of the vessel 'Charity', which had sailed from Jamaica in August 1694, and had been given up for lost a year ago. She had been driven by contrary winds to New York, where she had re-fitted; but on resuming her voyage she had encountered a violent storm, during which she lost all her masts, and then her rudder. She had drifted helplessly for five months, while all on board were reduced to eating raw hides. (On one occasion a rat was reserved for the captain, 'a rare dainty'.) At last she sighted the coast of Portugal, re-fitted, and arrived home with a cargo worth between £30,000 and £40,000.

Sometimes news would be obtained 'from a Ship arriving in the

Downs'. Ships sailing up the English Channel on their way to London would often take shelter in the Downs, while waiting for favourable winds to carry them round the North Foreland into the Thames estuary. The postmaster at Deal handled mail to and from shipping in the Downs, and this would involve rowing out to a ship with the mailbag, collecting the incoming mail, and no doubt chatting with the sailors and picking up scraps of news.[16] Since ships might be delayed in the Downs for several days, any information obtained in this way could be immediately sent on by the postmaster (who was usually the port correspondent) and reach London, weather permitting, by the Dover road in about twelve hours. In this way Benskin must have obtained the news, dated from Deal and attributed to 'the Master of a Vessel that Lately arrived from the Streights', that he published on 27 May 1681. At first sight this news, telling about a great fire in Geneva that destroyed about fifty houses, 'and greatly endangered several Vessels that Anchored in the Port', must seem incredible; but Benskin's printer had a chronic inability to spell, and 'Geneva' for 'Genoa' was for him a minor aberration.

Occasionally news from abroad came from English travellers returning home. On 30 December 1679, Harris reported that passengers from Dunkirk spoke of French soldiers being stationed in the ports along the coast. On 7 October 1681 the *Impartial Protestant Mercury* drew attention to fresh rumours that the English parliament was likely to be summoned to sit on the 28th of November, and gave as its authority 'a Person of Quality lately arriv'd from France', who said that 'he was told such a thing at Paris'.[17] On such precarious foundations much of the day's news was based. The determination of successive governments to release as little political news as possible led fairly frequently to English news being taken from foreign papers. On 13 September 1681 the *Loyal Protestant* announced:

We have advice by the *Harlem Courant* from Amsterdam of the 12th instant, That His Majesty of Great Britain's Envoy at the French Court hath presented a Memorial in favour of the poor afflicted Protestants of that Nation, setting forth, that his Master could not look upon the Prosecution of his Neighbour Protestants without concern, and therefore was resolved to give Protection with Immunities to all such as should fly to him for refuge . . .

Thompson may have had a threatening visit from a messenger of the press; for on 1 October, in what looks like an officially worded retraction, he stated: 'The Relation in the *Haerlem Courant* of the 12th is a meer fiction, there being not anything of Truth in that Report.' In the early eighteenth century the government of the day still tried to keep a tight control on the news it allowed to appear. In the first number of the *Evening Post* (6 September 1709) readers were promised a better account than any yet available of home news, which was so inadequately covered 'that we read more of our own Affairs in the Dutch Papers than in any of our own'.

When the *Evening Post* made this promise, however, Great Britain was still at war with France, and it was war news that readers were especially anxious to have, and to have without delay. We have seen how the packet boats were frequently held up by bad weather and the newswriters left to bite their nails. There was, however, another way by which news could have crossed the English Channel or the North Sea: it could have come by air. The men who had an imperative need for the latest war news, more so even than the newswriters, were the stockjobbers of Exchange Alley, who bought heavily before the news of a victory could reach the general public, and sold before the news of a defeat. In a pamphlet attack on stockjobbing Defoe asserted that

Sir H[arr]y F[urne]se in the late King William's Reign was able to maintain such a constant Intelligence in Holland, Flanders, Germany, Ireland etc. that he several times brought the King Accounts of Battles fought, Victories won, Towns taken etc. before the swiftest Expresses of the King's own Servants and Generals could arrive; and had once a Diamond Ring of £500 given him by the King for his early News.[18]

Defoe does not say here how Sir Harry, a wealthy financier and speculator, came to be so early with his news; but in his *Review* of 30 July 1709 he writes of stockjobbers deliberately putting about a false story that after the capitulation of Tournai the French were sending deputies to the Hague to sue for peace. Having raised the price of stocks by this fabricated good news, the jobbers 'no doubt SOLD OUT, as they found Opportunity immediately, without any Post, any Express, or any Possibility of its coming, Pidgeons and Daemons excepted'. To this hint of carrier pigeons may be added a more direct reference (in John Tutchin's *Observator*, 15 May 1706) to the use made of them: 'They tell me that Mr. Whiston's Pidgeons are all Dead, Flown away, or Enter'd into the French King's Service.' Some important news, then, may have reached London by pigeon-post, but if any such service was available to one or more of the newswriters, we should probably have heard about it from one of their sarcastic rivals.

From time to time some newspaper would obtain a scoop from one of the foreign embassies in London. The most famous leak of the early eighteenth century took place in 1711, when Henry St John transmitted a copy of the proposed peace terms to the Austrian minister, Count de Gallas, and he sent it to the *Daily Courant*, where it was published on 13 October. The Count was told he could no longer appear at Court, and the Emperor was asked to replace him with someone more suitable. There were other and less spectacular scoops obtained from contact with foreign embassies. On 11 August 1711 the *Gazette* had news of a victory gained by the Tsar of Russia over the Turks, and the *Evening Post* of the same date, stating that 'This Morning we had one Mail from Holland' published an account of the Tsar's victory in a Postscript. But Abel Roper's *Supplement* had already published the good news in its issue of 10 August, explaining that 'the following News from the Hague was dispatch'd by the Danish Envoy there to the Briel [the Brill; a small Dutch coastal town just south of the Hook of Holland], some hours after the Letters were sent away, directed to the Danish Envoy here'. This news had been received by express from the King of Denmark, who had received it by express from the Tsar. It appears, therefore, that the regular packet boat had sailed before the news of the Tsar's victory was generally known, and that the news had reached the Danish embassy in London through the dispatch of another vessel later in the day. (That the *Gazette* was able to announce the victory on the morning of 11 August would indicate that it, too, was indebted to the Danish embassy for the information.) The *Supplement*, then, had achieved a mild scoop. We know that Abel Roper had the assistance of 'a Danish gentleman' to translate the Dutch news for his *Post-Boy*, but this gentleman had died.[19] Roper was now publishing the *Supplement*, and if we want to guess how he obtained this news from the Danish embassy, the answer may be that he had acquired a second Danish gentleman to replace the first.

On Monday 2 January 1721 Berrington's *Evening Post* published a Postscript giving a detailed account of a Spanish victory over the Moors on the plain of Ceuta. This news had reached the *Evening Post* by way of the Spanish embassy in London:

On Sunday the first Instant, at five a Clock in the Afternoon, his Excellency the Marquis de Pozo Bueno, his Catholick Majesty's Minister at this Court, received by Express the following Account of a Third Victory obtain'd over the Moors by his Catholick Majesty's Forces.

Berrington's account ran to three and a half pages, and he thought it of sufficient importance to give almost the whole of his regular issue to it next day. If we ask why Berrington was favoured, among all the London newspaper men, with this exclusive information, the answer must be that he was one of the Roman Catholics then at work in the printing trade, and would therefore be likely to have a friend or acquaintance at the embassy of His Catholic Majesty.

The determination to be first with the news led at times to mistakes being made, but on other occasions to intelligent guesses that turned out to be correct. When the siege of Namur was reaching its climax in the last days of August 1695, the newswriters were eagerly waiting to announce the capitulation of the Castle. On Thursday 29 August the *Post-Boy* had a report dated 'Paris, August 26th.': 'Yesterday 5 Expresses passed through this City going to the Court of France, from the Mareschal de Villeroy; the Contents of their message are yet a secret, which makes us conclude that the Castle of Namur is reduced to Extremity.' On the same day the *Flying Post* reported in a final paragraph that 'the Discourse of the Town' was wholly concerned with whether the Castle had been captured, and added that 'according to our best Information, it is supposed to be in the Hands of the Allies', having been 'taken by Storm on Thursday last'. The information referred to consisted of 'some letters . . . brought by some Interested Persons on Saturday Morning last in a fisher-boat from Newport, which landed next Morning at Margate'. The Castle had certainly not been taken on Thursday last (22 August): the final assault had only begun. On this occasion, however, no harm was done, for in its next number the *Flying Post* was able to refer to the terms of surrender already published 'by authority', i.e. by the *Gazette*.[20]

In 1711 the *British Mercury* was not so lucky: it reported a colossal defeat of the French that had not taken place. In the summer of that year a large French army under the command of Marshal Villars lay entrenched behind an eigtheenth-century Maginot Line, running from Oppy in the west, through Arras, to Bouchain and Valenciennes in the east, while the bulk of Marlborough's army lay to the north of Arras. Marlborough was determined to wind up his campaign with the capture of Bouchain, and in the last week of July he carried out one of his most skilful manœuvres. He gave orders to his troops to march south-west, as if intending to attack the French at the western end of their heavily fortified lines, and Villars duly began to withdraw troops from the east to reinforce those apparently threatened in the west. When night fell, however, Marlborough ordered the English and Dutch army to turn round and march due east, and when day broke they were 'met by a message from Marlborough, announcing that the detachment under Generals Cadogan and Hompesch had traversed unopposed the causeway near Arleux, and were in possession of the French Lines'. The message also contained a polite request to the foot-soldiers: 'the Duke desires the infantry will step out.' In the next 16 hours they covered 36 miles, and without losing a single man, now lay between the French and Bouchain. A daring thrust then took Marlborough across the river Schelde, and the siege of Bouchain began.[21] This was a remarkable tactical achievement, but it was not what is usually described as a 'victory', and certainly not the sort of victory reported by the *British Mercury*.

On Sunday 29 July, the *Gazette* had published a supplement, giving an account of the manœuvres outlined above, and describing how the army had marched 'with great Chearfulness, and without Halting' for 24 hours. The account ended with the latest news then available: 'Brigadier Sutton left the Army on Thursday Night, at which time they were passing the Scheld, and he believes Bouchain is now Invested [besieged].' On Monday 30 July the *British Mercury* (which by this time must have been almost completely set for publication next day) managed to find room for a shortened version of the *Gazette's* report, and then proceeded to make its fatal blunder:

When Brigadier Sutton (who brought this News to the Queen) came away on Thursday Evening, my Lord Duke was preparing to attack the Enemy; of the happy Success of which his Grace has sent over an Account by Major General Evans, who arriv'd here Yesterday with a Letter to the Queen's Majesty, in which, as we are very credibly inform'd, his Grace had only Time to say, That Her Majesty's Army had gain'd a compleat Victory; and that Marshal Villars was THEN WITH HIS GRACE; referring for the Particulars to the Major General aforesaid: Which Particulars (according to our best Information) are, That besides Marshal Villars, his grace has taken 16,000 Prisoners, and amongst them 22 Battalions entire: That the Enemy's left Wing, and all their Horse, are entirely ruin'd, 160 Cannon, 120 Colours, 58 Standards, and all their Baggage taken, and the Army in Pursuit of the rest.

When the *British Mercury* next appeared on 1 August there was nothing for it but to publish a complete retraction: its heart-stirring account of a famous victory, with the enumeration of prisoners taken and cannon captured, was all a mistake. But its attempt to explain, and as far as possible justify, how it came to credit the Duke with a second Blenheim, throws some interesting light on the growth of a rumour. Where the report had first come from it was difficult to say, but it was probably 'occasion'd by Colonel Killigrew's passing thro' the City, being sent Express by the Duke of Argyle from Barcelona', with news that the Allied army in northern Spain had been reinforced by three regiments from Ireland, and now consisted of 25,000 men.

That Gentleman's Passage thro' the City (at a Time when every Body was in Expectation of great News) had given Occasion to the Rumour of a Victory. Some go so far as to say that some curious People call'd out to the Colonel, to know whether he came from Holland, and had brought good News to the Queen? and that some of his Followers, either to banter that Mob, or free themselves from their Importunity, answer'd, *Aye, aye.* Men's Imagination is fertile in supplying their Want of Information, especially in Matters of great Importance, and such as they are desirous of. They lump'd the Matter at once, and nothing less would serve but the taking of the French General, his Cannon, Baggage etc. and destroying all the Troops that could be suppos'd within the Reach of our Army. We have often had Surmises of Things which wise Men give little Attention to; but this Matter became in a Moment so general, and was every where related with such Assurance and so much Joy, and Persons of the best Rank assign'd as Authors of it, that it would have seem'd, in some Measure, criminal to have misbeliev'd it.

It can be added, in further extenuation of the *British Mercury*, that this extraordinary rumour blew up on a Sunday, when the streets were full of idle citizens ready to pass on what they hoped they had heard, and severally willing to accept the importance of one who brings good news. As the *Mercury* itself put it, 'How general [the report] was before 8 a Clock on Sunday, and how generally Credited, is not unknown about Whitehall, Westminster, and from thence to the Royal Exchange.' As it was a Sunday, too, and the presses were waiting to run off the next day's issue, there was little time for second thought; and a further inducement to go ahead with the story may be found in a report published by the *Post-Boy* on Tuesday 31 July that 'on Sunday in the Afternoon, the Guns at Lambeth were fired, and those at the Tower: the Evening concluded with Bonefires, Illuminations, Ringing of Bells etc.'

So far nothing has been said about the possibility that some newspapers had their own foreign correspondents. The Restoration papers of 1679–1682 do not appear, with one exception, to have had any access to private information from abroad other than those sources already considered. The exception is Smith's *Currant Intelligence*. When this paper was revived in 1681, it carried frequent reports from Paris, written in a familiar epistolary style, and dealing for the most part with matters of particular interest to an English reader. On 13 September it had news of an insult offered to Henry Savile, then a special envoy at Paris, and on 21 November of the satisfaction given him by the French King for the affront, and of a duel between Mr

Carnegy, son of Lord Southesk, and Mr Talmage, son of the Duke of Lauderdale. On 2 August 'the news we have here' was about 'the Prince of Orange's designing to come to England'. The length of most of these reports and their focus on English concerns, together with such expressions as 'It will be no less surprize to you than it hath been to us here', suggest that the information reaching the *Currant Intelligence* was coming from its correspondent, or at the least from a written news-letter. A long satirical piece published on 6 December seems to tip the balance in favour of its being an English correspondent living in Paris. The writer states that 'Our Apothecaries Shops are furnished with Medicines of all sorts . . . for the cure of the Body Politick', and goes on to name some. Those shops supply 'Dragon's Blood, that fills the Veins with Duty and Obedience to their Prince'; a purge 'that will certainly ease our Churchmen of such summs of Money and Estates as they have by their whining and dissembling got from the People'; an opium 'to lull asleep the Northern Crowns, that they shall not wake till it is either too late, or at least to no purpose'. If 'our' shops and 'our' churchmen may seem to indicate that a Frenchman is writing, the word could equally well be used by an Englishman living in Paris; and it seems hardly likely that a subject of Louis XIV (unless perhaps a Huguenot) would have described his country's policy as being one of lulling the northern crowns asleep, or have risked sending a letter with such sentiments through the French post. At all events, the *Currant Intelligence* had some sort of regular correspondent in France. It was also publishing from time to time, though not so frequently, similar communications from the Hague (e.g. 'We are not here a little alarmed at the Discovery of a Plot to seize the Person of His Highness the Prince of Orange.'), and also from Strasbourg (e.g. 'A Miller of a Village belonging to our University . . .').[22] Remembering that the *Currant Intelligence* was indebted to 'Mr. S---r of the Post-House' for its English country news, one may wonder whether the same person was not also in touch with his opposite numbers in Paris, Strasbourg and the Hague, and still further defrauding the Duke of York of his revenue.

It is only when we reach the second decade of the eighteenth century that we can be quite sure that any English newspaper (always excepting the *Gazette*) had got so far as to have its own regular foreign correspondents. De Fonvive, the able and successful writer of the *Post Man,* is sometimes cited as a journalist who had his own private sources of information from abroad. 'As to Foreign News,' John Dunton wrote in 1706, 'he has settl'd a good Correspondence in Italy, Spain,

Portugal, Germany, Flanders, Holland, etc.'²³ It would be wrong to brush this statement aside; but in 1706 the word 'correspondence' was not necessarily used for communications by letter. We need to know whether Dunton means only that De Fonvive had arranged to have as many foreign prints sent to him as were then available, or whether Dunton knew what De Fonvive had his own regular correspondents in the countries named. A man like De Fonvive would almost certainly have had friends and acquaintances in France and other European countries, and from them he might well have obtained information that he could use in the *Post Man*. But if some of his news came to him in this way, he kept very quiet about it; and if there are no good grounds for doubting that he had regular paid correspondents abroad, there is likewise no clear evidence to show that he had any. To this may be added, for what it is worth, a statement made in 1709 by the *General Postscript*. The writer of this paper took the easy way of attracting attention by making satirical and disgruntled remarks about almost all the other papers then appearing. Writing about the *Post Man*, he remarks of De Fonvive: 'He pretends to mighty Intelligence from Abroad. I believe indeed he may have settled some sort of Correspondence in Holland and Flanders, but that's all. He useth the Foreign Papers as the *Phanaticks* do the *Scriptures*, only takes that Part of 'em that will serve his Turn, and leaves out the rest . . .'²⁴ The question of De Fonvive's foreign correspondents must be left open.

A claim to have had several foreign correspondents was made by Abel Boyer. When two men quarrel, all sorts of interesting facts are apt to come to light. Boyer, a Huguenot who had come to England in 1689, had been writing the *Post-Boy* for the proprietor, Abel Roper, until the two men fell out. (The reason for their quarrel was probably that Roper wanted his paper to become more Tory, and Boyer, whom Swift once described as 'a French dog', was a convinced Whig.) Boyer was a useful man because he was perfect in French, but Roper dismissed him without warning in August 1709. Boyer therefore found a different publisher, started his own *Post-Boy*, and drew up a statement which he called 'Mr. Boyer's Case', to let the public know how unfairly Roper had treated him. In the course of his self-vindication he claimed that he had raised the circulation of Roper's paper by his industry in 'procuring private Letters, and several valuable Pieces not to be found in other Papers'. He would therefore continue to write the 'true' *Post-Boy*, and he had 'five or six Foreign Correspondents' whom he would continue to maintain.²⁵ Again we are left in some doubt about what sort of correspondents those were. 'Five or six' correspondents is an odd way of calculating their number: Boyer was making a careful statement to the public from whom he hoped to gain support, and if he really had regular correspondents abroad, we might have expected him to name the foreign countries or cities in which they lived, in order to show how admirably he was supplied with foreign news. Like De Fonvive, Boyer was a well-educated man; he had travelled in his youth, and completed his studies in Friesland, and had lived for some time in Holland. He may have had friends who kept up a learned or general correspondence with him; or he may, as he claimed, have come to an agreement with regular correspondents abroad, and put them on Roper's payroll. Again we cannot be sure.

Boyer must have taken some of his readers with him, for his rival *Post-Boy* survived till April 1710. Roper's *Post-Boy*, now intransigently Tory, entered on one of its most successful periods. Some years later it began to publish what it called its 'Hague Letter', ostentatiously enclosing it in proprietary points of quotation to establish exclusive rights to this source of foreign information. In the first days of May 1716 the *Gazette*, together with all the other newspapers well-affected to the Whig government, carried accounts of a victory gained by the Danes over the Swedes near Moss in Norway. In the summer of 1715, George I, as Elector of Hanover, had concluded a treaty with the King of Denmark, by which Bremen and Verden, then in the possession of Sweden, would be restored to Hanover in return for his joining the coalition against Charles XII. George I's ministers had gone so far as to make a show of strength by dispatching a fleet to the Baltic to protect British shipping. It was no wonder, therefore, that the defeat of a comparatively small Swedish force at Moss should be given prominence in the loyal Whig newspapers, and they reported the engagement with varying details, depending upon whether their account was dated from Copenhagen, from Hamburg, or from 'a West-India Ship which sailed the 30th. of April from Staverne in Norway'.[26] All this time the Tory *Post-Boy* remained silent about the Swedish defeat; but when its issue for 10 May appeared, it was almost wholly given up to Swedish and Danish news, and readers were told in a lengthy note why they had been kept waiting so long:

The Compiler of this Paper having been charged by his Enemies, if not suspected by his Friends, of Partiality to Sweden, because, since the Invasion of Norway by that Heroick King at the Head of his Army, he hath not run on in the common Strain of most of our English News-Writers in translating implicitly from the Dutch, and with them setting the Swedes and their Enemies backwards and forwards at Pleasure; he hath prevail'd with himself, in order to take off such an Imputation, to dedicate this one *Post-Boy* to the Service of all the Grumbletonians upon that score.

The reason why he had not done so sooner was that the reports were muddled and conflicting, some saying that the Swedish army was at Christiania, others, that it was somewhere else:

But the first of all is, that we have a due Deference to our worthy Correspondent at the Hague, whose last letter of May 15 [NS] hath these very Words: *L'on n'a ici point de leures nouvelles de ce qui se passe en Norwegue. Il y a bien des navires qui en arrivent, mais l'on n'ajoute pas grande croiance a celles qu'ils en apportent, parce qu'elles sont communément controuvées.* That is, 'We have here no certain Accounts of what passes in Norway. It is true, Ships do arrive from thence; but we do not greatly regard what News they bring, because it is commonly forg'd.'

The Hague correspondent was still keeping the Danes at bay in a letter published on 22 May. Whether the *Post-Boy* was subscribing for a written news-letter, or whether the Hague letters came from its own private correspondent, it is hard to tell; but in this case the second alternative is perhaps the more likely. When, on 7 May 1728, the writer of the *Post-Boy* felt compelled to answer objections being made to his news service, he reminded his readers of 'the Extraordinary Expence he [was] at in furnishing a *Hague Letter*, which gives the best Account we have of Transactions in the different Courts of Europe, the Interests of Princes etc.', and 'which undoubtedly exceeds any thing in the News way that comes to England'. It is true that 'extraordinary' could mean, and in the context of expenses still does mean, no more than 'extra', i.e. 'additional to what is usual'; and by 1728 the claim that the 'Hague Letter' exceeded anything comparable could certainly have been challenged. But it is also true that for some years, as the writer of the *Post-Boy* ruefully commented, this feature was 'transplanted and repeated by so many other News-Papers, some in Part, and some in Whole', that many readers had forgotten the paper in which it originated. At all events, although the 'extraordinary expence' of maintaining a foreign correspondent was more than most newspapers in the early eighteenth century would have been prepared to meet, a change was on the way.

In August 1719 a new weekly paper appeared, *The Thursday's Journal; With a Weekly Letter from Paris*. After about five months its name was changed with No. 22 to the *London Journal*, and the day of publication was altered to Saturday. (The Saturday journals were stealing the news it published so conveniently for them on Thursday.) The new journal was founded by John Trenchard, a gentleman of means, who had first attracted attention in 1697–8 by writing against standing armies in time of peace. The first number contained a manifesto, almost certainly written by Trenchard, dealing, *inter alia*, with what the public could expect from the new paper in the way of foreign news.

Particularly I am to intimate that as other Journals are in their foreign Articles filled only with publick Matters from Abroad, I shall in particular give them all the private Home News, as we call it, of the City of Paris, and of the Court there; of the Cities of Rome, Genoa and Amsterdam, and perhaps of other Cities and Courts too, as my Correspondence and Intelligence encreases, but in the very Stile I receive it, as you will see in the present Paper as a Specimen.[27]

The first three numbers, together with the fifth and the sixth, had a letter from Genoa; the fourth and the sixth, one from Paris; and the sixth, one from Leghorn. In the sixth number the reader was told: 'We have Letters from Paris, Genoa and Leghorn, written by English Correspondents settl'd in those Places, at our own Expence, which is more than any Author in the World ever had before, or any present Writer whatsoever can pretend to.' This forthright statement appears to dispose of such claims as Abel Boyer made for the *Post-Boy*, or others have made for De Fonvive's *Post Man*. For the first time we are told where the foreign correspondents lived, and we are also told that their expenses were met by the newspaper that published their reports. From now on the letters from Paris, Genoa and Leghorn are a regular feature. On 17 September there are two letters from Paris, and on 1 October, two from Genoa. Their news is almost always of matters that would interest the English reader: from Paris about John Law, the Scottish financier, and his speculative Mississippi scheme; from Genoa about supplies sent out from that city to the ships of Admiral Byng; from Leghorn about a Spanish galley with the Pretender on board. The very triviality of the news that occasionally reached Trenchard would indicate that his correspondents were under an obligation to send him some news every week, whether anything much was happening or not. In the early days they may have been paid out of his own pocket, but as the circulation of his paper climbed, such costs could have been met easily from profits.

For some time the renamed *London Journal* had no serious rival in its foreign news, but as time passed it was overtaken by the *Daily Journal*. At first this new paper was more concerned with building up its home news, but in due course it acquired an impressive number of its own foreign correspondents. A glance through its pages for the first two months of 1728 will show that on 11 January it had reports from

Lisbon and Kingston, Jamaica; on the 15th from Benicarlo, Cadiz, Rotterdam and Alicante; on the 16th from Oporto; on the 20th from Leghorn; on the 23rd from Amsterdam; on the 24th from Malaga; and on the 26th from Genoa and Barcelona. On 2 February it had correspondents writing from Naples and Marseilles, and on 6 March from Gibraltar. The foreign news of the *Daily Journal* at this time went well beyond anything of the kind so far provided. It was just at this time too that the paper advanced its price to 2*d.*, and attributed the increase to the heavy expense incurred in meeting the costs of a news service greater than that of any other paper. The news supplied by its foreign correspondents was sometimes not much more than port news, i.e. the arrival and departure of merchant ships, but nearly always, as with the news sent by the *London Journal's* correspondents, it related to incidents and events of special concern to English readers. Sometimes it was of more general interest. In August 1728 the *Daily Journal* published two long accounts on consecutive days, sent by 'one of our Correspondents on the Spot, which cannot be, but by our Means, communicated to the Publick', of the rejoicings in Madeira on the double marriages between Spain and Portugal.[28] When a newspaper is able to attribute a report to one of its correspondents on the spot, we are indeed entering the world of modern journalism.

The unusually high proportion of foreign to domestic news in the eighteenth-century newspaper demands some explanation. The *Daily Courant* and the *Post Man* tended to offer their readers little else; but even the more popular weekly journals, aimed at a less educated public, gave what may seem to the twentieth-century reader a disproportionate amount of space to solid slabs of foreign news, subtitled Italy, France, Spain, etc. and sometimes adding up to a third of the paper's contents. Did the newspapers do this because it was what their readers wanted, or because it suited their own convenience? By 1700 they had become geared to the arrival of the Dutch and French papers, and from these, with little trouble to themselves, they could get most of what they needed to fill their columns. News obtained from the foreign papers had the great advantage of being already collected, digested, and put into words. The writer of an English paper had only to translate that news, or have it translated for him, and make his own selection for English readers. No doubt it was news that should have interested a rational man; but how interesting was it, and how rational were those who read it?

In the first number of the *Daily Courant* Samuel Buckley gave his readers a paragraph of news dated from Rome:

In a Military Congregation of State that was held here, it was Resolv'd to draw a Line from Ascolie to the Borders of the Ecclesiastical State, thereby to hinder the Incursions of the Transalpine Troops. Orders are sent to Civita Vecchia to fit out the Galleys, and to strengthen the Garrison of that Place. Signior Casali is made Governor of Perugia. The Marquis del Vasto, and the Prince de Caserta continue still in the Imperial Embassador's Palace; where his Excellency has a Guard of 50 Men every Night in Arms. The King of Portugal has desir'd the Arch-Bishoprick of Lisbon, vacant by the Death of Cardinal Sousa, for the Infante his second Son, who is about 11 Years old.

This abrupt sequence of facts is typical of the foreign news provided by eighteenth-century newspapers. A modern editor would probably keep the item about the King of Portugal requesting that his eleven-year-old son should be made an archbishop, and even make a 'story' of it; but he would almost certainly scrap most of the rest. In his gentle way Addison ridiculed those among his fellow citizens who sat all day in a coffee-house reading the day's news in one paper after another, 'pleased with every thing that is Matter of Fact, so it be what they have not heard before'; who are equally delighted with a victory or a defeat, and who are 'glad to hear the French Court is removed to Marli, and are afterwards as much delighted with its Return to Versailles'.[29] In this playful mockery of undiscriminating readers Addison had been anticipated by his friend Nicholas Rowe, who alluded in 1703 to

> distant Battles of the Pole and Swede,
> Which frugal Citizens o'er Coffee read,
> Careless for who shall fail or who succeed.[30]

The hallmark of such citizens (whose first appearance and subsequent proliferation Addison attributed in 1712 to 'our late war') was an unselective and insatiable appetite for facts: facts which were interesting because they were new, not yesterday's facts. Addison and his fellow essayists had a new word for such readers; they called them 'quidnuncs', because they kept asking: 'What now? What's the news?'

If there were enough of those scatter-brained readers, they probably helped to increase a newspaper's circulation; though not if they read the free copy available in a coffee-house. Reliable evidence at this time of a widespread demand for foreign news is hard to come by; but on 15 November 1733 the proprietors of the *General Evening Post* announced that they had been receiving letters asking them 'to be more extensive in their Relation of Foreign News'. In response to those requests their paper would appear for the future in a larger size and in three columns, 'whereby the Publick will be supplied with more Foreign and Domestick News . . . than in any Paper whatsoever extant'. Addison was dead by this time; but if he had been alive, would he have greeted this announcement as a sure sign of cultural advance? Men like Addison and Pope had an ambivalent attitude to the newspapers. They undoubtedly read them, but they also regarded them as legitimate targets for ridicule: newspapers were not 'literature', and yet the literary upstarts who wrote them were threatening the standards of literature. Having occasion to put the versifier and hack writer James Ralph in the *Dunciad*, Pope pressed the attack home in a footnote:

This low writer constantly attended his own works with Panegyricks in the Journals . . . He was wholly illiterate, and knew no Language, not even French . . . He ended at last in the common Sink of all such writers, a Political Newspaper . . . and receiv'd a small pittance for pay.[31]

Addison, no doubt, would not have written about Ralph with such uncompromising contempt, but his attitude to newspapers was at best patronising. While he was willing to smile at the quidnuncs and their mindless patter about the latest news from abroad, he was even readier to ridicule the home news that the papers published. On one occasion he did this in a facetious proposal to start a daily paper that would publish 'all the most remarkable Occurrences—within the Verge [the territorial limits] of the Penny-Post'. He gives some examples:

By my last Advice from Knights-bridge I hear that a Horse was clapped into the Pound on the third Instant, and that he was not released when the Letters came away.

By a Fisherman which lately touched at Hammersmith, there is Advice from Putney, that a certain Person well known in that Place, is like to lose his Election for Church-warden, but this being Boat News, we cannot give entire Credit to it.[32]

So much for home news. But although foreign news was more or less immune from the charge of triviality, it could still be made to look slightly ridiculous by laughing at the half-educated readers of it, 'moving about in worlds not realised'. The implication is that for Addison (and readers of the *Spectator*) foreign news was something that a man of sense, and at least a few women, were capable of assimilating and evaluating. Yet if this interpretation is correct, it still leaves unanswered the puzzling question: What did readers of such papers as those of Mist, Read and Applebee make of the large and indigestible gobbets of foreign news that appeared, week after week, in their favourite journal?

145

CHAPTER 5

Politics

In the reign of Charles II political comment was at best a precarious activity, and at the worst a highly dangerous one. The King and his ministers had never come to terms with the newpapers, and would have have been glad to see the nation served only by the *London Gazette*. Their attitude was precisely expressed by L'Estrange in 1663: newspapers made the people 'too familiar with the actions and counsels of their superiors', and gave them 'not only an itch but a kind of colourable right and license to be meddling with the Government'.* In the days when the only newspaper he could buy was the *Gazette*, the thinking Englishman must often have contrasted his situation with that in the Low Countries, where anyone had the liberty to read the day's news in a considerable variety of papers. When, in 1679, Englishmen became accustomed to choosing which paper they would read, a habit was formed that was not to be easily broken.

It is true that in 1680 the King had successfully asserted his authority, and had succeeded in suppressing the interloping newspapers for several months; but the very fact that they began to appear again at the end of the year offers some indication of the pressure from below that he had to contend with. (How far they had the financial support of Shaftesbury and the Country Party is a question that has never been satisfactorily determined.) In the summer of 1681 the King's gradual adoption of a more absolute form of government enabled him, as we have seen, to control the newspaper press, and ultimately to stamp it out in the autumn of 1682. If, then, the newspapers published between 1679 and 1682 may sometimes seem to be unduly muted in their political criticism, it must never be forgotten that they were working under an authoritarian government. It was not only overt comment that such a government found objectionable and punished by arrests, fines and imprisonment: the mere meddling with public affairs, even when the news was true but not of a kind that the government wished the people to know about, was subject to the same harsh penalties. Few

* Cf. p. 97.

publishers or printers of newspapers in this short period escaped prison at one time or another; and for some, such as Nathaniel Thompson or Langley Curtiss, it became almost a second home.

If we look at the situation from the King's point of view, we may see good reason for his inveterate hostility to the newspapers: the nation was involved in a prolonged confrontation over the question of the succession, which was being fought out in his last two parliaments. In 1713 Daniel Defoe was to publish in quick succession three political pamphlets: *Reasons against the Succession of the House of Hanover*, followed by *And What if the Pretender should Come?*, and finally by *An Answer to a Question that No Body Thinks of: But What if the Queen should Die?* All three pamphlets were heavily ironical, for Defoe was a convinced Hanoverian, but they got him into deep trouble. The situation in the last years of Charles II was being repeated two generations later in the last years of Queen Anne. If the Queen were to die, who would succeed her – the Protestant Elector of Hanover, or the son of James II, the Jacobite (and Catholic) Pretender? Defoe was rather too young in 1679 to be writing political pamphlets, but if he had been a little older he might well have risked publishing one with the arresting title: *But What if the King should Die?* Between 1679 and 1682 it was the main political question of the day; the country was divided between those who favoured the King's Catholic brother, the Duke of York, and those who supported his Protestant son, the Duke of Monmouth. The treatment by the newspapers of those two key figures may help to show how far it was safe to go by way of comment, or by selecting and slanting the latest news about them for publication.

When the Duke of York arrived in Edinburgh as High Commissioner in late November 1679, the *London Gazette* gave one and a half columns to a glowing account of the warm welcome he received.[1] It was the function of the *Gazette* to present the royal family on all occasions in a favourable light; but even the Whig Harris, who was under no obligation to praise a Catholic duke, printed his Edinburgh correspondent's much shorter report estimating the train of gentry at 4,000. He added, however, that the number of militia (no doubt there to maintain order) was 12,000.[2] The Tory Thompson reported that the Duke had been 'magnificently entertained' by the Duke of Lauderdale, and that when he reached Edinburgh 'the Magistrates and Inhabitants used all the Pomp imaginable to make him honourably welcome, the Houses being all along adorn'd with Tapestry', and the people of Edinburgh greeting their High Commissioner 'with demonstration of much rejoycing'.[3] On 9 January Thompson reported that the Duke had been splendidly entertained by the Lord Provost and magistrates, and presented with a gold box. Harris's Edinburgh correspondent had nothing to say about a box, but concentrated instead on any incidents that tended to suggest the Duke's religion made him unwelcome to the Scots. On 3 February 1680 Harris published a report that 'some of the Common People in Scotland offered some affronts to the Duke's servants while they were at their Devotions, by throwing Stones at the Chappel Windows'; and, as further evidence of the tension aroused by his entourage in Edinburgh, related how 'one of his Royal Highnesses Servants being in company there with a Scotch Gentleman, did take too great freedom in villifying that People and Country, which the Gentleman so resented that he used him worse than the High Priest's Servant was treated of Old, for pulling out his Knife, he cut off both his Ears'. In his *Currant Intelligence* of 17 February, John Smith, who had his own Edinburgh correspondent, dismissed both those statements as 'malitious lyes'. Since Harris introduced the first statement by 'It is said', and the second by 'From Edinburgh we are told', we may perhaps take it that the balance of truth lay with the normally reliable *Currant Intelligence*.

It is clear, however, that the Duke of York aroused such different reactions that almost anything said about him was coloured by the writer's political sympathies. Apart from the *London Gazette*, the papers of Thompson, Benskin and John Smith could be counted upon to mention him with approval, or even with adulation: the Whig papers of Harris, Francis Smith, Curtiss and Janeway habitually treated him with hostility, and at times with covert or open contempt. When, with the King's permission, the Duke returned to London on 24 February 1680, he made the journey by sea. Four days after his arrival, the *Currant Intelligence* carried a report from its Edinburgh correspondent, dwelling on the anxiety of the good people about the high winds that had sprung up since he set sail. In the following year, when the Duke was again in Edinburgh, the same correspondent reported in late September: 'His Highness is a Pattern to all this Kingdom for sobriety and painfulness [careful attention to business], he never appoints any meeting of the Council, Exchequer, but he observes it to a moment.'[4] On 3 May 1681 Benskin's Edinburgh correspondent, remarking on the settled state of the northern kingdom, attributed it all to the Duke: 'His Royal Highness, by reason of his generous behaviour, and Princely deportment, has so far won the Love of this City as cannot be well expressed.'

Against such glowing tributes Harris was hard pressed to find adequate grounds for denigration. On 7 January 1681 he published a report from his Edinburgh correspondent that the Duke's court was 'very thin', and that he was beginning to find that 'the opinion of your Parliament doth greatly influence this Kingdom'. (Some weeks before this was written, the House of Commons at Westminster had given a third reading to a bill to exclude a Catholic successor from the throne of England.) But Harris had received other good news that must have especially delighted him. On 4 January he published a report that on Christmas day the Edinburgh students, 'with many of the City, made great Preparations for the burning of the Pope here'. The students had met with opposition from the magistrates, who had called out the guards, and the procession had been forbidden 'very early this morning at their utmost peril by Beat of Drum, and some imprisoned that promoted it'; but they were not to be overawed, and successfully burnt their Pope in the High Street 'over against the Archbishop of St. Andrews' Lodgings . . . to the great pleasure of the Protestants of this City'. The report concludes: 'At the long you will find our Nobility and Gentry as well as the People infinitely disposed to imitate England in speaking their abhorrence of Popery'. Such welcome news could bear amplification, and on 7 January Harris was able to add from his correspondent's next letter that the pope-burning 'had the approbation, not only of this Loyal Protestant City (manifested by loud Acclamations of *no Pope, no Pope*) but of the whole body of the People of Scotland'.

On this occasion Harris was not alone in reporting the anti-Catholic demonstrations in Edinburgh. On 5 January the short-lived *English Gazette* had given all of its first column to the pope-burning by 'our young Students in the College here'. A still more detailed report, which Curtiss printed as his first item, had already appeared in the *True Protestant Mercury* of 3 January. On 15 January he was able to give further information: several of the students had been arrested and threatened with the torture of the boot; and on the day after the pope-burning many citizens wore a blue ribbon and a gilded laurel in their hats, with the inscription 'No Pope, no Papist'. (The blue ribbon had recently been adopted as a distinguishing sign by the adherents of the Duke of Monmouth, and the cry of 'No Papist' pointed directly at the Duke of York.) The annual ceremony of burning the Pope on 17 November (the anniversary of Queen Elizabeth's accession) was something the London magistrates could not stop, even if they had been so inclined.[5] The King might not like it, but as Defender of the Faith in a Protestant nation he had put up with it. In Edinburgh the circumstances were rather different: the Scots, it is true, were predominantly Protestant, but since the King's brother was not only High Commissioner but a professed and devout Roman Catholic, a pope-burning procession was a direct insult to him.

To propose a toast to the Duke of York in a public place was either an act of folly or of deliberate provocation, liable to end in a breach of the peace. On 12 April 1681 Harris recounted how a captain and his friend drank a toast to the Duke of York in a coffee-house, and called upon the company at another table to do the same – 'which they refusing, the Captain threw a Glass of Mum [an imported German beer] in one of their Faces, upon which a Constable was called, who apprehended them, and carried them before a Justice of the Peace.' Speaking disrespectfully of the Duke occurred so often that it was well on the way to becoming a minor crime in the statute book. On 8 October 1681 both John Smith and Thompson report one such incident, when (as Smith has it) a Muggletonian called Nathaniel Powell was put on trial for 'speaking base, scandalous and reproachful words against His Royal Highness'. Less reticent, Thompson gives the man's actual words: he had called the Duke 'a Pimp and the Son of a Whore, and . . . the Cause of most of the Troubles in England'.

The strong anti-Catholic bias of the City gave the Tory Thompson occasion to print a humorous anecdote in his *Loyal Protestant* of 12 November 1681. Two female ballad singers in Bow Lane were singing a ballad about 'Young Jemmy' (the Duke of Monmouth), which was very well received. But when they went on to sing one about 'Old Jemmy' (the Duke of York), 'a little Zealous prick-ear'd Brother (a Man in Office to be sure) cried out, "Help, Neighbours, Friends, Brethren, Here's Popery going to be set up among Us; Oh, these vile Popish Strumpets, etc." ' He then arrested the two women, refusing their request to be carried before the Lord Mayor, saying, 'What, because you have got a Lord Mayor according to your own desire! No, I'le not go so far, I'le carry you to what Justice I please.' (The new Lord Mayor, Sir John Moore, was much more amenable to the Court than his immediate predecessors.)

The dislike, or even hatred, of Charles II's Catholic brother reached a symbolic climax on 25 January 1682, when some person or persons mutilated his portrait in the Guildhall by cutting off its legs a little below the knees. The Mayor and aldermen advertised in the *London Gazette* offering the unusually high reward of £500 to anyone who could discover the guilty party, since the mutilation of the Duke's picture could only be interpreted as 'in effect Malice against his Person'[6]. *The Loyal Protestant* of 28 January was no doubt enlarging on those words when it observed that the vandals were 'much troubled that they had not His Person within their power to act out the same malice upon as they did upon His Royal Father of ever Blessed Memory'. The Whig newspapers noted the outrage; but expressions of open satisfaction would have been too dangerous, and in any case the mutilation of the Duke's portrait spoke for itself.

To set against the Catholic Duke the Whigs had his nephew, the young, handsome, and, above all, Protestant Duke of Monmouth. The Whig newspapers made the most of him. Those Englishmen who believed that he would make a better king than his uncle were able to point to his victory over the Covenanters at Bothwell Bridge, and to his magnanimous treatment of the defeated rebels. On 17 July 1679 Harris had news from Edinburgh that Monmouth was pleasing all sorts of people there by 'his moderate and indifferent [impartial] carriage'. When he returned to London as the conquering hero, his uncle was no longer there: in view of the growing clamour for a Protestant succession, Charles had thought it best to have a cooling-off period, and had ordered James to withdraw to Brussels. But when Charles became seriously ill towards the end of August, his brother was advised to return to England, and he arrived at Windsor at the beginning of September, where he was affectionately greeted by the King. To counteract the growing popularity and importance of Monmouth, Charles had deprived him of his commission as general of the armed forces (conferred upon him when he was sent to Scotland), and now ordered him to withdraw for some time from the kingdom. Monmouth was unwilling to go, but at last, as Harris and Thompson both reported, he left for Holland on 24 September. How far the fortunes of Monmouth (and more particularly his relations with the King) had become matters for rumour and political concern may be seen from a curious report in Thompson's *Domestic Intelligence* of 16 September. The news appears as a 'stop press' item in much larger type than the rest of the paper:

Last night about six a Clock, a Person came Post from Windsor, with Orders and Money (as he said) for the Ringing of Bells for the Duke of Monmouth's being received again into His Majesties Favour, which was accordingly done at St. Margaret's Westminster, and other places; and wood prepared for Bonfires: But this is supposed by some to be a mistake, but in our next we may give a plainer account.

The plainer account never appeared. But already in 1679 the young Duke was being looked upon in some quarters as a satisfactory Protestant successor to the throne. The bells and bonfires reported by

Thompson may well have produced a spontaneous expression of Whig joy, but the false news that Monmouth had been restored to his father's favour may equally well have been manufactured by the Whigs as part of what was now becoming a well-managed campaign in support of the young Duke.

On 28 November Monmouth returned to London unexpectedly, and without the King's leave. Thompson just managed to give his readers the news in a final paragraph: 'This Morning at Two of the Clock his Grace the Duke of Monmouth arrived at Whitehall, whereupon there was Ringing of Bells and making of Bonfires for Joy.' Thompson was quite capable of suppressing facts when it suited him to do so; but on this occasion he appears to have had no inclination to tone down the welcome accorded to Monmouth, however annoyed the King might be with the unauthorised return of his disobedient son. (At this point in his newspaper career Thompson was a good deal less of a Tory than he later became.) *Mercurius Anglicus*, which came out a day later, was able to publish a rather fuller account: the Duke arrived incognito from Holland, and although 'it was very late at night before it was known about the court, yet such was the Affection of the people towards him, that they made Bonfires in the Palace Yard, etc. at 1 and 2 in the morning'. On the evening of the same day (the report continued) more bonfires were lit in the City, 'though one of our Domestick Intelligencers said, *He was yesterday gone from Holland in a Yacht up the Rhine for Cologne.*'[7] The newsman who had given this erroneous intelligence was none other than Harris, but he made some amends on 2 December with his own glowing account of the bonfires and rejoicing. Harris had clearly been misled by the *London Gazette*, which had published a report on 24 November from its Hague correspondent that Monmouth was about to visit Cologne. The odds are that Shaftesbury had stage-managed Monmouth's abrupt return to England, and that the news of a forthcoming trip to Cologne was intended to conceal his real intentions. Bells and bonfires at 2 a.m. would certainly suggest some previous planning: bell-ringers have to be assembled, and effective bonfires are not built in a few minutes.

The King, who could hardly have been pleased with a disturbance in Palace Yard at such an early hour, forbade his rebellious son to come to Court, and ordered him to return to Holland. On Monmouth's refusing to leave, Charles reacted sharply. On 1 December he gave orders that Monmouth should be stripped of all his offices and sinecures, and that they should be distributed to others. The impact of the newspapers of those harsh measures seems not to have followed party lines. On 9 December Thompson again took the side of Monmouth, relating how he had been visited by many persons of honour, or entertained at their houses, and how

those persons on whom his Majesty hath been pleased to confer his Places (divested from him) have been severally to wait upon his Grace, expressing a great deal of sorrow for his Majesties disfavour towards him, wishing a happy Reconciliation, and Restauration to all again. His Grace returned them thanks, gave them Joy of their Places, and said he was glad to see them conferred on such Honourable persons; and notwithstanding there were those that malign'd him, his innocency was sufficient to protect him from the worst of his Enemies . . .

For good measure Thompson also reported that the Duke was mourning the death of his youngest son, the Earl of Doncaster. In his next number Thompson announced that on the Duke's going to Sunday worship at St Martin's Church, the people 'rose from their seats, and some cried, *God bless the Duke of Monmouth.*' That this invocation was to become a recognised way of expressing one's political sympathies is suggested by a similar account in the *True Protestant Mercury* of 2 March 1681, when the same congregation cried, 'God bless the Protestant Duke.' For the present, at any rate, Monmouth was much in the news. On 3 February 1680 Thompson told his readers: 'His Grace the Duke of Monmouth is very well, and bears his afflictions as becomes him . . .'.

In the spring of 1680 Monmouth's name was kept before the public by the revival of a frequently repeated claim that he was the legitimate son of the King, and therefore the true heir to the throne. On this occasion the evidence of Charles's marriage to Lucy Walter was said to lie in a black box given by Bishop Cosin to his son-in-law, Sir Gilbert Gerrard, with instructions not to open it until the King's death. But Gerrard (so the rumour ran) had recently opened the box and found a sealed envelope containing a certificate showing that Cosin had in fact married Charles to Monmouth's mother. When Gerrard was brought before the King to deny the story, he asserted that he had never seen any such certificate[8]. The King, who had already twice proclaimed, in January and in March 1679, that he was never married to Mrs Walter, now repeated his declaration on 26 April 1680, and had it published in the *Gazette* on that day and repeated on 10 June, The newspapers fought shy of mentioning the black box: in view of the King's categorical denials the story was too hot to handle.

Encouraged by Shaftesbury, Monmouth made visits to various parts of the country, showing himself to the people and impressing them by his good looks, his affability, and his handsome retinue of followers.

On 17 February 1680 Harris reported one such visit to Chichester, where, after hunting in the neighbourhood, Monmouth was welcomed with bells and bonfires, and magnificently entertained by the Mayor and aldermen in their fur gowns, supported by the trainbands. On 24 February Thompson announced that he had been credibly informed that the account given by Harris was 'a strained discourse', and his report of the celebrations exaggerated. The most notable of those peregrinations or 'progresses' took place in the summer of 1680, when Monmouth made a prolonged tour of the west country. In *Absalom and Achitophel* Dryden described how the young Duke, moving through towns and villages 'with Chariots, Horsemen, and a numerous train', was received everywhere with shouts of joy; but he warned his readers that

> This moving Court, that caught the people's Eyes,
> And seem'd but Pomp, did other ends disguise.

What political use could be made of Monmouth's showing himself to the people may be illustrated by the story of a Somersetshire girl to which Harris gave prominence on 7 January 1681. This young woman was in a dreadful condition, with running sores in a hand and arm. Having tried the local physicians, 'who tampered with it for a time, but could do no good', she 'went likewise 10 or 11 Miles to a Seventh Son, but all in vain'. Her case seemed hopeless.

But now, in this Girl's great Extreamity, God the Great Physitian Dictates unto her, thus Languishing in her miserable, hopeless condition, what Course to take, and what to do for a Cure, which was to go and touch the Duke of Monmouth.

When the Duke appeared at Crewkerne, she pressed forward and caught hold of one of his wrists with her diseased hand, crying 'God bless your Greatness', to which Monmouth replied, 'God bless you.' Within a few days the running sores in her hand and arm had dried up, 'the bunch in her breast was dissolved', and 'her eye that was given up for lost is now perfectly well'. The account of her marvellous cure was signed by the minister of the parish and several others. If Monmouth had ever come to the throne, one of his royal duties would have been to touch for the King's Evil: what Harris was asking his readers to believe was that the young Duke had inherited his father's power to cure the King's Evil, and must therefore be his true and legitimate son.

It was easier for the Whigs to capitalise on the undeniable charisma of Monmouth than for the Tories to drum up much enthusiasm for the Duke of York. In the circumstances denigration of Monmouth was the safest response. It is true that he was (or had been until recently) the King's favourite son, but by 1681 it was possible to be critical of him, as Dryden was in *Absalom and Achitophel*. In the *Loyal Protestant* of 29 March, when the Oxford Parliament was in session, Thompson's correspondent there corrected a statement published in the *Protestant Oxford Intelligence* that Monmouth had arrived with a great retinue, and had been welcomed 'with many shouts and acclamations of the people'. In fact, Thompson was able to assure his readers, Monmouth was attended by a mere 30 followers, of whom only some were gentlemen, and the rest his servants:

Some of which Company began to make faint Essays of Humming (or applause) thereby to provoke others to do the like, both in Cat-street (through which he passed) and at his alighting at his Lodging; but they were not in the least seconded by any.

Was Thompson's Oxford correspondent a Tory don who remembered Shakespeare's *Richard III*? In that play (Act III, scene vii) Buckingham gives Gloucester a sardonic account of how he had tried to stir up the citizens to accept him as their king, dwelling on his victories in Scotland, and how like he was to his royal father in appearance and nobleness of mind. When the citizens remained dully unresponsive, some of Buckingham's followers had thrown up their caps, and 'some ten voices cried, "God save King Richard!"', but again without arousing any response. Any resemblance is probably coincidental, but Thompson's new willingness to denigrate Monmouth is significant. The way in which Monmouth was received by the people was becoming almost a way of reading the political barometer. Thus, on 24 July 1682, in a paragraph dated from Chichester, Benskin's *Domestick Intelligence* reported: 'His Grace the Duke of Monmouth, upon his return from taking his Progress in these Parts, was welcomed by a great number of Citizens, though not with so many as formerly . . .' Since Benskin's paper came nearer to being politically impartial than most, this balanced statement probably gives a true estimate of Monmouth's sinking popularity in 1682, and of the rapidly declining fortunes of the Whigs.[9] The last word may be given to Nathaniel Thompson. In his *Loyal Protestant* of 7 February 1682 he published a piece of royal news that he may well have thought would settle the question of the succession once and for ever:

It hath been whisper'd of late, that Her Royal Highness the Duchess of York is With child; but now we have it fully confirm'd, to the great Joy & Happiness of all true English-men; and we hope it will prove a Son, who (if it please God he survive His Majesty) may many years hence succeed in the English throne, and cut off all the vain hopes of Ambitious Pretenders.

Thompson was right about Her Royal Highness being pregnant; but when her time came she gave birth to a daughter, Charlotte Margaret, who, like her four predecessors, did not live for many months. Had she survived long enough, and if by some remote chance she had been brought up a Protestant, she would almost certainly have succeeded her half-sister Anne in 1714 as Charlotte, Queen of Great Britain, France and Ireland.

The forum in which the great debate about exclusion was carried on was the House of Commons; but the modern reader who turns to the seventeenth-century newspapers to find out what was happening in parliament will be sadly disappointed. As has already been noted, the House of Commons had strictly prohibited any printing of its votes or proceedings without special permission; but in any case, during the whole period from July 1679 to November 1682 when the unlicensed papers were appearing, parliament was in session for only about twelve weeks. And for most of those twelve weeks the papers had been stopped by the King's proclamation of 17 May 1680, and did not begin to re-appear until the very end of December. This situation, in which there was either a parliament sitting but no newspapers, or newspapers appearing but no parliament, meant in effect that parliament and the newspapers synchronised for only about two weeks. News of what was happening in parliament could still be had from news-letters, and was of course passed on by word of mouth in coffee-houses and taverns. From 1 November 1680, too, the *Votes of the House of Commons* had been officially published by order of the House, although the information they supplied was formal and meagre.

Such as they were, however, the *Votes* began to be used by Harris in his revived *Intelligence*, and by Curtiss in his *True Protestant Mercury*, both of which appeared on 28 December 1680. How far Harris and Curtiss could have claimed that they were not *printing* the votes of parliament, but only reproducing what had already been printed by order of parliament, would have to be left to a seventeenth-century lawyer to determine. But with a Whig majority in the House of Commons, only too pleased to have its proceedings given the maximum publicity, neither Harris nor Curtiss would have been in much danger. What is more interesting, however, is that both men not only made use of the *Votes*, but added on occasion strong editorial comments. On 11 January 1681 Curtiss gave the best part of a column to reprinting from the *Votes* the resolutions taken by the House on 10 January, ending with the statement that the Lord Chancellor had pro-rogued parliament till the 20th. But Curtiss had his own defiant addition:

At which time 'tis not doubted by any good Protestant Subjects, but they will again meet and *Sit*, to proceed (as hitherto, to the satisfaction of the whole Nation and Protestant World, they have done) to bring Traytors to Justice, secure (by the most and only effectual means) his Majesties Royal person, the Protestant Religion, our English Birth-rights, and all his Majesties Dominions from *Popery*, Domestick Conspiracies, Fatal *Councils*, Arbitrary *Violence*, and Forreign *Invasions*. For which every true English man will in the Interim zealously implore Heaven, and Cordially say Amen.

On the same day Harris also announced the prorogation to 20 January, and added his own pious hopes:

When it is not doubted but such Lawes will pass as shall effectually secure against the design of the Popish enemies of his Majesty and the three Kingdomes to the satisfaction of all his Majesties Protestant Subjects.

The one occasion on which the newsmen appear to have made a genuine attempt to produce their own parliamentary reports was at the meeting of the Oxford parliament in March 1681. Their accounts of the proceedings, brief and imperfect though they may be, are a measure of the political crisis, and of the importance attached to the decisions then being taken. At this time there were five unlicensed newspapers appearing twice a week, all of them carrying the word 'Protestant' in their titles, and three of them deeply committed to a new parliament immediately tabling another bill to exclude the Catholic Duke of York from the succession. Three of the five papers had been started since the King dissolved parliament on 18 January 1681. Francis Smith's *Protestant Intelligence* appeared on 1 February, to be followed by Thompson's *Loyal Protestant* on 9 March. One day later the importance that Oxford was about to assume was underlined when Benskin brought out (in London) the first number of his *Protestant Oxford Intelligence*.

On Saturday 19 March, the King, accompanied by Nell Guin and the Duchess of Portsmouth, attended a performance of Charles Saunders' *Tamerlane the Great* at the Oxford playhouse. On Monday 21 March Charles opened his new and last parliament in the Geometry School. The tone of the Whig newspapers may be seen from Francis Smith's sardonic observation in his issue of 28 March: 'Last week His Majesty was pleased to be present at the acting of a Play called *Tamberlaine the Great*, and upon Monday last His Majesty was to see a Comedy called *Plain Dealing*'. If this cutting remark, with its allusion to Wycherley's comedy of *The Plain Dealer*, was Smith's own, it does him credit; but since he did not publish it until 28 March, it may have been going the rounds at Oxford and have reached him in due course from his Oxford correspondent. At all events it was not long before the plain dealing commenced. On Friday 26 March the Commons resolved to impeach Edward Fitzharris, and on Saturday the expected bill to exclude the Duke of York was brought in. Sunday passed, and on Monday morning the Commons resolved that the Exclusion Bill should be read a second time 'tomorrow morning' at 10 o'clock. But tomorrow morning was too late: Charles had decided to enact his own comedy of plain dealing. This time there was no question of proroguing parliament; it was abruptly dissolved. On 31 March the *London Gazette* gave the substance of the King's brief announcement to the Lords and Commons: 'His Majesty told them, That their Beginnings had been such that he could expect no good success of this Parliament, and therefore thought fit to Dissolve them.'

On 24 March the *Gazette* had announced that (instead of the normal three days a week) 'there goes and comes a Post every day from Oxford'. The Commons had also ordered that their *Votes* should be published every day. There is, however, clear evidence that on this occasion the newspapers did not wait for the official *Votes*, but had their own sources of information. In Harris's *Domestick Intelligence* of 29 March the parliamentary news is scattered through the whole issue, and appears to have been set by the printer as and when it reached him from Oxford. The later paragraphs, it is true, may have come from the *Votes* of 26 March; but the opening paragraph is clearly based on an independent report:

Oxon. Our Letters from thence say, That the Honourable House of Commons taking into their consideration the great danger His Majesties Person is exposed to, from such as are engaged in the Horrid Popish Plot: Amongst other Remedies against such danger, it was proposed as an Expedient, that James Duke of York should be Excluded from all things but the Regency, and that all the other Rights belonging to the Succession of the Crown should revert to the Princess of Orange. And it was proposed, that the said Duke of York might be confined from coming near England by several hundred miles. But we hear that after all, They gave Orders for a Bill of Exclusion to be brought in against him, to prevent his inheriting any of these Imperial Crowns, but no such Bill is yet brought in.[10]

There is nothing in the *Votes* about the Duke of York being allowed to act only as a regent while all the other rights should belong to his Protestant daughter Mary, the Princess of Orange; nor is there anything about his being 'confined from coming near England by several hundred miles'. Harris, however, was correctly reporting what had occurred: in the debate preceding the introduction of the 1681 Bill

those suggestions were put forward as 'expedients'. He must have obtained this information through someone who was present when the
debate took place, and the most likely source would be a member of
parliament. After the House had resolved on Saturday morning to
bring in a third Exclusion Bill, it adjourned till 5 p.m. It looks
therefore as if Harris's correspondent, without waiting for the afternoon session, when the Bill was given its first reading, had caught the
post with the all-important information that a bill *was* to be introduced,
and was being debated. The news that the Bill had been given its first
reading did not appear till Harris's next number on 1 April, by which
time parliament had been dissolved.

The Oxford parliament did not last long enough to show how far
the Restoration newspapers might have been prepared to go in reporting its proceedings. In the reign of Queen Anne, Abel Boyer began to
include cautious parliamentary reports, including speeches, in his monthly *Political State of Great Britain* (1711–29), and got away with it,
possibly because his reports were not strictly contemporary. Boyer's
example was followed by *The Historical Register* in 1716, and in 1732
by *The Gentleman's Magazine* and *The London Magazine*. In 1738 the
House of Commons reasserted its sole right to publish its own proceedings, and threatened any offending newswriter, publisher and
printer with the utmost severity of the law. Their debates, however,
continued to appear in an ingenious disguise: in May the *London
Magazine* began reporting them as transactions of the Roman Senate,
and in June the *Gentleman's Magazine* followed with 'Debates in the
Senate of Magna Lilliputia', written up, or sometimes composed, by
Samuel Johnson. It was not until 1771 that the right to publish
parliamentary reports was finally conceded.[11]

When the parliaments of Charles II were prorogued or dissolved, the
King ruled the country with the help of his ministers and the Privy Council. All Privy Councillors had to take an oath of secrecy, and when the
business was highly confidential the Council 'sat close', even the clerks
being asked to withdraw.[12] In spite of those precautions a surprising
amount of Council business was leaked, and found its way into the
newspapers. Unlike the House of Commons, the Council appears to
have been unable to stop the unauthorised disclosure of its proceedings, and the newswriters seem not to have been in awe of the
possible consequences to themselves. It is true that Council business
was sometimes reported in the *Gazette*, and could then be safely
reprinted by other newspapers. On 20 January 1680 Harris published
a sensational account of a plot, involving Colonel Blood and one Philip

Le Marr, to accuse the Duke of Buckingham of sodomy; and since the charges concerned so prominent a member of the nobility, the Council asked the Attorney-General to examine the witnesses and report on his findings. The report was published in the *Gazette* of 5 April, and duly reprinted verbatim in Smith's *Currant Intelligence* next day.

As often as not, however, the newspapers were relying on their own secret sources when they published details of Council proceedings. How far they were prepared to go may be seen from a short report in Thompson's *Loyal Protestant* of 12 November 1681:

There being this week a Cabinet-Council held for considering the Dutch Ambassador's Negotiations, we are now advised that His Majesty's Answer to him was to this effect: That he had well considered of the League, and was willing himself to enter into it; and withal advised him to pursue the League with the German Princes; and if the French King should make any further pretensions in Flanders, he would take such measures as would no way prove satisfactory to him.

Thompson's informant had indeed given him the substance of the King's reply to the Dutch ambassador on 8 November. The only point left vague concerns the measures the King said he would take if the French invaded Flanders: he had promised the ambassador that he would summon parliament. At this time Charles was relying on secret subsidies from Louis XIV: he had accordingly shown the French ambassador his reply, and at the same time assured him that the promises made to the Dutch ambassador would not be carried out.[13] Thompson little knew on what dangerous ground he was treading.

Some newspaper reports of Council proceedings are remarkably detailed. On 31 May 1681 the *Impartial Protestant Mercury* gave the whole of its front page to reporting the appearance before the Council of James Magrath, the latest in a long line of mendacious Irish witnesses. Magrath found his way into the Tower on 25 May, succeeded in gaining admittance to the Earl of Danby (then a prisoner there), and told him he could produce persons who would show that Sir Edmund Berry Godfrey had hanged himself. Danby prudently called for the Constable of the Tower, who handed the Irishman over to the Secretary of State, Sir Leoline Jenkins. Next day Magrath was called before the Council and went to pieces under examination, confessing that his whole story was a fraud, and that he had been bribed by Mrs Cellier (a Roman Catholic midwife) to swear to it. The news of his appearance at the Council had been briefly reported in Smith's *Currant Intelligence* of 28 May, but three days later the *Impartial Protestant Mercury* report gave the questions put to Magrath and his answers in considerable detail. All this time the *Gazette* had kept quiet about Magrath, but in view of the way in which the facts had been leaked, the editor was forced to publish a belated official account on 2 June.

When Shaftesbury was arrested on the morning of 2 July 1681, examined by the King in Council, and committed to the Tower, the *Gazette* dealt with the whole business in eight lines. Several other papers, however, gave fuller accounts of what passed in Council, including the *Loyal Protestant* and the *Impartial Protestant Mercury*, both of which quoted or paraphrased some of the words spoken by Shaftesbury in answer to the charges brought against him. According to the *Currant Intelligence*, Titus Oates provided Shaftesbury with his dinner on that day, and it may have been through Oates that the *Impartial Protestant Mercury* got hold of the words said to have been uttered by Shaftesbury to the Council: 'That were he guilty of those Crimes laid to his Charge, he was more fit for Bedlam than the Tower'.[14]

The leaking of Council proceedings, however, was so frequent that there were clearly well-organised sources of information. One such source was a Mr Netterville, a shadowy figure whose name occasionally makes brief appearances in the State Papers. In September 1681 we find a query 'whether Netterville has been examined about giving intelligence to Cotton and Claypoole, dispersers of newsletters, and from whom he has the transactions of Court and Council which he communicates to them.'[15] When William Cotton was interrogated in October 1683, he made a long statement about how he obtained his news. 'If I had not foreign news to begin with, . . . I came in the morning to Mr A. [?] or Mr. Netterville, and if I had any of them, we began with that.' Later he mentioned two other sources:

Hancock has great intelligence both from Court and Council, and therefore I believe some considerable person furnishes him. . . . Combes has great intelligence and often what is private . . . He must have some considerable information from Court . . .[16]

Claypoole and Hancock, then, had their contacts at Court who were prepared to pass on state secrets for a consideration. Access to the Court of Charles II was not difficult if a man was fashionably dressed, and carried himself with the air of a gentleman. Mr Netterville may have been such a one, but if so, he probably knew a courtier of more importance, a Restoration Rosencrantz or Guildenstern, who was freely accepted in those circles where indiscreet political discussion is carried on, and where talkative peers or gentlemen in their cups betray secrets without realising that they are doing so. This scenario is, of course, purely hypothetical; but it remains true that a small stream of confidential information trickled more or less steadily from Court and Council into the newspapers.

Deprived of almost any chance to report parliamentary proceedings, the Restoration papers had an important part to play in publicising petitions for parliament to meet. Since the King kept proroguing his parliaments, this became almost the only way of exerting pressure on him. The first step in what was to become a well-organised movement was a petition presented by 16 peers on 7 December 1679, and printed by *Mercurius Anglicus* and by Harris and Thompson in their respective papers. The object of this petition was to ensure that parliament, which had most recently been prorogued till 26 January 1680, would not be prorogued again when that day arrived. The wording, however, was respectful and tactful, beginning with 'Sir, We are here to cast our selves at your Majesties feet', and going on to beg that the King would consider the great danger to his own person and to the Protestant religion, and effectually make use of his 'Great Council the Parliament'. It was their humble advice and earnest petition that parliament might sit 'at the time appointed', and that he would allay the fears of his subjects by giving 'publick notice and assurance thereof'. Later petitions were to repeat the fears of the people for the safety of the King and of the Protestant religion. Charles, who deeply resented unsought advice from his subjects, could hardly tell the peers to mind their own business, but contented himself with remarking that he wished everyone might take as great care for the welfare of the state as he did.[17]

How the peers' petition came to be printed so promptly in the newspapers we can only guess; but as the text was given in full, it would appear that it was sent to them by one or more of the noble lords concerned. At all events it was only the prelude to an outbreak of popular petitioning that showed all the signs of being fully organised. The King was quick to realise what was happening, and on 11 December the *Gazette* printed his proclamation against tumultuous petitioning, now being carried on by 'divers evil disposed persons . . . for specious ends and purposes relating to the Publick, and thereupon to Collect and Procure to the same the Hands and Subscriptions of multitudes of His Majesties Subjects . . .' Forms (it continued) were being drawn up and sent into the country to be signed; and letters had been intercepted, 'wherein the persons to whom they were addressed are bid to get as many Hands as they could to the said Petitions, saying, That it mattered not though they were neither Gentleman or Freeholders, but that they should be sure to get as many Hands as they could.' The King had therefore summoned the Lord Mayor and aldermen to attend a meeting of the Council, and had made it clear that he expected them to stop those who were now going about to procure signatures, and not to let them or those who signed go unpunished.

But this was more easily said than done: the proclamation appears to have been widely ignored. On 13 January 1680 Sir Gilbert Gerrard, accompanied by Shaftesbury's friend Francis Charlton and several other gentlemen, presented the King with a monster petition from the inhabitants of London, Westminster and places adjacent. According to Harris, who gave the text of the petition in his issue of 16 January, 'His Majestie made this Gracious Answer, *I know the substance of it already. I am Head of the Government, and will take care of it,* and then received the Petition, it being a great Roll of above 100 Yards in length, and carried it away in His Hand.' What Charles carried away in his hand was presumably a copy of the petition itself. On this occasion the first paper to give the news was *Mercurius Anglicus,* which appeared on 14 January; it had nothing to say about the King giving a gracious answer to the petitioners, but reported that when 'Mr Smith the Counsellor offered to read it, and began some part', the King stopped him, and said he knew what it contained. On 16 January Thompson noted that the King was seen to express a particular dislike of Sir Gilbert Gerrard's being concerned in promoting the petition. What the King said to Gerrard had already been spelled out in the *Gazette* of 15 January: '*He did not expect to find one of his name, and particularly him, in such a thing, and that he was very sorry for it.* Whereupon Sir Gilbert would have said something to the King, but His Majesty turned away, and would not hear him.'

Unfortunately the editor of the *Gazette,* Robert Yard, had not got all his facts right. In citing the names of the petitioners who accompanied Gerrard at the presentation he had included 'Mr. Desborough' and 'Mr. Ireton'. It looks as if some Whig had deliberately planted false information on him, or some Tory with a misguided sense of humour. John Desborough, Cromwell's brother-in-law and one of his major-generals, was still living in Hackney in January 1680, although he was to die later that year. He may have been the person referred to in Yard's report, or it may have been one of his sons. Henry Ireton, the regicide and Cromwell's son-in-law, had died in 1651, but he had a son and a brother still alive. All this is beside the point, however, since neither a Desborough nor an Ireton was present when the King accepted the petition. This was made clear in Harris's *Domestick Intelligence* of

16 January, where the final item is an advertisement denying the report 'falslie and maliciouslie published in the Gazette', that Desborough or Ireton had been present, and giving the full list of those who had. On 19 January Yard was compelled to print a letter from Gerrard and Thomas Smith denying that there was any truth in the statement about Desborough and Ireton being 'any way concerned in the delivery of the said Petition', and adding the scornful conclusion: 'We do conceive you did not take your Instructions from your own view, nor any others that were present.' Yard could only explain that the error 'had its rise from those that affirmed they saw those two Gentlemen'. Plucking up his spirits a little, he recovered some lost ground by asserting that their mistake was 'not so great as theirs who gave out that the King returned a most gracious Answer'.

For some time now Harris had been giving the readers of his paper a progress report from various parts of the country about the way the petitions were going. On 6 January he had such reports from Somerset, Devon, Wiltshire and Yorkshire. When Thomas Thynne, accompanied by Sir Walter St John and Sir Edward Hungerford, handed over the Wiltshire petition on 22 January, with its 30,000 signatures, the *Gazette* on 26 January gave a full account of their frosty reception:

His Majesty was pleased to ask them whether they had their Directions from the Grand Jury. Mr. Thynne answered No. His Majesty was pleased to reply, Why say you that you come from the County? You come from a Company of Loose and Disaffected People. Adding, What do you take Me to be? And what do you take your selves to be? I admire Gentlemen of your estates should animate People to Rebellion and Mutiny. You would not take it well I should meddle with your Affairs, and I desire you will not meddle with Mine, especially with a Matter that is so essential a part of my Prerogative.

Here we have the royal view of extra-parliamentary activity in the seventeenth century. To Charles those organised petitions for parliament were simply rabble-rousing. If Thynne and his Whig friends had collected 30,000 signatures in Wiltshire, most of them, in those days of a restricted franchise, must have come from men who had no right to vote in a parliamentary election; and even gentlemen and freeholders had no right to tell him when to summon or dismiss his parliaments.

On 9 January Harris had given his readers an interesting glimpse of how signatures were being collected for petitions. An Essex correspondent sent him news from the little village of Ovington about an attempt 'to Stifle the Petition for sitting of the Parliament, which was recommended by the Knights of the Shire of Essex'. After sermon and prayers one morning, the minister of the parish, Mr Thomas, had asked the congregation to stay behind to sign the petition. When news of this reached the Bishop, he summoned Mr Thomas to appear before him; but 'several gentlemen of worth' certified that he was sick, and could not undertake the journey. The Bishop then demanded that 'at his Peril he must send his Lordship the Petition with the hands taken to it, and the Letter that recommended it to him; to which he answered that it was out of his power, and hath since heard nothing further'. As Thompson reported on 27 January, the Essex petition was duly presented by Colonel Mildmay, a son of the regicide, and the number of signatures was said to exceed that from any other county.

While Harris was revelling in the petition movement, and giving it much of his space, Thompson was torn between his disapproval of such almost rebellious pressure on the King and his journalistic urge to report the news. He succeeded in satisfying both impulses. On 6 January he reported that 'the chief discourse at present is about Petitions', and went on to describe how 'Tables, Pen, Ink and Petitions have been placed upon the Royal Exchange at Change time, and people invited to subscribe them'. A little earlier, on 30 December and 2 January, he had given news of the ineffective steps being taken to stop the collectors of signatures, and of their successful defiance of the magistrates.

In so far as he could, however, Thompson did his best to stress the case against petitioning. How hard he was working to discredit the Whig petitions may be seen from several items he published in his *Domestick Intelligence* for 30 January. From York he had received word of fraudulent practices in the collection of signatures. Being informed that some of his servants had signed the petition, the Archbishop of York questioned them about it; but all of them, except the coachman, denied that they had subscribed their names. On further enquiry, the constable of the town confessed that he had either written in the names himself or got others to do so. From Bristol, Thompson had a story about a nonconformist minister who was promoting the Somerset petition and sent the constable out to collect signatures. When the man returned he found the minister in bed with the wife of one of his parishioners. On 17 February Harris dismissed this tale as a 'notorious lie'; but no doubt it had served its purpose. Another of Thompson's items in this same issue is certainly reliable. As the King was proceeding to Westminster on 26 January to meet (and dissolve) parliament, a goldsmith from Taunton with the appropriate name of Mr Dare, thrust himself forward with yet another petition. He had chosen an unpropitious moment, and Thompson reported that he was 'severely checked' by the King. Finally, in an amiable exercise of satirical fantasy, Thompson announced:

It is reported that several Schools in and about London have petitioned his Majesty, that he will be pleased to give them the late Petitions to make Kites of; which, if granted, it is supposed the Westminster Scholars will have them, as being particularly [in] his Majesties favour.

(Some months earlier the King had extended his royal pardon to several Westminster boys who had been involved in the murder of a bailiff.)*

Soon after the petitioning movement began, some of those who were opposed to it, or alarmed by it, felt the need to mount a counter-attack, and began to draw up addresses to the King abhorring the practice. The subscribers to these addresses were soon to be known as 'Abhorrers'. As early as 29 December 1679, Thompson had a brief notice in his *Domestick Intelligence* about a petition being prepared 'in opposition to that for the sitting of Parliament'. Oddly enough, it was left to Harris in his paper of the same date to spell out what was happening. Under a heading 'The Loyal Protestant Association' he printed what appears to have been a public notice for a counter-address:

We whose names are hereunder Subscribed, out of a Sense of our Duty both to Church and State, and to witness our detestation of all Illegal and undutiful practices, do hereby unanimously declare unto the World, that we abhor the thought of any such Confederacy, and that we will have nothing to do in the Agitating, Promoting or Subscribing of any such Petition as aforesaid, in Opposition to his Majesties Royal Will and Proclamation.

Since the promoters use the word 'abhor', this may be the real beginning of the abhorring movement. The following day *Mercurius Anglicus* also referred to the Loyal Association against petitioning, 'which those who are zealous for say These Protestors are bare-fac'd Papists, or such in Masquerade'. Before long the movement against petitioning began to show results; but the Abhorrers were more distinguished by their social standing than by their numbers. They were mainly men of substance, holding important office – Grand Juries, Mayors and corporations, Justices of the Peace.

On 26 January 1680 the *Gazette* reported that the Mayor, aldermen and burgesses of Bridgwater had dissociated themselves from various petitions now 'going about this County and Borough . . . in which we humbly conceive there are some things derogatory to the King's

---

* Cf. p. 72.

Prerogative'. A similar declaration was made by the Grand Jury and all but four of the Justices of the Peace: warrants had been issued against the promoters of the petition, and one man had been indicted. Similar repudiations were reported by the Grand Jury of Essex in the *Gazette* of 8 April, and by the Grand Jury of Westminster on 19 April. All this activity must have had some effect. No doubt it gave loyalists the feeling that they were doing something, and not leaving the initiative entirely to the Whigs; but 'utterly disowning' and 'abhorring' were at best negative gestures of support.

For all the effect the Whig petitions had on expediting the recall of parliament, they may be said to have failed; the King was to keep the members dangling their heels until 21 October 1680. Yet the organised petitioning from all over the country enabled the Whig opposition to keep the exclusion issue alive. As an exercise in political publicity, therefore, petitioning was undoubtedly successful. It had the advantage, too, of being available at any time to keep up the pressure. When the parliament that had met at last on 21 October was prorogued on 10 January 1681 until the 20th, it is significant that the Whigs did not wait to see if the King would keep his word, but immediately prepared for the worst. On 18 January the *True Protestant Mercury* announced that the Lord Mayor and Recorder had waited on the King with a petition that parliament should meet on the day appointed, only to receive the King's evasive reply, that 'he was well satisfied with the Loyalty and Affection of his City of London'. On 22 January the same paper reported that similar petitions had reached the King from Exeter and Honiton. But by then Charles had already dissolved parliament, and called another to meet at Oxford on 21 March.

The choice of Oxford for what was to prove his last parliament at once provoked a protest from the Whigs, who would infinitely have preferred Westminster, where they were close to their supporters in the City. On 29 January Harris gave all of his front page and part of his second to reporting a speech by the Earl of Essex, and a petition by Essex and 15 other peers that parliament should not be moved to Oxford. The *True Protestant Mercury* of the same date gave this news more briefly, but also reported that some 1,000 London watermen, anxious to avoid a loss of lucrative custom, were said to have subscribed to a petition that parliament might sit as usual at Westminster.

Harris made use of another and odder argument against the move to Oxford. On 1 February he gave his readers a long and sensational story about a young woman called Elizabeth Freeman (usually referred to as the Maid of Hatfield). On 24 January she had seen the apparition of a woman in white, who had said to her: 'The 15th day of May it is appointed for the Royal Bloud to be Poysoned.' The apparition re-appeared next day, and this time gave her a more specific message for the King: 'Tell King Charles from me, and bid him not remove his Parliament, and stand to his Council.' A third time the apparition appeared, telling her not to be afraid, but to 'do [her] message'. On 5 February the *True Protestant Mercury* reported that she had gone to London and found her way to Whitehall, but had not been admitted to the royal presence. She had, however, retold her story to several people, and on her way home the spirit reappeared and told her that 'her obedience was accepted'. She may have aroused the curiosity of Charles, or even his apprehension, for on 16 February the same paper reported that she had appeared before the King and Council. The King listened to her story, asked her a few questions, 'and was pleased to bid her, *Go home and to serve God, and she should see no more such Visions.*' Some months later, Thompson printed in the *Loyal Protestant* a long advertisement in which Robert Stephens, one of the messengers of the press, asserted that Harris and Francis Smith were concerned in publicising the Maid of Hatfield's vision.[18] They had not actually concocted the story, for it was corroborated by the local schoolmaster and several other inhabitants of Hatfield, but they had seen how it could be used to discourage the holding of parliament in Oxford, and there may well have been an element of suggestion employed at some stage on a hysterical young woman. In dismissing her bogus prediction on 19 May, Thompson added that she was now said to be distracted, and that application had been made to admit her to Bethlehem Hospital. She had served her turn. There remains, however, one teasing question. On 15 April Harris's readers were told that the Maid had again seen the vision, and that it had 'appointed her' once more to present herself to the King. What Harris or his newswriter had in mind we shall never know, for with the issue of 15 April his paper came to an end. There were several good reasons why his *Domestick Intelligence* might have been stopped by authority, but this resuscitating of the Maid of Hatfield may have been the last straw.

In the weeks immediately preceding the opening of the Oxford parliament, the newspapers were full of the election returns. Here again the Whig opposition kept up the pressure by the addresses of instruction that were drawn up for their elected representatives, and once more the newspapers played an important part by printing many of those in full. Although in content and wording those addresses vary a little from one county to another, any intelligent reader could hardly have failed to notice that the similarities were so marked as to suggest a common origin. Among the Shaftesbury papers, as it happens, there is a draft of instructions to newly-elected or re-elected members of parliament that was obviously intended as a model to be used on such occasions. On 25 February, for example, Harris has an account of the unanimous re-election of the two Knights of the Shire for Essex, and then proceeds to give in full the address presented to them in the name of the freeholders. The two members are requested 'to Assert our just and ancient Rights and Priviledges, and particularly that of Petitioning . . . Endeavouring to secure the Meeting and Sitting of Frequent Parliaments; To destroy and root out Popery, by securing us against all Popish Successors, and particularly by passing a Bill against James Duke of York . . .' In the same issue Harris found room to print the address (along similar lines) delivered to Arthur Onslow and George Evelyn, the two Knights of the Shire for Surrey. *Smith's Protestant Intelligence* was even more active in publishing such addresses, sometimes giving almost a whole issue to them. It seems reasonable to suppose that the Whig managers not only organised those addresses, but saw to it that they were forwarded for publication in the Whig papers. They were, in fact, a sophisticated exercise in Whig propaganda. Ostensibly it was the people, or at any rate the freeholders, who were instructing their representatives to safeguard their liberties and to secure the passing of an Exclusion Bill, but the initiative had come from above. 'In form,' it has been said, those addresses 'were an appeal by the people, but since they were in no sense spontaneous, they represented in fact an appeal to the people.'[19] When, on 8 April 1681, the King issued his *Declaration to all his Loving Subjects*, giving the reasons why he had dissolved his last two parliaments, loyal addresses soon began to reach him. The *Loyal Protestant* of 10 May did not fail to note how quickly the political wind had changed, and to draw the appropriate conclusion:

It doth now appear that those Petitions and Addresses published in the Names of several Counties and Corporations were *Mis-Representatives* and not *Vox Populi*; For we now abound with Addresses, Letters and Congratulations of a different nature.

The changed political climate after the King's *Declaration* was indeed remarkable, and the loyal response seems to have been rather more spontaneous than the Whig petitions had been. It was the turn of the silent majority to go over to the attack, for now that the King had given them an unmistakable lead, they were prepared to back him up with their unqualified support. Loyal addresses thanking him for his gracious *Declaration* poured in from every corner of the country, and since many of them naively echoed the well-penned words of the King they must have been easy to compose. For many weeks the *Gazette* printed many (perhaps most) of the addresses in full, and carried little other news. To cope with this abnormal flow of material special measures had to be taken. Something could be done in the early days by increasing the depth of the page and reducing the size of the type; but before long four-page issues became common. Successive issues from 23 to 30 June are all double numbers, in small type.

Those addresses were presented to the King in the names of cities, towns, burghs and counties, by Mayors and bailiffs and aldermen, burgesses, freeholders and Grand Juries; but loyal addresses were also drawn up by the London apprentices and by those of Southwark and Westminster, and even, if we may believe the *Impartial Protestant Mercury* of 14 June, by the cooks and chandlers of Salisbury.[20] On 30 August Thompson, who printed the address of the Westminster apprentices in full, reported that it contained more than 5,000 signatures. Concerning one of those signatures he told his readers (27 August) an ironical story about a broker who had taken his apprentice to task for signing the address of the Westminster apprentices, and beaten him severely for it.

The Boy to excuse himself, said, *Sir, I not only thought it my Duty to His Majesty, but also that it would suit with your own inclinations; your self having subscribed to the late Address to His Majesty from the Inhabitants of the City and Liberties of Westminster. – Sirrah,* (replied the Master) *I did it to please a good Customer.*

The extensive coverage that the *Gazette* gave to the loyal addresses was not repeated in the unlicensed newpapers, but they did receive considerable attention; not only from Thompson's *Loyal Protestant*, where it was to be expected, but from Benskin's *Domestick Intelligence* and Smith's *Currant Intelligence*. Benskin's first number appeared on 3 May 1681, and contained news of a loyal address from the Mayor and aldermen of Windsor (one of the earliest), and another from Southampton. Benskin had a painstaking and very loyal correspondent at Windsor, who continued to send him news of the latest addresses all through May and June. On 13 July he reported that since his last there had been ten more – 'so that by this we may see that God has bowed the Hearts of all the People, unless it be such as love to fish in Troubled Waters'.

Unlike the *Gazette* the unlicensed papers had not the necessary space to print loyal addresses, and those that were in sympathy with the Whig opposition would have had no desire to do so. Yet room was found on several occasions to publish the entire text of an address. One of the earliest and most extravagantly loyal of those addresses reached the King from the city of Norwich, and was published by John Smith in his *Currant Intelligence* of 7 May. It took up all of the front page, and part of the first column on the second. The King was congratulated on maintaining the rights of his subjects, 'their Liberties and Properties against the Arbitrary proceedings of the House of Commons in their two last Parliaments, and their Unlimited and Illegal Imprisonments'. He offered the unanimous thanks of the citizens of Norwich for giving those parliaments 'such timely dissolutions', and was assured that 'the Convening of Parliaments to any place, Managing, Proroguing and Dissolving the same' was 'the unquestionable Right of your Majesty'. Smith was now in trouble: on 18 May the *True Protestant Mercury* reported that the Grand Jury of Middlesex had 'found a bill' against the printer and publisher of the Norwich address, 'as reflecting upon parliaments'.[21] The Whigs were fighting back. In the event, Smith reprinted the address with comments in his issue of 11 June – a gesture of defiance in the circumstances. Meanwhile, on 3 June, the *Impartial Protestant Mercury*, in a paragraph dated from Norwich, reported that most of the citizens were delighted with the action of the Grand Jury. This may well have been so. Like so many other cities at this time, Norwich was deeply divided politically, and the loyal address 'reflecting upon parliaments' may have been forced through by the Earl of Yarmouth, who exercised considerable power locally.[22]

The King's *Declaration* undoubtedly gave his loyal subjects genuine satisfaction; but it also brought over a number of waverers, and even some of those who had signed a petition for parliament only a year ago were now ready enough to subscribe their names to a loyal address. Yet if the Whigs were on the defensive, they were far from giving up the fight. Since Harris had been silenced, their two most effective newspapers had been the *True Protestant Mercury* and the *Impartial Protestant Mercury*, and both sneered frequently at the loyal addresses. In doing so they often employed the same tactics as the Tories had used to discredit the Whig petitions: many (it was suggested) were induced to set their hands to a loyal address who would never have thought of doing so on their own. On 14 June the *Impartial Protestant Mercury*, claiming that the idea of the London apprentices submitting a loyal address had been broached by Nathaniel Thompson, went on to assert that 'some unthinking Lads' had been 'drawn in by Implicit Creed (the paper being denied to be read to them)', and that most of those who set their names to it were not apprentices at all, but 'Ruffians and

Beggerly Vermine, drawn in by Pots of Ale'. On 21 June the same paper reported that the Lord Lieutenant of Kent, having ordered a general muster of two foot regiments, invited the officers to dinner, and then unexpectedly presented them with an address to sign. Some were unwilling to do so, but in the end most of them complied.

In such circumstances it was only natural that some cynical observers took a sceptical view of all loyal addresses, but it was dangerous to say so openly. Benskin reported (23 June) that when two men were heard to mock at loyal addresses, 'some Gentlemen of note . . . very fairly Cained them, and brought them to a Confession of their Errors.' On 25 July and again on 4 August, the *Gazette* announced that for speaking scandalous words at Lyme Regis against addresses in general, 'and particularly of that which was presented to His Majesty by the Gentlemen of this County', a man had been indicted by the Grand Jury to appear at the next assizes, and obliged to find security of £1,000. Such an announcement in the *Gazette* was clearly intended as a warning to other scoffers. The King's amiable habit in the summer of 1681 of rewarding loyal addressers with a buck or a doe for a celebratory dinner was perhaps a contributory inducement to draw up an address. It cost him little to cull from one of the royal herds of deer. On 2 August Thompson reported that the King had ordered two of the fattest bucks in Hyde Park to be sent to the London apprentices for a dinner to celebrate their loyal address.[23]

While the *Gazette* was seeking to give the impression that the addresses reaching the King were the expression of a spontaneous and nation-wide loyalty (as to a considerable extent they probably were), the Whig papers were equally determined to show that the nation was still deeply divided. On 3 June the *Impartial Protestant Mercury* reported that there was disagreement in Coventry whether to send a loyal address or petition for a parliament, and that the aldermen were not meddling with either side.[24] A satirical note crept into some of the Whig stories about loyal addresses failing for lack of support. On 22 June the *True Protestant Mercury* told its readers that when an address was being promoted at Richmond in Yorkshire, the Mayor, who had no wish to become involved, 'refused to meddle with it, saying, *Those that medled least, had least to answer for.*' In the same issue Curtiss had a story about the Mayor of a small town in Devonshire, who was very zealous about promoting an address, and received considerable support from the townsmen,

but an Honest Country Farmer moved to give his Opinion, which was granted; then he told them, *They had troubled his Majesty with too much Ink and Paper already*, and so advised to send something more welcome, and laid down a bagg of Twenty pounds in money upon the Table desiring each one to do the same, but all the rest of the Loyal persons fell off, and left his alone, so that neither Address nor Money was agreed upon.

Curtiss must have had some appreciative readers in St Martins le Grand, for in his next number he was able to report that when the inhabitants of that liberty were invited to subscribe to a loyal address the major part were against it, 'and some of the most considerable of them offered to lay down £5 a man, for his Majesties present supply, if those Loyal Gentlemen that were so forward in Addressing would do the like, which they refused to do.'[25]

The extent to which the nation was divided by the King's *Declaration*, one half of his loving subjects wishing to thank him for it, and the other half determined to ignore it, is nowhere better seen than in the behaviour of the Inns of Court. Since lawyers are accustomed to thinking for themselves and weighing the evidence, the benchers were not to be stampeded into an easy acquiescence, and attempts to promote loyal addresses in the various Inns met with considerable resistance. On the evidence published by the Whig and Tory papers, both sides were winning, but such addresses as eventually reached Charles were far from being unanimous. On 10 June, Janeway's *Impartial Protestant Mercury* reported that there had been a heated debate at the Inner Temple on a proposal to thank the King for his *Declaration*, and that the question had been postponed for further discussion. On a subsequent debate the motion for an address was 'laid aside'.[26] In his issue of the *Loyal Protestant* for 14 June, Thompson tried to put a better face on what was happening at the Inner Temple: it was simply a question of the Templars having to deal first with urgent business; but many had asserted that if the motion for an address were to be put they would vote for it. So much for Janeway, whose paper Thompson dismissed as a 'Seditious Bog-house'.

At the Middle Temple there was again sharp disagreement. On 17 June Janeway reported that some people had lately collected almost 20 signatures, 'but what use they intend to made of it, we know not.' In his next issue he gave the whole of his first column to explaining what had then occurred. Those in favour of an address tried to rush it through by summoning a Hall before the opposition had time to assemble. But when a vote was taken, those against prevailed; whereupon those for an address withdrew and composed one of their own, which was presented to the King. Much the same appears to have happened at Gray's Inn. In view of the part played by the *Impartial Protestant*

Mercury in denigrating addresses, it is not surprising to find *Heraclitus Ridens* noticing on 14 June 'how Dick Janeway plies it both against wind and tide, and what pains he takes to lessen the Loyal Addresses'.

The determination of the newswriters to put their own political construction on almost every event makes them an unreliable source of information for the modern historian. He must often, at least, be prepared to read between the lines. When, for example, at the trial of Shaftesbury on 24 November 1681, the jury brought in its famous *ignoramus* verdict, almost all the historical evidence emphasises the loud demonstrations of satisfaction in court. According to the *True Protestant Mercury* 'there was great Shouting in the Court and places adjacent', and Smith's *Currant Intelligence* reported that 'an extra-ordinary great Shout was given by the People both in the Court and Yard'. What Nathaniel Thompson or his reporter heard was hissing: when the verdict was announced, 'a general *Hiss* went throughout the Court'. No doubt the truth is that the Whigs present in court behaved like Whigs, and the Tories like Tories, and that it is never easy to hiss effectively when other people are cheering loudly. The issue may be left with the *Impartial Protestant Mercury:* 'There were some disloyal affronters of the Law, supposed to be Papists, that were so impudent as to *Hiss*, but the generality of the many hundreds present gave an applusive exclamation.' In the circumstances this may be accepted as surprisingly honest reporting.[27]

Unlike the proceedings of parliament, city politics could be, and were, reported fully, with the bias appropriate to the paper in which the news appeared. Between 1679 and 1682 the elections for Lord Mayor and the two sheriffs were dominated by the determination of the Whigs to maintain their hold in the City. Until the autumn of 1681 all went well for them; but then, in spite of strong opposition from Sheriff Pilkington and others, Sir John Moore, a non-party man amenable to pressure from the Court, was elected Lord Mayor. On 13 October he sent the Recorder of London, accompanied by the two Whig sheriffs (Pilkington and Shute), to Whitehall, to ask if His Majesty would do the City the honour of dining at the Guildhall. In accepting this invitation, the King improved the occasion with a distinctly acid reply, which was duly reported in the *London Gazette*:

Mr. Recorder, An Invitation from my Lord Mayor and the City is very Accept-able to Me; and to shew that it is so, notwithstanding that it is brought by messengers so unwelcome to Me as these two Sheriffs are, yet I accept it.

The big shock for the Whigs came in the summer of 1682 when the new sheriffs were being elected. The Whigs were confident that their candidates would be chosen as usual; but, by leaning heavily on the Lord Mayor and by other devious practices, the Court succeeded in having the first poll nullified, and in a second poll two Tory candidates were declared elected. Those breath-taking events were fully recorded in the newspapers.

By this time, too, the papers had a new and nation-wide issue to engross their attention: the so-called *quo warranto* proceedings against municipal charters. One after another those charters were surrendered, reviewed by carefully selected lawyers, and returned in a form more to the liking of the King and his ministers. When at last London received its new charter in 1683 the unlicensed newspapers had all been suppressed. In the general tightening of control that began in 1681 there was no place for the uncontrolled dissemination of news.

As the King gradually asserted his authority over Shaftesbury and his party, the most serious sufferers were to be the Dissenters, who now took the place of the Catholics as the main victims of religious persecution. As early as 21 February 1681 Francis Smith complained indignantly about the prosecution of Norwich Dissenters in accordance with a statute of 35 Elizabeth[28]. This statute had been repealed by the previous parliament, but the King had seen to it that the bill should not be presented for his assent. Throughout 1681 the Judges on circuit, Grand Juries and Mayors were demanding the presentment and prosecution of Dissenters according to the law, and the newspapers kept reporting the results. All over the country, and in Bristol especially, conventicles were broken up; preachers and members of their congregations were arrested and fined, and, in the event of non-payment, the fines enforced by distraint of goods and chattels. On 18 October Smith's *Currant Intelligence* gave two columns to an address by Jeffreys to the Justices of the Peace for Middlesex, demanding the strict execution of the law against conventicles. On 13 December the *Loyal Protestant* reported that the Mayor of Sandwich had been reprimanded by the Council for not prosecuting the local Dissenters.[29]

By 1682 the harrying of the sectarians had become even worse. In July of that year an informer called John Hilton, known as Captain Hilton, had started a very specialised newspaper, *The Conventicle Courant*, in which he recorded the successful prosecution of Dissenters in and around London, and this periodical ran irregularly until February 1683. Hilton was paid by results; and in a petition to the King for back pay he claimed that, by his own efforts against conventicles, fines totalling more than £10,000 had been levied in London, and more than £7,000 in Westminster, and that he had employed fifty or more persons every Sunday and on some other days in tracking down conventicles.[30]

As a curious instance of how this climate of persecution might affect an individual citizen we may take the treatment of Richard Farrington between 1681 and 1682. Farrington, who had sat in the Oxford parliament as one of the two members of parliament for Chichester, was known to be well-disposed to Dissenters, and (if we may trust Sir Roger L'Estrange) his wife attended a conventicle there[31]. From the *Impartial Protestant Mercury* of 5 July 1681 we learn that the overseers of the poor in Chichester and the churchwardens, of whom Farrington was one, had been carrying out a distraint on the goods of such persons as had refused to pay the rate fixed by the parishes for poor relief. Among the delinquents was the aged Bishop, Guy Carleton, who had fought for Charles I in the Civil War, and had recently been rewarded with the bishopric. When the churchwardens went to his palace to present their demand, he refused them entrance. As a consequence of his obduracy, 'a Distress was made on Two Cows, Two Horses, and three Mares of his Lordship's', and they were offered for sale. From a sense of duty, perhaps not unmixed with pleasure, Farrington was present at the auction. As, in his capacity of churchwarden, he was watching the proceedings, one of the Bishop's servants 'presented a Pistol close to Mr. Farrington's Breast, and swearing, *Dam him*, he had particular Order to kill him', pulled the trigger, 'but by God's Providence the Pistol did not fire'.[32]

Some months later, on 10 November, Thompson published a letter in his *Loyal Protestant* from one 'J.J.', of whom he admitted he knew nothing. The writer of this letter reported that 'a great quantity of Arms were found in Mr. Farrington's house, where many of the most eminent Dissenters frequented'. On being questioned, Farrington first said the arms were for the militia, and then that they were for his own defence, in case the French should land. On the following day the *Impartial Protestant Mercury* put the record straight. A raid had indeed taken place, led by the two head-constables, without a warrant, and supported by the Bishop's clerk, a customs-house officer, and a great rabble. They had searched the house on the pretence of looking for prohibited goods, and had found none. As for the arms, all they discovered were 'two or three Rusty Basket-Hilted Swords, prepared, 'tis believed from their antique Shape, against the Spanish Invasion in *Eighty Eight*'. Mr Farrington was bringing actions against those over-busy trespassers.

A year later Farrington found himself involved in a more serious incident, which led to a charge of his being an accessory to murder. On Sunday 6 August 1682, his coachman, John Davies, committed assault and battery on an informer called Richard Habin who had been breaking up conventicles, and the man was so badly hurt that he died soon afterwards. On 15 August the story appeared in Thomas Vile's *London Mercury*, Thompson's *Loyal Protestant*, and L'Estrange's *Observator*. Vile's account was strictly impartial, but L'Estrange had seen the chance of an attack on the Dissenters, and made the most of it. John Davies had attacked Habin 'by the Order of his Master (as they say in the Town)' and 'without any Provocation'. He knocked the man down, trod on him, and followed him with blows on the head. 'This was done in the *Open-Street*, by *Fair-Day-Light*, near 100 Lookers on; 4 or 5 in Mr. Farrington's *House* that could not but see it; And yet no Interposing.' Thompson's version was also loaded against Farrington: the coachman was 'encouraged . . . nay, commanded' to beat Habin.

In the *True Protestant Mercury* of 22 August Curtiss published a letter from Chichester in which his correspondent gave a very different version of what he called the 'accident'. Habin was one of two 'scandalous and infamous' informers who were making money from prosecuting Dissenters found at conventicles, and taking money from others in return for not prosecuting them. On the day in question Habin had been drinking, and as he passed the house of Mr Farrington ('a worthy Gentleman') he broke the windows with his stick. The coachman, coming from the stable, remonstrated with him, and Habin replied with threatening language; whereupon the coachman wrested Habin's stick from him and struck him on the head four or five times. Habin ran to the Mayor's house, but not finding him at home, 'ran to the B[ishops]s, where his head being dressed, it is said (though drunk before) he drank more, and then went to sleep in the stable, where he dyed.' The emphasis here is all on Habin's excessive drinking: some surgeons who had examined the wounds in his head said *they* were not the cause of his death.

In the meantime L'Estrange had been acquiring fresh information, apparently from more than one willing correspondent. On 26 and 28 August he elaborated considerably on his first account. We now learn that on the Sunday before the fatal attack, while the coachman was escorting his mistress to the Stockbridge conventicle, they met with Habin. What is said to have followed may be true, but sounds suspiciously like pure invention. When the coachman saw Habin, '*What* (says he) *shall we never be Quiet for ye? You'd have Your Brains*

177

*Knock'd out if you were Right serv'd; and if ever you come again, I'le do
it my self.*' The case against Farrington is also amplified. When he was
asked by the Mayor for the coachman's name, he 'absolutely Denyed
the Knowledge of it at first, but upon *Second Thoughts*, told it.' To say
the least, it is highly improbable that Farrington, a man experienced
in public affairs, should tell the Mayor he couldn't remember his own
coachman's name. As for the broken window, it was examined by
'divers Credible Persons', who all agreed 'it was *"Broken from within
the House"*'. And when the coachman was beating Habin, Farrington
'did not only look out of his *Window*, but go to the *Door*; and call to
him to lay on, and Beat him Stoutly'. Lest readers of the *Observator*
should fail to register the full significance of what Farrington was alleged to have said, L'Estrange had 'lay on' and 'beat him stoutly' printed
in black letter.

In the event Farrington was tried on 16 November for abetting John
Davies in murder. A short account of the trial appeared in the *Loyal
Impartial Mercury* of 17 November. The chief witnesses for the prosecution were a child of twelve, and one William Crossingham, 'a
fellow that gets his living by running of errands'. The Lord Chief
Justice was not impressed, and directed the jury to find Farrington not
guilty. Had Farrington been a Tory and a good Church of England
man it is unlikely that a charge against him would ever have been
brought.

When newspapers were revived in 1695 they were noticeably less par-
tisan than those of the years 1679 to 1682. Whigs and Tories were still
at variance, but the issues separating them had become rather blurred
by a division within the Tory party, which was split between those who
still favoured the old regime or had reservations about the legitimacy
of the new King's claim to the throne, and those who were now firmly
committed to the Protestant settlement of 1689. It is impossible to
estimate accurately the size of the Jacobite minority which was
prepared to risk all for the restoration of James II, but early in 1696
an unsuccessful plot to assassinate King William was a reminder that
they were still a menace to peace and prosperity. The subsequent trials
of the chief conspirators were fully reported in the newspapers. The
Flying Post and the *Post-Boy* carried long accounts on 12 March of the
trial of Robert Charnock, and of that of Sir John Friend on 24
March. The *Flying Post* gave the whole of its issue of 26 March to the
trial of Sir William Parkyns; and his execution and that of Sir John
Friend on 13 April were again fully reported.

The assassination of the King would have been a prelude to the invasion of England, but this too failed; the disaffected in England and Scotland waited for the landing of the invasion force from France, and the invasion force waited in vain for a rising in England or Scotland. Few of the King's subjects seem to have loved him, or even to have liked him (though there were some exceptions, notably Daniel Defoe). Yet as the reign of William progressed, more and more Englishmen came to realise that they would have been much worse off without him. This was a period of re-adjustment, when old habits and expectations and loyalties were giving place to new. The Toleration Act of 1689 had made life less difficult for the Dissenters, although it no doubt increased the intolerance of the intolerant. For some time after the Revolution the King had tried to rule with mixed administrations of Whigs and Tories. From time to time he used his royal veto on bills that had passed both Houses of Parliament, but he behaved much more like a constitutional monarch than Charles II had ever done.

At all events, in the last decade of the seventeenth century there are signs of a new willingness to listen to reasonable arguments for one course of action or another, and not simply to vilify or abuse political opponents. The House of Commons, it is true, remained jealous of its privileges, and an incautious journalist might still be summoned to appear before the Bar of the House to be disciplined; but such occasions usually resulted in little more than the huffing and puffing of outraged members, and an abject apology would normally settle the matter. The final lapse of the Licensing Act, however, was far from ushering in a period of political licence; the law against seditious libel could still be invoked to deal with anyone who was thought to have gone too far. Even so, reasoned comment was now more generally tolerated; in wartime more so than might have been expected.

A modern historian has drawn attention to what he calls, fairly enough, a 'leading article' in the *Flying Post* of 3 March 1696.[33] The writer of this article (almost certainly George Ridpath) was concerned about the dangerous threat of invasion mentioned above, and with the inadequate preparations for meeting it. He was, or appeared to be, well informed about the steps being taken by the French: Louis had approved the plans for invasion, the Duke of Berwick had been in England making secret plans for it, and James II intended to accompany the invading fleet in person. Reconnaissance had shown that the French had assembled a large fleet, and (in a phrase that a twentieth-century leader writer would have been glad to hit on) the harbour at Calais was so crowded with masts that it looked like a wood in winter.

Everything seemed to favour the French: Scotland was blaming England for the failure of its colonial scheme on the isthmus of Darien, and England itself was in the middle of a financial crisis brought on by the recoinage. And what were we doing about all this? A large part of the navy was being drawn off to escort a valuable convoy from the Mediterranean, leaving the Channel inadequately protected, and the troops that could defend England if the French landed were stationed abroad fighting in a foreign war . . . It was all strong stuff in the 'Something must be done about it' vein to which we are well accustomed today, but which was unfamiliar to newspaper readers in 1696. Such interference in public affairs by a mere newspaper would never have been tolerated in the reign of Charles II; it was indeed this sort of meddling in government affairs that L'Estrange had sought to make impossible in his days as licenser of the press. L'Estrange was now in his seventieth year, and some years earlier he had suffered an apoplectic stroke that nearly proved fatal. If a copy of the *Flying Post* for 3 March had fallen into his hands he would have been in danger of another stroke; but on that very day he was arrested and committed to Newgate on suspicion of being involved in the assassination plot. At all events, this outspoken article in a London newspaper was a symptom of the growing emancipation of the press. In the words of the historian just mentioned, 'In no other European state was such a reasoned exposition of a critical situation available for the public.'

When the political thermometer rose in the reign of Queen Anne, it was some time before the full effect was felt in the newspapers. The sharply differing views of Whigs and Tories were rather to be found in the rich pamphlet literature of the period, and in essay papers such as John Tutchin's *Observator*, Charles Lesley's *Rehearsal* and Defoe's *Review*, all of which fall outside our field of reference. As the war drew to an end in 1711, most of the papers became politically polarised, the Whig *Flying Post* attacking the Tory *Post-Boy*, and the *Post-Boy* hitting back at the *Flying Post*. In 1711 the *Post-Boy* found itself facing a new adversary, the *Protestant Postboy*, which stated its aim as being to act as 'an Antidote against the Poysonous Assertions and Insinuations of the said *Post-Boy*, by Detecting the Spring from which they flow'. The *Daily Courant*, which had begun by being apparently impartial, moved to total commitment with the Whigs. The intensity of political feeling in those months was comparable to that in the years immediately following the Popish Plot. In addition to writing political essays for the Tory *Examiner*, Swift may have contributed occasionally to the *Post-Boy*. If we may believe the *Protestant Postboy* of 25 September 1711,

Roper's paper was being helped by the former authors of the *Examiner*, 'particularly by an ambitious Tantivy [High Church Tory], whose Towring Hopes of Preferment having been disappointed in Ireland, turn'd Cat-in-Pan'. Swift certainly had dealings with Roper, and it is possible that on 10 November he contributed to this leading Tory newspaper the long and well-written article on the proposed peace.

In the last years of Queen Anne's reign, when the Tories were in power, Whig journalists and printers were subjected to a considerable amount of harassment; and when the political situation was reversed in 1714, it was the turn of the Tory journalists and printers to suffer. Yet Ministers of State, however much they might be exasperated by political criticism, had not the same power to suppress the newspapers as Charles II had exercised in the autumn of 1682, and if they had made any such attempt there would almost certainly have been a public outcry. Accordingly they proceeded more cautiously, but vexatiously, by issuing warrants for arrest, and subjecting the authors, printers and publishers of newspapers to examinations by one of the under-secretaries. Many of those examined were never brought to trial, but were set free after a short imprisonment. Others were granted bail, and released after giving sureties for their good behaviour. Surprisingly, a prisoner was sometimes allowed the use of pen, ink and paper, and might carry on, or at least supervise, his newspaper while still in custody. Others were tried, found guilty and fined, or, when the offence was considered more serious and an example was thought desirable, sentenced to stand in the pillory. The real hardship came when the victim of the government's displeasure was unable to find his securities or pay his fine, in which case his imprisonment might be prolonged.* For the most part, however, the policy appears to have been to frustrate and disrupt the publication of newspapers, and so encourage them to be more cautious in what they published, rather than to go to extremes and risk public discontent.[34]

There was one sort of political offence for which little mercy could be expected: any open expression of Jacobitism was dangerous. The death of Queen Anne, the last of the Stuart monarchs, had been followed immediately by the proclamation of George, Elector of Hanover, as King. A Protestant succession was assured; the Whigs were now in control, but many Tories were suspected of nursing a secret loyalty to the king across the water. The rebellion of 1715 was to show how few active Jacobites there were in England, and most of those who had any

* Cf. p. 213.

inclination that way were in favour of 'letting I dare not wait upon I would'. Still, there was a sufficient number of disaffected Tories ready to take a furtive delight in any gibes at the new Hanoverian king, and they expected the Tory newspapers to provide them with the opportunity. George I was in no hurry to meet his English subjects, and did not reach London until more than six weeks after his accession. On 7 August 1714 the *Post-Boy* announced: 'We patiently expect the safe Arrival of the King.' On 10 August the *Flying Post* drew attention to the loaded word 'patiently', and on the same day the *Post-Boy* issued a correction: 'N.B. In our last, in the London-Article, for patiently, read impatiently.' It is hard to decide whether 'patiently' was a genuine misprint, a joke of the printer, or a deliberate sneer.

At all events, it is easy to find latent Jacobitism coming to the surface in the next few years, by way of innuendo and implication. On 4 June 1715 Mawson's *Weekly Journal*, reporting the celebration of the King's birthday, laid some stress on the precautions taken to prevent disloyal disturbances. The paragraph that followed drove the point home:

The Next Day being the Anniversary of the GLORIOUS RESTAURATION of King Charles II, the same was observed with greater Rejoycings than ever was known, since that GLORIOUS DAY on which that Monarch made his Publick Entry in 1660.

Mawson was balancing on a tightrope here, but he had his safety net: if any exception were taken to the juxtaposition of two such contrasting paragraphs, he could plead that he was only reporting what had happened. Similarly, on 25 October 1718, Mist reported that 'Monday being the anniversary of his Majesty's Coronation', the Lord Mayor had ordered the beadles of the City parishes to warn the inhabitants to keep their servants and apprentices within doors, 'to prevent any Tumult or Riot, as has formerly been committed; by which means there was no disturbance.' So long as the journalist took the advice of one of Applebee's correspondents, 'Be the Story your Province; leave the Reflection to the Readers',[35] he could get away with a good deal. Innuendo was infinitely adaptable. On 9 August 1718 Mist told his readers that one Robert Harrison had stood in the pillory at Whitechapel for crying out 'King James for Ever!', and that 'one man throwing Dirt at him, the Mob obliged him to go down on his knees to ask him Forgiveness, and several gave him Money'.

How serious a view the government took of any open manifestation of Jacobitism may be seen from some prosecutions in 1716. When Mawson's *Weekly Journal* came to an end in 1716, his friends con tinued to support the Jacobite interest in *Robin's Last Shift*, and when that came to an untimely end, in *The Shift Shifted*, both with the subtitle of *Weekly Remarks*. The upshot of their seditious activities was that Isaac Dalton was indicted for publishing 'a libel called *Weekly Remarks*', containing several expressions 'highly reflecting on His Majesty and the government'. He was also charged with saying, while a prisoner in Newgate, 'King George is a rogue, God damn him', and with giving the soldiers on guard a shilling to drink the Pretender's health in the name of King James. At the same time George Flint admitted to being the author of the *Weekly Remarks*, and Dalton's sister Mary to being the publisher of *Robin's Last Shift*. Dalton was sentenced to one year's imprisonment, and to find sureties for his good behaviour for three years. His sister and Flint received similar sentences. Later in the same year Dalton was indicted again for publishing *The Shift Shifted*, and sentenced to another year's imprisonment after he had served his first term, and to stand in the pillory at Newgate. Mary, wife of George Flint, was given one year for being concerned in the publication. Flint escaped from Newgate, and fled to France. In view of his behaviour in Newgate, Dalton was perhaps lucky to get off so lightly.[36] He was more fortunate than the young printer, John Matthews, who was hanged at Tyburn in 1719 for printing a Jacobite pamphlet, *Vox Populi, Vox Dei*, calling upon the people to cast off their Hanoverian King and restore the Stuart dynasty in the person of James III.

In the 1720s and 1730s the most notable development in political controversy is to be found in the refinement of satirical techniques. Faced with the dangers inseparable from overt criticism, the newspapers were driven to use the more indirect modes of satire. In an essay 'Of Libels' Thomas Gordon enumerates some of the ironical approaches that may be employed with comparative safety. He cites first the animal fable in the manner of Aesop, where the wicked minister is 'a wily Fox, set over an honest Flock of Sheep to guard them from Dogs and Vermin', but instead of that, worries them to death. Equally ancient and effective is the mock panegyric, where you praise a statesman for virtues he does not possess, or, 'if Money or Provisions are scarce, thank God and the Government for the *Plenty* which [the nation] enjoys'. A favourite modern mode is the historical, where you find examples of pride, avarice and corruption in great men of the past, and encourage the reader to make the contemporary application hmself.[37] (One of the most devastating examples of the historical parallel is to be found in No. 27 of the *Examiner*, where Swift makes use of the known character of Marcus Crassus to denounce the avarice of Marlborough.) These and other modes of satirical onslaught were used to good effect against Walpole and the royal family by the writers of the *Craftsman*, who carried the art of innuendo and *double entendre* as far as it would safely go, and on a few occasions too far. Compared with the *Craftsman* and its sophisticated and often brilliant satire, the seventeenth-century newspapers were primitives. Their writers may have been willing enough to wound, but they had much to learn about how to strike.

With the coming of the weekly newspapers, too, there was more space available to develop a political argument, and the popular essay papers of Addison and Steele and their successors had accustomed a growing public to the pleasure of sustained and reasonable discussion. In such papers as the *London Journal* and the *British Journal* the long political essay was probably as important to most readers as the news. Many of the men who now wrote for the newspapers, such as George Ridpath, John Trenchard, Thomas Gordon and Nicholas Amhurst, had been educated at an English, Scottish or Irish university; and among those who helped Amhurst with the *Craftsman* were Bolingbroke and William Pulteney. In the 1720s and early 1730s, when an important section of the newspaper press was bought by the government and subsidised, it suited the opposition to sneer at Walpole's hirelings as dull and incompetent. Yet some of them were able men. Writing for him in the newly-acquired *London Journal* Walpole had Bishop Hoadly; and in the *Daily Courant* he had his own brother Horatio, Francis Hare, Bishop of Chichester, and Dr Henry Bland, headmaster of Eton and later Dean of Durham. Nothing like this was happening in the days of Benjamin Harris and Nathaniel Thompson.

CHAPTER 6

The newspaper men and women

1

This final chapter falls into two main sections. In the first, an attempt is made to put some flesh on dry bones by considering, in such detail as the known facts make possible, the lives and misadventures of some newspaper men and women of the late seventeenth century. This is mainly a story of risks taken and authority flouted, and of the retribution and suffering that all too often followed. In this early period the newspapers were far from being the fourth estate of the realm. In much the same way as the actors had been considered rogues and vagabonds in the first half of the century, so the newspaper writers and publishers were given short shrift when they came up against those in authority. They could, and often did, annoy the government of the day; but their words did not strike terror into the men in office. When they offended they were dealt with summarily, and there was no public outcry about the punishment meted out to them. Their readers expected them to be bold and outspoken; yet, when they suffered the consequences, their supporters melted away.

The second section is concerned with the undefined and often casual organisation of the newspapers. If we ask, 'Who did what?' and 'Who was responsible for what was printed and published?' the answers inevitably introduce an element of speculation, and certainly do not disclose a uniform pattern of responsibility. Any attempt to discover what was going on must be made in the context of seventeenth-century printing conditions, with due regard to the small number of persons involved in producing each issue of a newspaper. We must not think of last-minute changes in the make-up of the front page when an important piece of news came in; of the disciplined arrangement of the news in separate sections, each with its own editor; of endless copies of each edition rolling rapidly off the press for bundling and distribution. We must think rather of a few men endeavouring to bring order out of chaos, and sometimes struggling to find enough copy to fill the four columns at their disposal. Since a clear indication of what was actually happening is hard to obtain, and has often to be deduced from the results, some evidence has occasionally been drawn from comparable conditions in the early eighteenth century.

The little we know of those early newspaper men is nearly always related to the occasions when they were in trouble, and it is therefore not possible to give a rounded view of their lives and characters. Nathaniel Thompson, for instance, may have been a good husband and a kind father, but all we know about that side of his life is that he was a married man. Yet even with such scattered and inadequate facts as are available in the contemporary newspapers and in public records, something can be done to show what precarious lives those newspaper pioneers lived, and, whatever their motives, the sort of eager or dogged persistence that drove them on.

Benjamin Harris was in business by 1674, when he published Benjamin Keach's *War with the Devil*, which reached a seventh edition in 1683, and which Dunton believed would sell 'to the end of time'.[1] Had Harris, an anabaptist, restricted his stock to such godly works, he would have led a quieter, if less interesting, life. But with the discovery of the Popish Plot, if not earlier, he began to live dangerously, and threw himself into the religious and political controversy that ensued. From its earliest numbers in July 1679 his *Domestick Intelligence* was vehemently anti-Catholic; and Harris reported the various occasions on which Catholics were arrested, suspected of fire-raising or of committing some other crime. On 14 July he gave his readers a story about several Papists and one Protestant drinking together in the public house of 'a small village' in Dorsetshire, and how 'they fell into discourse concerning the horrid Plot'. The Catholics denied that there was any plot, and 'spoke with all scorn and contempt imaginable of Mr. Oates and his Evidence'; but being unable to controvert the proof offered by the Protestant, they 'resolved to use the most Invincible and Infallible Argument of the Catholic Church, and as we hear barbarously murdered the Protestant, whereupon they were immediately apprehended, and committed to Prison for the same'. No doubt other stories set in small and unnamed villages were going the rounds at the time, but Harris had nothing further to tell his readers (not even a 'we hear') about what ultimately happened to those homicidal Catholics. For some months he seems to have avoided being called to account for the tendentious news he often published in his paper, or for the dangerous comments he sometimes made. As we have seen, he had been careful not to make any criticism when, at the trial of Sir George Wakeman on 18 July 1679, Lord Chief Justice Scroggs had directed the jury to find a verdict of not guilty. That it still rankled in his mind, however, was soon to become clear.

The first hint that Harris had gone too far was given by Thompson on 27 January 1680: 'On Saturday last [24 January] Mr. Harris, a Bookseller, was committed, for incerting some matter in his Intelligence which gave displeasure to the Lord Chief Justice.' Almost anything appearing in Harris's *Intelligence* might have given offence to Scroggs, but the matter referred to was his report on 20 January that 'Articles of high Misdemeanor were offered by way of complaint to the King's Most Excellent Majestie . . . by Dr. Oates and Captain William Bedlow, against the Lord Chief Justice Scroggs'. If Harris had stopped there, he would have been safe enough: he was publishing true news, however unwelcome it might be to Scroggs. Unfortunately he went on to add a provocative comment:

Therefore if any have been oppressed or injured by the said Lord Chief Justice, they will be speedilie Heard, if they in time come in; the cause will it's thought be heard the beginning of February.[2]

To issue such an invitation to his readers Harris must have been living in a state of euphoria: the hated Scroggs, he must have felt, was about to get what was due to him, for Oates and Bedloe were still riding high in popular esteem; and so far as he himself was concerned, if by any chance he was brought to trial for what he had written about the Lord Chief Justice, his political friends would see to it that he had a Whig jury who would bring in an *ignoramus* verdict. In the event the charges brought against Scroggs were heard and debated before the King in Council, and on 22 January the *Gazette* reported that the Lord Chief Justice had been vindicated on all counts, and the matter dismissed from the board.

Here we come on a missing link in the chain of events. When Harris was led into the court of King's Bench on 5 February 1680 and found himself facing the Lord Chief Justice, the charge he had to answer had nothing to do with anything he had published in his *Domestick Intelligence*, but set forth that 'the said Benjamin Harris did maliciously and designedly to scandalize the King and Government, cause to be Printed, and Sold, a late seditious Book called, *An Appeal from the Country to the City, for the Preservation of His Majesty's Person, Liberty, Property, and the Protestant Religion*'[3]. At what point Harris learnt that he was to be tried on this serious charge, and not for an indiscretion in his *Intelligence*, we do not know, but he could have had very little time to prepare his defence. The short period that elapsed between his committal to prison for what he had published in the *Domestick Intelligence* of 20 January and his trial on 5 February suggests that the government may already have collected enough evidence to prosecute him for publishing the *Appeal*, and merely used his attack on Scroggs to get him into safe custody while the crown lawyers were perfecting the case against him.

The work for which he was now to stand trial was admittedly seditious, for it advocated setting aside the lawful succession of the King's brother James in favour of the Duke of Monmouth, whom Charles had publicly declared to be his illegitimate offspring. But in what sense was Harris the 'publisher' of this pamphlet? The *Appeal*, as we now know, had been published in early October 1679, and although Harris may have been a prime suspect, the government does not appear to have had any evidence to connect him with it when it first appeared. On the contrary, several other people had been arrested for selling it, including Nathaniel Thompson's wife Mary.[4] To this may be added a statement in Luttrell's diary, that after Harris had been sentenced he 'had very hard measure; for he was not the first publisher of it, but one Nathaniell Thompson; but this Harris bore all'.[5] A pamphlet arguing the case against the Catholic James succeeding to the throne is hardly one that we should expect to issue from Thompson's shop; but Thompson was unpredictable, and in 1679 his references to the Duke of Monmouth in his *Intelligence* had been noticeably friendly.

Since Harris was not being accused of treason he was allowed counsel for his defence; and the case they made out for him was that he was not the *first* publisher of the *Appeal*, and that in selling it he had no malicious design to scandalise the King as the indictment sought to make out. That was the best they could do, for the crown had called several witnesses to prove that the pamphlet had actually been sold in his shop, although one of them, Mrs Grover, testified under cross-examination that it had been in print before she saw it in Harris's shop. One of his counsel told the court that it had been 'publickly sold in other Booksellers Shops before we had it, and so we thought in a way of trade we might do the like'; and another explained that his client 'seeing it running up and down the Town, he gets some of them, and suffers them to lie up and down in his Shop, and this only as a common thing to get Money'. Unfortunately for Harris, the crown called 'the printer's man', who testified that he had printed the pamphlet for Harris, and the Recorder made the most of this:

Mr. Recorder. And what, did you do it in the Daytime, was you not at it in the Night?

Printer's Man. Yes, I was upon it in the Night.

Mr. Recorder. Ay, it was a deed of Darkness, and so fit for Night-Work.[6]

After he was sentenced, Harris had an advertisement inserted in his *Domestick Intelligence* stating that he did not know who had written the

Appeal; that he had never received any copy of it from Titus Oates, either in manuscript or in print, and that the first he had ever seen of it was 'a Printed Book in Quarto, of four sheets of Paper, commonly sold about the Town, some considerable time before he sold any of them'.[7] Before the jury retired he had tried to address them, but was forbidden to do so. What he had in mind to say to them was probably what he put in his advertisement of 17 February. There are, in fact, two 1679 editions of the *Appeal*, one in quarto and the other in folio, and the second of those was presumably the one printed for Harris.[8] That it was not the sole reason for his indictment is suggested by two outbursts from Scroggs in the course of the trial. When one of his counsel, William Williams, assured Scroggs that Harris was 'a Man of other Principles than to do such things', the Lord Chief Justice brushed this argument aside:[9]

There is scarce any but [Francis] Smith that is so factious a Seller of Books as Harris.——All your *Domestick Intelligences* are so; for which, you know, you have forfeited your Recognizance almost in every Book.*

In his final summing up Scroggs returned to Harris's newspaper, and told him that 'all Writers of News, though not scandalous, seditious, nor reflective upon the Government or the State; yet if they are Writers (as there are few others) of false News, they are indictable and Punishable upon that Account'. Strictly speaking none of this was relevant to the charge against Harris of printing and publishing the *Appeal*. One might conclude that Scroggs was still smarting from the treatment he had received in the *Intelligence* of 20 January; but it may be more reasonable to suppose that the sentence he was about to pronounce was a cumulative one, intended to cover past as well as present offences, and more especially to put an end not only to the newspaper that Harris had illegally revived on 28 December in defiance of the King's proclamation, but to any other newspapers that might follow his example. If so, the attempt failed. Harris, however, 'bore all': the pillory, a year's imprisonment, and the fine of £500 that he was unable to pay. If he did have a Whig jury, it was not a very resolute one. On being asked for its verdict, it found Harris guilty only of 'selling the book'; but after a little brusque bullying by Scroggs it quickly found him guilty as charged.[10] The verdict that Scroggs eventually obtained from the jury must have come as a shock to Harris. That he had indeed been buoyed up by an unshakeable confidence had emerged early in his trial, when

---

* The word 'book' was commonly used at this time to denote a news-book, i.e. newspaper.

one of the crown witnesses, Robert Stephens, testified to having on several occasions seen copies of the *Appeal* in Harris's shop. 'And I have asked him,' Stephens continued, 'Why he would so publickly vend them? . . . and he said, *He had several Thousands to stand by him.*'[11]

Harris's day in the pillory was something of a triumph. The friends that he had counted on to stand by him turned up in sufficient numbers, and 'he and his party hollowed and whooped, and would permitt nothing to be thrown at him'.[12] But having protected him from being pelted with garbage in the pillory, those friends thought they had done all that could be expected of them. No one came forward to pay his fine of £500, and until it was paid he would have to remain in prison, whether he had served out his year's sentence or not. When Scroggs was presiding over the trial of Henry Care on 2 July 1680 he reflected on this circumstance with grim satisfaction. Recalling the jubilant behaviour of Harris's friends standing round the pillory, he went on to spell out the hollowness of such support:

But those People that did then attend him leave following him in a Gaol for *five Hundred Pounds*, which may be five shillings a piece had discharged him of, if they had been as free of their Purses as they are of their Noises and Acclamations. So that in Truth, they are only violent against the Government whilst they can make Shouts and Noises, but if it comes once to deliver a man from a penal Sum they will let him rot in Gaol. For so Harris sent to me, that *his Party had all forsaken him*, and no man would give him any thing.[13]

There is no evidence to suggest that he was kept a close prisoner, and if he had the usual privilege of receiving visitors he was probably able to exercise a general control over his *Domestick Intelligence* from prison. At the end of his trial, when he was being handed over to a tipstaff to be taken to the King's Bench Prison, Harris had 'earnestly beseech'd his Lordship that he might be sent to any other Prison, and named Newgate three or four times, but it was not granted to him'.[14] The King's Bench Prison had a poor reputation, but it seems likely that Harris was asking to be sent to Newgate because it was much more accessible to anyone he might wish to visit him. The prison to which he was being sent was in Southwark, and to get there entailed crossing London Bridge and then walking for a considerable distance along the south bank. If his business was not to be ruined, and more particularly if he was to carry on his paper, he would need the help of his wife and Nathaniel Crouch, who was now in charge of the paper, and they could reach him much more conveniently at Newgate, not many minutes' walk from his shop.

What finally forced Harris to suspend publication of his *Intelligence* can only be surmised, but it is possible to make a good guess. On 30 March his paper contained a statement that Lord Chief Justice North, then on circuit, had declared 'that the Act of Parliament for the Conviction of Popish Recusants ought to be put in force against none but Papists', and not used to harass Protestant Dissenters. North had said no such thing, as he made clear on 12 April in the *London Gazette*. The opening words of his advertisement, 'Whereas in a licentious Pamphlet, Entitled *The Protestant Domestick Intelligence* . . .', will indicate his uncompromising repudiation of the words attributed to him. Ever since May 1679, when the small body of Dissenters in parliament had voted unanimously in favour of the Exclusion Bill, the King's attitude to the dissenting community had hardened, and a new persecution was about to begin. Once again Harris had burnt his fingers badly, not merely by publishing false news, but by interfering in matters of state. In apologising on 13 April for his error, he explained that the offending paragraph had been taken from another paper, *Mercurius Civicus*; but he may have been told that enough was enough, for with his next issue on 16 April he suspended publication.

There now followed in December 1680 the apparently unconstitutional intervention of the House of Commons, when orders were sent to the Marshal of the King's Bench Prison to release Harris, and he resumed publication of his *Domestick Intelligence*.* Meanwhile, on 22 December, the House of Commons had resolved to impeach Scroggs, and the House of Lords concurred. In the issue of his revived *Intelligence* of 14 January, Harris advertised a pamphlet which may have been a rushed job, *The Triumphs of Justice over Unjust Judges . . . Humbly Dedicated to the Lord Chief Justice Scroggs*, boldly issued as being 'Printed for Benjamin Harris'. The old euphoria had returned. How long he remained at liberty is another unsolved problem. There is evidence that he was still at large in February, and that the Council knew where he was to be found. The evidence comes from a long advertisement inserted in the *Loyal Protestant* of 12 July 1681 by Robert Stephens. As a messenger of the press, Stephens had been sent to Hatfield by an order of Council 'in February last', to find Francis Smith and Harris in connection with 'the *Vision*, which these Persons are concerned in the Printing'. It will be recalled that in an attempt to dissuade the King from holding his next parliament in Oxford, Harris had published the dire warnings of the Maid of Hatfield in his *Domestick Intelligence*, and they were republished in pamphlet form as

---

* See p. 17.

A True and Perfect Relation of Elizabeth Freeman. According to Stephens, Harris and Smith did not wait for him to take action when he reached Hatfield. They arrived with a constable at eleven o'clock at night, and tried to break his door open with two staves, 'charging him with Felony and Treason, giving him very reproachful words, and saying, *They had good Sheriffs, and good Juries, and need not fear what could be done by any Prosecution*; and set a Watch at his door all night; but as soon as morning came, and he sent for some Friends, they vanished.'[15]

However long Harris may have remained at large, he was certainly back where he belonged when he wrote from prison on 29 June 1681 to Secretary Jenkins, enclosing papers 'of a pernicious consequence' that had been sent to him to be printed; and he was still there in September, when he wrote to the King asking for remission of his fine and for his liberty.[16] Annexed to his letter was a declaration that he was heartily sorry for having published any work against the government, and that, if he were set free, he would disclose how he obtained the first copy of the book for which he was now suffering. Harris must have been growing desperate, for so far he had not tried to obtain his release by informing on others.

In spite of his enforced absence from his printing house he was able to keep his press at work. Unless, as is possible, someone else made use of his imprint, he published in 1681 *A Scheme of Popish Cruelties; or, what we must expect under a Popish Successor*. On 22 March 1683, after the unlicensed newspapers had been finally suppressed in the previous November, he brought out a new periodical with the provocative title of *Domestick Intelligence*. It was, however, an advertisement paper 'published gratis every Thursday for the Promoting of Trade'. For a man who had staked his future so heavily on a Protestant succession, the peaceful accession of James II in February 1685 was a disaster, and the rapid failure of Monmouth's rebellion some months later must have shown Harris that he could have little future in England. When he next turned up, it was in Boston, Massachusetts. Between 1689 and 1692 his imprint appears in a number of official publications for the State of Massachusetts. In 1695, if not earlier, he was back in England, in time to take advantage of the final lapse of the Licensing Act. Inevitably he started a newspaper, but it had a short life.[17] He was more successful with his *London Post*, started in 1699, but he had now to compete with a number of other newspapers run by men better educated than himself. In 1711 he was printing a new paper, *The Protestant Postboy*, published by Sarah Popping. A warrant for his arrest was issued on 3 October of that year for printing this 'Scandalous and Seditious Libell', and when he obtained bail on 6 October it was as printer (*typographus*): he had probably no control over the contents of the paper.[18] Some years earlier he had been turning a dishonest penny by pirating the almanacs of John Partridge, the astrologer. In Partridge's *Merlinus Redivivus* of 1713 there is a sarcastic reference to 'honest Ben', and with that the record on Harris appears to close.[19]

The career of Nathaniel Thompson was no less troubled than that of Harris, but it followed a different pattern. Unlike Harris, he never underwent a long term of imprisonment, but he was constantly harassed by presentments by grand juries, arrests, indictments and short periods in custody. He appears to have started his career as a printer in Dublin, but later settled in London. It must have been about this time that Langley Curtiss 'had the kindness to put Cloaths on [Thompson's] Back, and to pay for them when he was not in a Condition of doing it himself, nor had yet the Honesty to repay it since', and that this 'Popish Trinculo' found himself 'in Newgate for printing Cart Loads of Popish Books'.[20] Between 1676 and 1677 he was printing libels against the government; but by the time he started his *Domestick Intelligence* in 1679 he had become, and was to remain, a loyal supporter of the Court party. In 1685 he looked back ruefully on what his loyalty had cost him:

And, without ostentation I may say, I printed my News-Papers and divers other Pamphlets (that always vindicated the King and Government) to undeceive the People, who were daily impos'd upon by Curtis, Smith, Harris, Care, Vile, Baldwin, Janeway, etc., when no body else would or durst. For this the Malice of the Factious Party swell'd so high against me, that they, with the assistance of a certain Instrument (who swore through two Brick-walls before Oates appear'd) caused me to be imprison'd six times, so that above six years I was never free from Trouble, having seldom less than 3 or 4 Indictments at a Sessions against Me; at other times Informations in the Crown-Office, which villainous contrivances of their Agents cost me at least £500 in Money, besides the loss of My Trade and Reputation.[21]

In his *Domestick Intelligence* of 6 February 1680 Thompson published what may appear to be a harmless paragraph about the London apprentices:

Several Apprentices in and about the City of London (not well understanding what they did) having been perswaded to subscribe a Petition to his Majesty for the sitting of the Parliament, afterwards understanding how his Majesty resented that way of proceeding, have, upon better consideration, to shew their dislike of what they have done, resolved in solemn manner to sacrafice the

Rump, that the present Age may keep in memory the practice of '41, and not walk by their president [*sic*].

If we read this in its historical context when the Whig petitions calling for a new parliament were reaching Whitehall, we can see that the stated decision of the prentices 'upon better consideration' to 'burn the Rump' instead was (as it was intended to be) provocative. The political ritual of burning the Rump, symbolical of the remnants of the old Long Parliament dissolved by Monck in February 1660, was a Tory way of showing loyalty to the King, now being bombarded with petitions for a parliament. Even so, Sir William Waller, a Middlesex justice and a son of the parliamentary general of that name, was stretching a point when he had Thompson arrested and taken off to the Gatehouse Prison on a charge of treason 'for having been privy to a Treasonable Conspiracy of the Apprentices in levying war against His Majesty and encouraging them in it'.[22] Waller, notorious for his harrying of the Catholics, probably thought it would be better to have Thompson behind bars. Thompson himself attributed his arrest to the fact that for some weeks he had been exposing Waller's incompetence as a magistrate. Waller, for example, had been hoping to arrest a man called Bedingfield, and finding a cobbler of that name at Newark he had him committed to the Gatehouse; but the Bedingfield he wanted had already died in the Gatehouse, and the body had been identified by Waller's friend Titus Oates.[23]

For the present, at least, Waller was 'drest in a little brief authority', and he had used it. But he continued to provide Thompson with excellent copy. Readers of the *Domestick Intelligence* were told that Thompson had offered bail of £1,000, and that it had been rejected; but he was able to reassure them by stating that Waller had not refused him the use of pen, ink and paper, and that he intended to continue with his 'same faithful account'.[24] On 29 March he wrote to Sir Leoline Jenkins asking him to expedite his petition to the King and Council for a speedy trial.[25] On 3 April Smith's *Currant Intelligence* reported that he was still in the Gatehouse; but relief was on the way from an unexpected quarter. On 8 April it was announced in the *Gazette* that the King had turned Waller out of the Commission of the Peace; and on the following day Thompson had the pleasure of giving his readers some details about this over-busy and eccentric magistrate, who had at last pushed his search for incriminating information too far:

He did frequently in the night time take out of the Gate-house one Maurice Hickey (who is committed by the King and Council for High-treason) to the Tavern, and there spent 20s. at a Reckoning, and kept him till 4 or 5 of the clock in the morning, under pretence of an order of Council . . . But God be thanked, that was the last, and an honest man may now walk or sleep quietly in his bed in Middlesex, without being taken up for Treason, and committed without examination, till he can get time and evidence to make it out.

The dismissal of Waller probably led to the charges against Thompson being dropped; but two weeks later he allowed himself to become involved in the parochial politics of St Bride's, in the ward of Farringdon Without. His information had been supplied by a Mr William Badcock, who was apparently of the opinion that the vestrymen of St Bride's were a self-perpetuating rump who ran the affairs of the parish very badly. Even by seventeenth-century standards the long story Thompson published in his *Domestick Intelligence* of 23 April could not have been of very much interest to most of his readers, and the simplest explanation of why he published it at all would be that he got Badcock to pay for its insertion. But it was of the deepest interest to the injured vestrymen, who brought a libel action against both men and obtained damages of five marks (about £3) against each of them.[26]

In February 1681 Thompson was indicted for printing *The Presbyterian Pater Noster*; in August the London Grand Jury presented his *Loyal Protestant* as a scandalous paper 'tending to the Advancement and Introduction of Popery, and to the Suppression and Extirpation of the true Protestant Religion': and in October he entered into a recognisance 'to answer the printing of several late published pamphlets of which he is accused'.[27] Thompson's various pamphlets are difficult to identify since he often attributed them to other publishers. On 2 September 1681 the *Impartial Protestant Mercury* claimed that a half sheet purporting to give the last speech of Stephen College and published by A. Banks was 'wholly a Cheat and Forgery, and was in truth Printed by that Notorious Thompson'. But his most impudent exercise in this kind of deception (scarcely deception since it was so patently a joke) was to publish in 1682 *A Letter to Mr. Miles Prance* as being 'Printed for M.G. at the Sign of Sir E.B.G.'s Head near Fleet-Bridge'. The imprint of Langley Curtiss had been for some time 'At the Sign of Sir Edmundbury Godfrey's Head, near Fleet-Bridge', but earlier he had published from Goat Court. The 'M.G' in Thompson's spurious imprint stands for 'Mayor of Goatham', the nickname given to Curtiss by the jocular Thompson and habitually applied to him in his *Loyal Protestant*. Referring to the Prance letter on 4 March, Curtiss let the world know he had nothing to do with it:

But we must further take notice of the strange Villany of this Nat. Thomson, in fathering the Printing of it upon Langly Curtiss, at Sir Edmundbury Godfrys

Head, near Fleet-bridge, none in London giving that Sign but him; and this he hath frequently done, when he hath put forth any notorious Libel, as this is.[28]

What was 'strange villainy' to Curtiss was no doubt an excellent joke to Thompson and his friends.

So far, his troubles had been more or less routine for anyone who dabbled as much in politics as he did; but with the publication of *A Letter to Mr. Miles Prance* by John Farwell (or Farewell), and of *A Second Letter* by William Paine, he had chanced his hand once too often, and became the latest victim of the hysteria surrounding the Popish Plot. The letters rebutted in detail the evidence given against Green, Berry and Hill, the three men who had been hanged in 1679 for the murder of Sir Edmund Berry Godfrey, mainly on the perjured evidence of Miles Prance, who was himself a prime suspect, and who in 1686 was to confess that all the evidence he had given was fabricated. In addition to publishing the two Letters, Thompson reinforced their argument in the *Loyal Protestant* of 7 and 11 March, with such comments as 'the Fraud and Blind put upon the World' at the 1679 trial, and the pious hope that 'though a Lie may prevail for a time and eclipse the Truth, yet at length Truth will shine forth, with the assistance of that God who is the Author of Truth it self'. Stylistic evidence would suggest that those were further contributions from Farwell or Paine. What Thompson wanted his readers to believe was that Godfrey had committed suicide. With the King steadily reasserting his authority over his subjects, Shaftesbury losing ground, Oates banished from the Court and his pension withdrawn, Dugdale and other perjured informers discredited, Thompson may have felt that the time had come for a complete exposure of the myth of the Popish Plot. If so, he had misjudged the power that the Plot still exercised over men's minds.[29]

On 20 June 1682 he stood with Farwell and Paine in the dock of the King's Bench court, listening to Serjeant Maynard describing him as one who constantly printed libels 'against the Religion established, and the Justice of the Nation'. Two Whig sheriffs were still in office, and they presumably picked a hostile Whig jury; but it is unlikely that on this occasion it made much difference. When asked for their verdict the jury did not trouble to retire, but found all three defendants guilty as charged. In his summing-up Lord Chief Justice Pemberton made it clear that their real crime was to have cast doubt upon the authenticity of the Popish Plot. Had they succeeded in making out that Godfrey had committed suicide, 'all of them would have cryed out the Popish Plot was a sham, nothing but a thing raised by the Protestants against the Papists, and all the Plot must have gone for nothing'. And that to Pemberton, and no doubt to the majority in the court, was quite unthinkable.[30] On 3 July Thompson and Farwell were each fined £100 and sentenced to stand in the pillory for an hour 'with this Writing over their Heads: *For Libelling the Justice of the Nation, by making the World believe that Sir Edmondbury Godfrey murdered himself*'. Paine was let off with the fine of £100, 'since the court did not conceive him altogether so guilty', perhaps because, unlike Farwell, he had not taken up the court's time with a pertinacious defence, or perhaps, because he seemed too much of a gentleman in his appearance for the pillory.[31] On 5 July Thompson stood in the pillory for what must have been one of the longest hours of his life. According to one account he was 'severely pelted with dirt, stones, etc.'; and according to another, 'the small shot began to fly with rotten eggs and dirt, and when they hit Thompson they cried, "Thompson, Farewell!", and when they hit Farwell, they cried, "Farewell, Thompson!" . . . Thompson had ten times more dirt thrown at him than Farwell.'[32]

On 16 July 1682 Thompson paid his fine and was set free. But on 30 October Narcissus Luttrell noted that he was 'again committed to prison'. When he revived his *Loyal Protestant* in February 1683, it had not run for long before he was in trouble again: on 14 March he was summoned to appear before the Privy Council for publishing false news from Scotland, and sent to his old home from home in the Gatehouse Prison.[33]

Having reached, it must be hoped, less troubled waters in the reign of James II, he published in 1684 *A Choice Collection of 120 Loyal Songs*, and in 1685, *A Collection of 86 Loyal Poems*. He died in November 1687.[34] His life had been a prolonged struggle in a hostile religious and political environment. As a member of a persecuted minority he had been subjected to brutal abuse by his numerous opponents, and he had received little consideration from those whose cause he was trying to support. He always gave as good as he got, and sank at times to depths of merciless defamation; but in an age of scurrilous and often dull controversy he showed wit and liveliness, and the flair of a natural journalist. He may have died before his time, but at least he was spared the experience of living through the abdication of a Catholic King decisively rejected by his subjects.

When in 1661 L'Estrange begun his career of tracking down seditious printers and publishers, one of his first victims was the anabaptist bookseller Francis Smith, who had printed a volume of prodigies called *Mirabilis Annus*. Discovery led to Smith's spending the better part of the next two years in prison. His life is well documented, for he left several narratives of his sufferings, including *An Account of the Injurious Proceedings of Sir George Jeffries* and *An Impartial Account of the Tryal of Francis Smith*. Apart, however, from his politically important but short-lived paper, *Smith's Protestant Intelligence* (1 February – 14 April 1681), he was not primarily a newspaper man. The only other periodical publication with which he was connected was *Votes of the House of Commons*, of which, for services rendered, he was appointed printer in October 1680 by a Whig-dominated House of Commons. On the day that his newspaper was suppressed he appeared before the King and Council, and was committed a close prisoner to Newgate 'for some words he had spoken, as if he would never leave writing news till he had reduc'd this kingdome to a commonwealth'. It seems too much to suppose that he spoke those words before the King in a sudden burst of anger; and since he was admitted to bail in June, and discharged for want of prosecution in July, it looks as if there was insufficient evidence to convict.[35] Earlier in that year he had been indicted for publishing *A Speech of a Noble Peer* [Shaftesbury], but the jury brought in a verdict of *ignoramus*. In November, however, he was found guilty of reprinting and publishing the same pamphlet, but was not present in court[36]. About this time he fled to Holland. When he returned to England he avoided arrest for some time, but in March 1684 was apprehended by the City Marshal and returned to prison. There he remained, until in February 1685 James II was pleased to remit his fines and grant him a pardon.

It was common practice in the seventeenth and eighteenth centuries for printers and publishers to receive active assistance from their wives. This was certainly true of Francis Smith and Langley Curtiss. In the King's Bench on 7 February 1680, two days after Harris had been sentenced in the same court, Smith was charged with publishing *Some Observations upon the late Tryal*, commonly known as *Tom Ticklefoot*, a pamphlet criticising the conduct of Lord Chief Justice Scroggs at the trial of Sir George Wakeman. Since Scroggs was the injured party he did not preside at the trial himself, and his place was taken by Judge Thomas Jones, thought to be subservient to the crown and not remarkable for his lenity. The Recorder, Jeffreys, aggravated in his characteristic way the seriousness of the charge, and particularly frowned upon those 'idle Busy-bodies . . . who cannot, or will not be pleas'd because (forsooth) every thing does not go according to their mind and fancy'. Smith, who was ill and absent from court, heard none of this, but his wife was present in his place. His experienced counsel, William Williams, knew that the case was hopeless, and that the best course was to try to mitigate the sentence. 'My Lord,' he explained, 'the poor man, my Client, is a languishing, sick and dying man, and one that is almost ruin'd; if any Submission will serve the Turn, he will give all the Submission that is fit for a man to give . . .' Here Mr Fettiplace, who was also retained as counsel for Smith, broke in and told the court that no such order had been given him by his client; but at this point Mrs Smith took charge, and addressed the judge:

My Lord, my Husband is very sick and weak, and is not able to come himself, or else he would have done it; but I ask'd Mr. Williams if it were not best to submit to the Court.

Inevitably the jury found Smith guilty; but Judge Jones, impressed perhaps by the wife's humble good sense and her very proper acknowledgment of the authority of the court, promised that he would intercede on her behalf with 'my Lord [Scroggs], who is a person of that pity and compassion that he loves no man's Ruin'.[37]

On the same day in the same court, and again with Judge Jones on the bench, Jane Curtiss appeared, by direction of Scroggs, to answer the charge of publishing *A Satire against In-Justice: or, Scroggs upon Scroggs*, and pleaded not guilty. She may have been present at the morning session and learnt from that, for she behaved perfectly, and explained that she had acted without really knowing what she was doing:

I was ignorant in the matter, and knew no such thing; my Lord, my Husband, an't please your Lordship, was in the Countrey a hundred miles off of me, in Lincolnshire.

She promised that he would come and make his submission, and ended effectively with her own:

In any thing that I have done, I know not my self guilty; and if I am, I beg your Lordship's pardon with all my Heart, my Lord, or any bodies else.[38]

In view of later developments when she was running the *True Protestant Mercury* competently in her husband's absence, this projection of herself as a poor ignorant woman completely out of her depth must have been something of an act. She may indeed have been an attractive woman, and have aroused a dormant sense of gallantry in the judge. In the only description we have of Curtiss, Thompson calls him 'a middle-siz'd Fellow, . . . the Bridge of his Nose somewhat lower than ordinary', and adds, 'with a lusty pair of Brow-antlers' (the traditional

way of calling a man a cuckold).[39] More probably, the lenient treatment of these two women by the court may have been due to the fact
that their cases came on so soon after the severe sentence on Harris,
and word had reached the judge from above that further exemplary
sentences might cause a reaction against the government. That this
may be the true explanation is suggested by an uncharacteristic intervention by Jeffreys: when the judge promised Mrs Smith that he
would be an intercessor to Scroggs on her husband's behalf, Jeffreys
added: 'And as far forth as I can contribute to it, I will do the same.'[40]

Curtiss had a way of disappearing for extended periods. On 16 April
1681 the *Loyal Protestant* reported that he had been summoned to
come before the King and Council on 12 April, but that, although
called for 'divers times', he failed to appear. On this occasion
something serious must have happened, for there was a complete break
in the publication of the *True Protestant Mercury* between 16 April
(No. 32) and 30 April (No. 33). So long a gap in the normal publication
of a Restoration newspaper is unprecedented. It may be possible to
suggest a reason. In his newspaper of 19 March, after referring to the
arrival of Scroggs at Oxford for the sitting of Parliament, Curtiss went
on to add:

This day likewise (but whether in Company with his last mentioned Lordship
or not, we do not hear) went down Mr. Sheridan who intends to shew himself
at Oxford in a *Bravado*, but his Journey lies farther, viz. for Ireland, wisely
judging . . . the Air of that Kingdom to be more agreeable to his Constitution
in *Parliament Time* than that of England.

On 9 April Thomas Sheridan had an advertisement inserted in the
Loyal Protestant, quoting this paragraph, and adding that he would
speedily be returning to London, when the author and publisher of this
libel would be questioned, perhaps by Lord Chief Justice Scroggs,
'whom they have so basely traduced'. The prospect of having to face
legal proceedings from both Scroggs and Sheridan may have convinced
Curtiss that he would be well advised to lie low for a time.

He was in trouble again in 1681 for publishing *The New Popish Sham
Plot*, designed to implicate Lord Danby in the murder of Sir Edmund
Berry Godfrey. Danby asked that Curtiss should be kept in custody
until he had given bail of £1,000, but the court reduced the bail to
£500. On 6 June he appeared before the Council, but the Council
'having matters of greater Importance before them', 'appointed him to
attend the Council *de die in diem*'.[41] It looks as if the Council had in mind
his tendency to disappear. It was characteristic of Nathaniel Thompson
to take a keen interest in the misfortunes of his journalistic rivals, and to

keep the readers of his *Loyal Protestant* informed about them. On 22 June 1682 he reported that Curtiss had 'lately stept aside, but for what particular reason is yet unknown'. He followed this on 6 July with news that Curtiss had fled, and that a reward of £10 had been offered for anyone who would disclose where he was.[42] On 19 August Thompson again stated that Curtiss had absconded, and that his wife, 'that Doxy the Mayoress of Goatham', was carrying on his paper. Meanwhile, in the *Observator* of 5 July, L'Estrange had remarked that the *True Protestant Mercury* was no longer the work of Curtiss, 'nor Mrs. Curtiss neither, for that Paper is only Harry and the Sybill in a kind of Intellectual Copulation'. The sibyl is Jane Curtiss, and Harry is Henry Care, who had been writing for the *Impartial Protestant Mercury* until it ceased publication on 30 May, and was now helping Mrs Curtiss, in the absence of her husband, to produce the *True Protestant Mercury*.

On 5 July Mrs Curtiss had published a long account of the trial of Aaron Smith, the Whig lawyer who had given help to Stephen College in his trial at Oxford. The next day Thompson reported that she had been summoned to appear for publishing words that reflected on the court in its management of the trial (the report in the *True Protestant Mercury* contained abusive comment on both the Lord Chief Justice and Jeffreys), and that 'her Plea was, she did it for Profit, as others, but could not tell who it was that sent her the Copy'. On 8 July she herself (or Henry Care) reported that she had appeared before the Lord Chief Justice, 'not for maligning the conduct of the trial, but for selling it'. (Judges had, or assumed, copyright in the published report of any trial over which they had presided.) On the same occasion she also asserted that her husband had not fled from justice. But in any case he was certainly not to be found, and Mrs Curtiss was not the woman to disclose his whereabouts. He is said to have spent part of this time printing, in some country retreat, the first part of Samuel Johnson's *Julian the Apostate*,[43] a work that was to bring the author a term of imprisonment. Yet all this time Mrs Curtiss kept the Whig flag flying; and the *True Protestant Mercury*, as outspoken as ever, continued to appear until it finally closed down on 25 October.[44] By that time she was in deep trouble. On 28 October Thompson had the satisfaction of reporting that she had been arrested on a warrant for publishing and dispersing several notorious and scandalous libels against authority, and had been imprisoned in the King's Bench. The days of a Whig jury were over.

Langley Curtiss continued to walk on the edge of danger. In October 1683, some months after the execution of Lord Russell for his real or supposed complicity in the Rye House Plot to assassinate the King and the Duke of York, he published an inflammatory broadside on Lord Russell's ghost, *The Night Walker of Bloomsbury*. He was found guilty, and sentenced on 21 April 1684 to stand in the pillory in Bloomsbury Market, to pay a fine of £500, and to remain in prison till the fine was paid and security given for his future good behaviour.[45]

The closing down of the *Impartial Protestant Mercury* on 30 May 1682 had been a turning point in the campaign of the government against the newspapers. Janeway, brought before the King and Council in the previous October for publishing false news, was ordered to be prosecuted, and was allowed bail. When at last he came to trial on 16 May 1682, a staunch Whig jury found him not guilty.[46] It is possible to supplement the bare verdict from the *Loyal Protestant's* report on 18 May: when the Lord Chief Justice, astonished at this verdict, told the members of the jury that unless they believed the evidence given to be perjured they must find Janeway guilty, 'some of the Jury (after a little pause) answer'd, They had done according to THEIR Consciences'. But the lawyers had been learning a good deal from previous experience, and on this occasion they found an answer to the verdict of a packed jury: Janeway had given bail for his good behaviour to the Court of Exchequer, and now on 1 June it estreated his recognisances. In one of his news-letters Muddiman gave an account of what then followed:

Janeway finding himself and his bail clapped up in gaol upon his misde-meanour without the hope of being released by a London jury, and knowing by the experience of Ben Harris how slow the Party are in redeeming the Brotherhood from tribulation, made his application to the Attorney General, and so far prevailed as to gain his and their liberty upon engagement to trade no more in the publishing seditious or treasonable pamphlets. And upon that account it is that you want the *Impartial Protestant Intelligence*.[47]

Janeway's two authors, Vile and Care, reacted differently to the collapse of their newspaper. Vile, who was the more moderate of the two, had started a new paper on 6 April 1682, the *London Mercury*, and managed to keep it running until 17 October, when the messengers of the press were finally closing down all the newspapers. In an editorial note, repeated more than once, he promised 'until stopt by Authority' to give a true and impartial account of 'such matters as are reasonably fit for such Papers to intermeddle withal, alwaies avoiding Reflexions either on Church or State, Publick Transactions, or Particular Persons . . .'[48] It might seem to be a recipe for failure, but Vile's paper was well written and must have received some support. Thompson, who had a particular dislike of Vile, mentions his brief imprisonment towards the end of July on 'a Writ of *Outlawry* at the Suit of the King', but does not tell us what offence had been given.[49] On the evidence of the news appearing in his paper, Vile was keeping his promise to be discreet. On 12 September he advertised that a 'Printing House, with two Presses, good sorts of Letter, and all necessaries, will be Let, or the Materials Sold. Farther Information may be had of T. Vile . . .' If the two presses were his own, we may take it that he was preparing for the worst; but as things were going in the autumn of 1682, it must have been a buyer's market for printing presses and type.

Vile's publisher was Richard Baldwin. Discretion was not a quality associated with Baldwin at this early stage of his career, but he, too, may have begun to trim his sails. He had started two newspapers of his own: *Mercurius Anglicus*, which lasted for three numbers from 10 to 17 October 1681; and the *Protestant Courant*, which ran for six numbers from 24 April to 13 May 1682. In his last number of *Mercurius Anglicus* he rather jauntily told his readers that he had been arrested for printing and publishing a pamphlet called *No Protestant Plot*, and had answered that the copy was sent in a letter by an unknown hand, and if there was anything dangerous in it, 'it was more than he knew, having never read the said book; and that his design in Publishing of it was no other than to get Money in the way of his Trade'. This response led to his being kept in custody until 25 October, when he was released on bail, but bound over to be prosecuted next term.[50] His *Protestant Courant* was no more successful. On 6 May 1682 he accounted for its non-appearance on the previous Thursday by explaining that

some of the *Tory Popish Crew*, finding that it had got the general good approbation of all unbyassed *English Protestants*, and despairing of totally suppressing it, were resolved to try an *Experiment* on the *Printer*, which they did, and detain'd him so long in *Merry Company*, that he wanted time to finish the Paper by the day appointed.

The drunken printer was replaced by one who could hold his liquor. But worse was to follow. On 16 May the *Loyal Protestant* reported that Baldwin, having inserted several scandalous reflections on Sir William Dodson and others in his issue of 13 May, had been ordered to appear at the King's Bench Bar. Asked to name the writer of the scandalous paragraph, he refused to do so and was committed to prison. Thompson believed that he had destroyed the manuscript copy to conceal the name of the writer, which he said he had forgotten.[51] The young Baldwin evidently had his fair share of impudence, but was learning his lesson the hard way.

Of the Whig newspaper men, the last to go was Henry Care. When Janeway gave way to irresistible pressure in May 1682, Care, as we saw, transferred his pen to the *True Protestant Mercury*, and brought aid and comfort to the desperate Jane Curtiss. He had been writing his anti-Catholic *Weekly Pacquet, Or Advice from Rome* since December 1678, and had been found guilty on 2 July 1680 for a satirical passage reflecting on Scroggs the previous year; and while writing for the *Impartial Protestant Mercury* (in which he enjoyed referring to the Pope as 'His Un-Holiness') he had been prosecuted for a passage in the issue of 28 April 1681.[52] On the whole, in view of the frequent provocation he was prepared to give, he had escaped lightly. In October 1682, when he was indicted for writing against the Lieutenancy in his *Weekly Pacquet*, he was reported as 'not to be found',[53] although he succeeded in carrying on the paper until 13 July 1683. By this time, however, he had decided to make overtures to the government, and to ensure his own future safety by promising disclosures; in short, by turning informer.[54] When Captain Walcot was tried on 12 July 1683 for his complicity in the Rye House Plot, a letter he had written to Sir Leoline Jenkins was read out in court, in which he offered to make discoveries to the King about his fellow conspirators. 'I shall be ten times abler to serve him,' he assured Jenkins, 'than either Mr. Freeman, or Mr. Care; for they [the plotters] will trust neither of them'.[55] Care, having turned his coat, did nothing by halves, but dipped his pen in fresh ink and wrote with the same facility for the other side. Like Walpole's clerical journalists two generations later, he showed himself to be one of those who are

> Prompt or to guard or stab, to saint or damn,
> Heav'n's Swiss, who fight for any God, or Man.

His reappearance in the reign of James II, when he became the author of the semi-official weekly, *Publick Occurrences Truely Stated*, has already been noted. His business was now the exact opposite of what it had been in the reign of Charles II: it was to defend a government 'daily Exposed by false Reports: every thing liable to Misconstruction Trumpetted through the Kingdom, and dressed up in all the ill Colours that Malice or Mis-imploy'd Witt can invent'.[56] At least one seventeenth-century reader was dissatisfied with the results: on a copy of this newspaper in the Bodleian file he scrawled his acid comment: 'This is called ye jesuites Pisse pot thrown by Henry Care in ye Church of England men's faces'.

The day-to-day life of authors, printers and publishers was made more precarious by the government's use of informers. On 6 November 1679 a proclamation appeared in the *London Gazette* for the suppression of seditious or treasonable books and pamphlets. A reward of £40 was offered, with a promise of the King's gracious pardon, to any hawker who would give information leading to the discovery and conviction of the bookseller or printer from whom he had received a seditious book or pamphlet, and likewise to any bookseller or printer who would make known the name of the author. There is little evidence from the Restoration period to suggest that booksellers and printers were willing to betray their authors, although under persistent and menacing examination some would give way to pressure. In the eighteenth century, however, the informer (usually a printer who had obtained pardon for his own indiscretions on a promise to talk) became all too common a figure, especially in the early years of the new Hanoverian monarchy. On 1 March 1716 a newspaper called *Weekly Remarks and Political Reflections* appeared with a new printer, and readers were told that they 'need not wonder that the Printer is chang'd, when they consider that the Author is sent to Newgate on the first Printer's Information'. The author was George Flint, who continued to write the *Weekly Remarks* in Newgate until he was deprived of pen, ink and paper. Printers who informed were unlikely to obtain other employment for a considerable time, and had to be looked after by the government that had intimidated them. A memorandum dated 10 August 1719 from James Craggs, one of the two Secretaries of State, shows how it was done:

Having occasion to employ John Smith a Printer in detecting Printers and Publishers of Seditious Libels, and his family being thereby deprived of the benefit of his labour which was their only support, I desire that till he can return to his business you allow his wife half a crown a day for the maintenance of herself and their Children.[57]

We can follow the slimy trails of the informers in the State Papers. Among their victims in 1719 were the young printer John Matthews and, some months later, Elizabeth Powell. When Matthews was found guilty on 31 October 1719 of printing the treasonable pamphlet, *Vox Populi*, and hanged for it some days later, the chief witnesses against him were two of the workmen in his mother's printing house: a young apprentice, William Harper, and an ageing journeyman, Lawrence Vezey. Both had been arrested and kept in prison by the Crown, but a letter from Harper to the under-secretary Delafaye, in which he mentions 'your Inestimable promise to me', indicates that a deal had been struck. Three weeks later, nothing having been done for him, he wrote to Secretary Craggs, asking for a sufficient compensation for the loss of his friends and employment, to save him from entire ruin.[58] Eventually he appears to have got it, for on 12 October 1720 he writes about laying out the money he has received on a printing house. Vezey, on the other hand, had no future to provide for. In January 1720 the Society of Journeyman Printers had deprived him of his membership, and by June he was dead. His funeral on 22 June showed what the printing trade thought of him. When his coffin was carried to the graveyard at Islington, a mob, mostly composed of printers including a younger brother of John Matthews, rushed to the open grave and filled it, as one contemporary report puts it, with 'nastiness'.[59]

Mrs Powell was no stranger to trouble. In March 1716 she had been committed to Newgate for publishing *The Orphan*, a paper that probably did not survive the first number. (Some time before this her printer husband, Edmund Powell, had absconded, and a price of £100 was set on his head.) A week later she was released 'in Commiseration to the extream Poverty of her and her numerous Family', but before she was set free she had promised not to offend again.[60] They did not know Elizabeth Powell. On 7 April she published *The Charitable Mercury*, and again there is no record of more than the first number. In view of her brief introductory notice this is not surprising; it would have been wiser to begin less provocatively. She had obtained the assistance of several gentlemen (her readers were told) to enable her to carry on a weekly paper for her own benefit; there would be nothing in it offensive to the state, for 'a burnt child dreads the fire', and 'to speak ill of grandees' is to run oneself into danger. On the other hand, 'whosoever will speak well of them, must tell many a Lye.' The government must have thought that such uncompromising words were hardly what one would expect from a reformed character, and that they inspired no confidence in the gentlemen who had offered her their assistance. Mrs Powell still had her friends, however, and in November 1718 she was able to start *The Orphan Reviv'd; Or, Powell's Weekly Journal*. It was said to be 'written by Pitty's [William Pittis], a poor drunken Wretch'. It suffered a check on 22 January 1719 when she was examined about her 'scandalous weekly paper', but it survived for 76 numbers.[61]

All this was as nothing compared to her next act of defiance. On 6 February 1720 Read's *Weekly Journal* announced that 'yesterday morning' Mrs Powell had been apprehended for high treason, and Applebee's of the same date reported that 'the Widow Powell, who had absconded some Months, for reprinting the Pamphlet call'd *Vox Populi, Vox Dei*, was apprehended by the King's Messengers at a House in Aldersgate-

Street, and carry'd to Westminster, where she is close confin'd'. According to Edward Holloway, a journeyman printer who had worked for Mrs Powell but now turned King's evidence, she had asked him to reprint *Vox Populi* 'about the time of Matthews being hanged' because 'it would go off very well at that time'[62]; and helped by John Hoyle, also a journeyman, he had done the job for her.[63] Some time after this Mrs Powell decided to disappear. The information that finally led to her arrest almost certainly came from Holloway: on 1 February he wrote to under-secretary Delafaye telling him that the way to find Mrs Powell was to 'give orders for the taking her Daughter into Custody'; for 'the Mother having so great Respect [regard] for her, I believe she will certainly surrender, because her Daughter shall not be kept Confined.'[64] Having caught Mrs Powell the government did not seem able to decide what to do next. In a lengthy memorandum on her case, dated 21 July 1720, the legal officers were still mulling over it, and presumably considering how (and perhaps whether) they should try to secure a conviction. They noted the testimony of Holloway that Elizabeth Powell had engaged him to print *Vox Populi*; but against that they very fairly set the evidence of Hoyle, who stated that he had been employed by Holloway to print the pamphlet, and not by Mrs Powell. If one's sympathies are with Mrs Powell, a widow woman with many poor children to feed, the reasons given by Hoyle for making this statement will probably carry conviction. In his deposition he had sworn as follows:

That about Eleven at night Mrs. Powell in whose House they wrought came up into the work room that night that they were printing the said paper, and finding them at work asked what they were doing; to which Holloway answered they were upon a Job for himself. She reply'd then she must be paid for the use of her Tools and they must find Fire and Candles, and they desired her to send up a Peck of Coals and a Pound of Candles which she did accordingly and went to Bed; and this Examinant did not see her again till the next day at noon, after they had done printing the said Paper.[65]

Mrs Powell, of course, may have been a wily lady and have arranged with Holloway that she would come up to the work room and feign ignorance of what was going on there, but Holloway was hardly the man to fall for that trick. Equally, Hoyle may have known all the time that he was doing the job for Mrs Powell, and not for Holloway, and then, when the law caught up with all three, have resolutely refused to betray her. To solve this problem we should need to know more about Mrs Powell than we do. Holloway, at any rate, had made his peace with the government, and was safe from prosecution. On 19 November 1719 a warrant had been issued for Hoyle's arrest on a charge of high treason, for printing *Vox Populi*, and one for James Alexander on 17 December, for writing and publishing it.[66]

2

So far little has been said, except incidentally, about the way in which the newspapers were organised; how they were compiled, printed and distributed, and who was responsible for each stage of the process before the finished product reached the reader. Did Benjamin Harris, for example, write for his *Domestick Intelligence*, or merely supervise each number; did he also print and publish it, and if so, was he the proprietor of the paper as well? The same questions may be asked about the relationship of Nathaniel Thompson to his two newspapers, and that of Langley Curtiss to the *True Protestant Mercury*. What had Henry Care, Thomas Vile and Richard Janeway to do with the *Impartial Protestant Mercury*, and who owned that newspaper? Did John de Fonvive own the *Post Man*, and George Ridpath the *Flying Post*? Any attempt to arrive at the right answers must allow for the numerous permutations and combinations in contemporary practice, and to the absence on some occasions of any reliable evidence.

In seeking to resolve those and other questions it will sometimes be necessary to look forward to the newpapers of the early eighteenth century, where clear evidence of what was happening is rather more plentiful. But first we may return again to the year 1679, when a number of booksellers, with no previous experience in periodical journalism, began to offer the public printed newspapers. Men like Benjamin Harris and Nathaniel Thompson had to feel their way along from one day to the next, learning from their mistakes and profiting from their accumulating experience. They could, it is true, benefit from the example of the men who were writing news-letters, of whom Muddiman was only the most distinguished. Thompson, as we have seen, employed one such man, Benjamin Claypoole, who is mentioned in 1683 as one who sent a few news-letters into the country,[67] and in the *London Gazette* of 11 December 1679 as 'one Claypoole, who writes the *Domestique Intelligence*'. That this was not Harris's paper but Thompson's, is made clear by a note in Narcissus Luttrell's copy of a contemporary catalogue of books and pamphlets. Opposite Harris's *Domestick Intelligence* he wrote: 'Writt by one Nath. Crouch; it gave great offence in many things to those in authority'; and opposite Thompson's paper of the same name, 'Writt by one Claypool, and tending as much to villifye the dissenters'.[68]

The situation is made more uncertain by the absence of the word 'editor' in any contemporary reference to the newspapers of the seventeenth and early eighteenth centuries: when a newspaper offended those in authority, no one described as an editor was ever mentioned in a warrant or indictment, and strictly speaking, no such person then existed. An 'editor' was someone who prepared a new edition of an author's work (with special emphasis on producing an authoritative text), as Pope was to do for Shakespeare in 1725 when he discharged what he called 'the dull duty of an editor'. Even in this sense the word had only recently become current.

Of Nathaniel Crouch at this period almost nothing is known, except that he was prosecuted for a piece of false news in Harris's *Domestick Intelligence* of 12 March 1680. He seems, however, to have kept out of serious trouble. In the early eighteenth century he was credited by John Dunton with being the author of the *English Post* (1700–09?), and of collecting his news 'with so much accuracy and judgment that he is only outdone by the *Post Man*'.[69] A less kindly comment was made by another writer in 1709: 'The *English Post* I suppose must be writ by some Melancholy Gentleman that writes a Paper for his own private Use, for indeed I don't see of what Use it can be to any Body else.'[70] By this time Crouch had also become a voluminous author, producing under the name of Robert or Richard Burton numerous popular biographies, histories and other miscellaneous works. It is odd that so quietly industrious a man should have become involved in so intransigent a paper as Harris's *Domestick Intelligence*. According to Muddiman, Harris wrote the paper himself,[71] and there are some virulent passages, including the attack made on Lord Chief Justice Scroggs for which he was committed on 24 January 1680, that could only have come from his own pen. It is true that in a petition for his release from prison in September 1681 he asserted that 'he never was the author of anything he ever published',[72] but in making this statement he may have been thinking only of books and pamphlets. On the whole it seems more likely than not that he had a hand in writing, and also supervised, what appeared in his paper; in which case he would be at once author, printer, publisher and owner of his *Domestick Intelligence*.

Like Harris, Thompson appears to have been much too active a man, and far too deeply involved in contemporary politics, not to have been personally responsible for much of what he printed and published. We are not required to believe that the unreliable Claypoole did more than supply him with some of his news. The motives that induced Thompson to start his own *Domestick Intelligence* were largely political: his paper was to be an antidote to the anti-Catholic extravagance of Harris. At the very least Thompson must have written the accounts of his involvement with Sir William Waller and the attack on himself by young

Charlton, not to mention the other fairly frequent reports of his personal troubles: no one else would have been sufficiently interested to do so.[73] On the more uncertain grounds of stylistic evidence, one may see his hand in many of the satirical passages in his two newspapers, especially in the constant and sometimes scurrilous abuse of Langley Curtiss and his wife, and the frequent attacks on the *Impartial Protestant Mercury*.

John Smith's *Currant Intelligence* was both printed and published by him, and since he changed the title to *Smith's Currant Intelligence* halfway through the first series he presumably owned it. If we are to believe Thompson, he knew nothing about the news he printed, but obtained it from someone in the Post Office.* The same person may have provided him not only with his domestic news, but also with the considerable amount of foreign news appearing in the paper. It is true that in the *Currant Intelligence* of 6 April 1680 Smith is referred to editorially as 'John Smith (Author of this Intelligence)': but 'author' is probably used in this context as 'the person who originates or gives existence to' (OED), i.e. the founder of the paper. The more notorious printer-publisher, Francis Smith, may also be considered to have been the proprietor of the paper that carried his name, *Smith's Protestant Intelligence*, and in all probability was also its author. Writing on 19 April 1681, however, after this paper had been abruptly suppressed by the government, Muddiman observed that 'those that knew him do not believe it was altogether his'.[74] Smith may, therefore, have had a willing helper (perhaps someone in the Shaftesbury circle), although he was quite capable of writing the paper on his own.

The procedure with the *Impartial Protestant Mercury* was quite different. When the nominal publisher, Richard Janeway, was in trouble in May 1682 for publishing an offending paragraph, he stated that Henry Care and Thomas Vile were the authors of the paper. He also entered a petition in which he stated that he was a bookbinder, and was employed by Care and Vile to publish the *Impartial Protestant Mercury* for them. He had nothing more to do with the paper than to receive and distribute copies of it, account to Care and Vile for the proceeds, and 'be paid for his pains'. Notes for the paper were sometimes left at his house, usually unsigned, and he sent those to Care and Vile, who inserted what they believed to be true and inoffensive. The domestic news was supplied by Jasper Hancock, a writer of news-letters. From this it would appear that the true proprietors of the paper were Care

* Cf. p. 116.

and Vile, who probably translated the foreign news, and acted as editors of the paper.[75]

Of Benskin's *Domestick Intelligence* we have no information that would make it possible to pronounce on its authorship. When he had occasion to make an announcement about an earlier venture, the *Impartial London Intelligence*, he referred to himself as 'the Exhibiter of this paper',[76] which would seem to be Benskin's English for 'publisher'. His *Domestick Intelligence*, 'printed for T. Benskin', is referred to in January 1682 by Thompson as 'Brown and Benskin's Intelligence',[77] which suggests that by then Benskin held his paper in joint ownership. On 22 January he advertised *The Life, Bloody Reign and Death of Queen Mary* as being 'Printed for D[aniel] Brown and T. Benskin.' On 13 June 1682 Thompson mentioned a new paper, *The Loyal Impartial Mercury*, which, he asserted, was 'Printed for Benskin's Wife and Published by himself'. On this occasion Thompson must have been guessing, and guessing wrong. The words 'printed for' usually suggest ownership by the person named, and the imprint for the first number of *The Loyal Impartial Mercury* reads: 'Printed for E.B. and Published by T. Benskin'. But E.B. was not Elizabeth (or Esther, or Eleanor) Benskin; for in the second number the imprint is 'Printed for E. Brooks', and so continues to the end of the run. It was never likely that Benskin, if he was a good husband, would choose to involve his wife in the political risks of ownership at a time when the government was taking increasingly severe measures against the proprietors of newspapers. But that still leaves no explanation of why, with the second number, Benskin's name disappeared as publisher. Had there been a misunderstanding between Benskin and Brooks (a bookseller)? If so, it seems possible that when Thompson told the world in his *Loyal Protestant* that E.B. was Mrs Benskin, Brooks decided to come out into the open and also to be his own publisher.

The owner, or owners, of a newspaper are not always easy to trace. When an eighteenth-century gentleman decided to start an essay paper, the imprint, as often as not, would read 'Printed for the Author', and he would meet the printer's bill and the costs of distribution out of his own pocket. If he caught the taste of the town and his paper was taken in by the coffee-houses, he might entertain his readers for several months with his lucubrations, and even make a profit. The large number of essay papers that lasted for only a few issues indicate not so much a drying up of the author's inspiration as of his ready cash.

Even with newspapers, which could hardly be started in such a casual fashion, a considerable number in the early eighteenth century survived for only a few recorded issues. Yet others, started in all probability by the enterprise of one man, weathered the early difficulties and continued to appear for several decades. Since the *Post Man* was 'Printed by F. Leach for the Author' we may assume that De Fonvive not only wrote the paper but also owned it. When the first number of the *Daily Courant* appeared on 11 March 1702 it carried the imprint: 'LONDON. Sold by *E. Mallet* . . .', but on 20 April this was changed to 'Printed and Sold by *Samuel Buckley* . . .'. It seems unlikely that Elizabeth Mallet was ever the proprietor of the paper she sold, and much more likely that it was owned from the start by Buckley, who was both a printer and publisher. We know that by 1708, if not indeed from its foundation, it was jointly owned by a club of booksellers,* one of whom may have been Buckley. He was certainly the author or compiler of the paper. Abel Roper certainly owned the *Post-Boy,* and one of his contemporaries asserted that it was 'a Composition both of Bookseller [Roper] and News-Writer [Abel Boyer]'.[78] In the *Flying Post* of 6 August 1713 a correspondent remarked on the close similarity of news items in the *Post-Boy* and in Berrington's *Evening Post,* and added: 'I am told Mr. Abel Roper is the Proprietor of those Papers, or at least receives three full Halves of the Profit of 'em.' He may have been right; but it is perhaps more probable that the frequent repetition in the *Evening Post* of paragraphs that had appeared the same morning in the *Post-Boy* (often with slight variations in the wording) was due to Berrington's practice of collecting his news from the morning papers.[79] George Ridpath of the *Flying Post* was probably another owner-author. In 1694 he was quoted as saying that it was part of his business to write news, by which he was able 'to imploy and maintain three or four'.[80] No one seems to have doubted that *Mist's Weekly Journal* (as it was re-named in 1725) belonged to Mist, but there are few indications that he wrote for it. On 18 January 1718 Read's *Weekly Journal* enumerated Mist's 'nonsensical Scriblers' as 'Foe [Defoe], Seddon, and the debauch'd Author of the *Entertainer,* a poor unbeneficed Parson'. When examined on 4 June 1720 about some numbers of his journal that had given offence, Mist admitted to the 'authorship' (i.e. the editing?) of three of them, but not to that of another 'which he had entrusted to the care of Mr. Dan'l Defoe being himself gone a Journey into the Country'.[81] Earlier, in November 1718, when attributing another contribution to Defoe, he admitted having made 'some few Alterations in transcribing the same, not altering the Substance'.[82] From this it would appear that when he was not

* Cf. p. 31.

in prison or absent in the country, Mist had more or less effective control of what went into his paper. To say that he edited it is probably to say too much.

Some evidence has already been given of daily papers being owned jointly by a number of shareholders.* Such joint ownership was not confined to the dailies. When, on 17 November 1733, the *General Evening Post* announced a change of policy, the statement was made not on behalf of the proprietor, but of the proprietors. On 24 November 1719, when Thomas Warner, the publisher of the *St. James's Post* and the *St. James's Evening Post*, was under examination, he named Thomas Walker as the writer of the domestic news for both papers, and stated that Walker was employed by himself (Warner was a bookseller), by Read (a printer), and by Taylor, Osborn and Bell (all booksellers). Some of those men were also partners in the publication of books requiring a considerable capital expenditure. In naming himself and the others as Walker's employers (that is, as owners of the two papers) Warner made a significant statement that was obviously intended to absolve them from all blame, and this was duly minuted:

They do not direct what shall be put into the said Papers, but leave that entirely to the discretion of Debeere as to the Foreign News and of the abovementioned Walker as to the Paragraphs of the Domestick News.[83]

When offence was given, the well-to-do proprietors of the newspapers seem rarely to have been called to account. There were some exceptions, like Nathaniel Mist, who continued to flout the government and suffered for it. So, too, did Thomas Sharpe, who was both printer and proprietor of the *Freeholder's Journal* (1721–22), a well-written weekly journal that criticised the government severely and effectively. On 25 April 1722 he was betrayed by Edmund Curll, who had become a particularly unpleasant informer. Curll wrote to Lord Townshend about the current issue and about a libellous letter intended for the next week's issue. He had apparently intercepted this letter through the good offices of 'the Publisher, one Payne, who is a very honest man', and wholly ignorant of the paper's contents 'till he has it sent to him by Mr. Sharp, the Printer and Proprietor of it'.[84] Sharpe was committed to prison, and kept there until he could find sureties for his good behaviour. The government's policy at this time was 'to fall upon printers and publishers'; if they were financially ruined, the authors of the libels would be effectively silenced.[85]

* See pp. 31–2.

Occasionally the government tried a different approach. When, in 1722, it was thought necessary to put an end to the damaging 'Cato's Letters' then appearing in the *London Journal*, the under-secretary Charles Delafaye got in touch with its proprietor, Elizee Dobree. From the surviving correspondence in the State Papers there are no signs that Dobree was intimidated in any way. His correspondence with Delafaye (sometimes in English, sometimes in French) is polite but not servile, the letters of a businessman prepared to do a deal. In what he called 'A Computation of the *London Journal*' he estimated the average sale at 15,000 copies, and the profits at £960 a year. He did not mince his words in calculating the adverse effect on both sets of figures if his journal became a government organ: 'By turning off the Strength of Expressions & thereby Lessning the Sale to ab^t 7 or 8,000 there would be little, or, no profitt at all.' He expected the sale to drop to 8,000 or less, and accordingly proposed that the government should pay him £800 a year, 'to be paid att the signing of this agreement', although he would still be £160 out of pocket by the sale.[86] On what terms the final settlement was reached we do not know; but the whole affair appears to have been conducted as a normal business transaction. Was this perhaps a special case? It is odd to find Dobree alternating between English and French in his letters to Delafaye. Both men had French names, and it is possible that both may have come from the Channel Islands. If so, they were probably known to each other, and this could account for an element in their correspondence that would nowadays be called 'old school tie', and for the apparent leniency with which the proprietor of a highly troublesome journal was treated.

If the author, publisher or proprietor of a newspaper was in trouble with authority or with an injured party, the usual practice was to blame someone else. On 30 July 1681 the *Loyal Protestant* carried a statement that an order had been made in Council 'prohibiting any payments to be made to the Lord Ranelagh or his Deputy as Treasurer of Ireland'. Thompson published an apology on 9 August:

Through inadvertency in my absence, a Discourse was incerted in mine of the 30 of July last, relating to Right Honourable the Lord Ranelagh, which I understanding to be false, thought it my duty to satisfy the world, that the substance of that story was taken out of one of the publick News Letters, daily spread about the world, and never intended (by me) as any prejudice to his Honour.

The inference to be drawn from these words is that Thompson normally supervised what went into his paper. On this occasion the culprit was almost certainly Claypoole, if he was still working for Thompson.

The person most often blamed for false, libellous or seditious news was the printer. In actual practice he was often the only one left in charge of a newspaper. Newswriters and others might come and go during the day or the evening; but the printer had to be there all the time the paper was being made up, and sometimes, when copy was scarce, had to use his own judgment about what to include. In January 1724 Mist explained how an offensive letter had appeared in his journal; it had been inserted by the printers, who had searched a drawer in his office for copy needed to fill up the paper.[87] Some years earlier, when a paragraph reflecting on a foreign prince was published in the same journal, James Bettenham 'whom he [Mist] intrusted to take Care of his Business in his Absence', had been arrested on the premises. Bettenham was a printer.[88] In 1722, during another and more prolonged absence of Mist, his journal was left in charge of a young and inexperienced apprentice printer called Doctor Gaylard. ('Doctor' was apparently his Christian name, for it appears in his signature in 1722 on a letter and petition to Lord Townshend.) On 21 April Gaylard had allowed a paragraph to appear stating that some politicians had started a rumour about 'a certain person' (i.e. the Pretender) having left Rome. Called to account for this blunder, Gaylard explained that as he had often been obliged to be absent attending to Mist's affairs, he 'did not always see every Article that was put into the said Journal, but left the same to the Care of the Press-men Employ'd about the same'. The home news was generally taken from the public papers or reached him from correspondents by the penny post, and he had no idea that anything was being published that would offend the government.[89] A similar explanation was offered by Thomas Read when he was examined about a paragraph published in the *St. James's Evening Post* of 17 July 1729. He had nothing to do with the paper himself, but it was printed by his father, James Read, who had gone to Boulogne to see his daughter, and left the paper in charge of a journeyman, whose name he did not know.[90]

Sometimes the printer was left in charge with general instructions on what to put in the paper. When, on 26 April 1729, the *London Journal* published an article 'To the People of England' that seemed to strike the wrong note for a paper now subsidised by the government, enquiries were naturally made. It turned out that James Nott had been printing the paper for the past five or six weeks because the regular printer, William Wilkins, was out of town, no doubt on a well-deserved holiday. The article in question had been brought in by James Pitt, 'who does now and then help them to a paper', and Nott had inserted it 'in pursuance of a general Order from yᵉ said Wilkins to receive such papers from yᵉ said Pitt whenever he should bring any'.[91] What happened on this occasion to Pitt, who wrote for various government papers under several pseudonyms, we do not know. (Incidentally it emerged from the questioning of Nott that Wilkins not only printed the paper but had been given the whole direction of it by the government.)

A flagrant example of the printer being left to fend for himself occurred in the *Weekly Medley*, an ill-run journal conducted by William Bond. When his issue for 14 November 1719 appeared, it included the only three pieces of domestic news the printer found in the *St. James's Post* of 9 November, and one of these related to John Matthews, hanged at Tyburn a few days earlier. In this paragraph Matthews was described as an 'unhappy and deluded youth' who had for several years been 'instructed by Mr. Orme, a Nonjuring Parson', and had confessed to having been 'unhappily drawn in by the Nonjurors' to do what he did. Although there is nothing to show that Bond was an active Jacobite, his *Weekly Medley* was certainly not Hanoverian, and it had been characterised by Read's *Weekly Journal* as 'seditious': if Bond had known that a paragraph attacking the nonjurors was about to appear in his paper he would certainly have stopped it. But he had not known, because as a man of letters he was concerned only with 'the front' of his paper, and left the news to his inferiors. In his next issue he made it clear that the paragraph had been inserted without his knowledge, and he dissociated himself from his blundering printer in no uncertain terms:

I declare to the World, and declare solemnly in the Face of it and Heaven, that I was an utter Stranger to that Paragraph 'till I was charged with inserting such a Calumny, when the Paper was published, when it was too late to be recalled. If any careless unregarding Person that attends the Press will steal Paragraphs from the Thursday's Post, Flying Post, or from Papers if possible more base and detestable, I hope I shall not stand chargeable with the Crimes he is guilty of.

Whatever else they may or may not have been responsible for in a newspaper, the printers do appear to have been left in sole charge of the advertisements. Since those were normally unexceptionable, the publisher did not see any need to check them, and the author felt free to give his mind to higher things. Advertisements could therefore be left to the printer, one of whose recurring problems was to ensure that all the available space in each issue was filled: he could set advertisements as they came in, and have them ready for use as the need arose. But this convenient transfer of responsibility to the printer sometimes led to trouble. When Abel Roper was challenged about an indecent advertisement that had appeared in his *Post-Boy* he is said to have replied: 'I am not answerable for advertisements; I know nothing of it.'[92] So, too, when a reader complained in 1718 about obscene advertisements in the *St. James's Evening Post*, readers were advised on 24 April that 'such have been taken in without the Consent or Knowledge of the Author or Publisher', but an undertaking was given that the offence would not be repeated. On 5 September 1729 an advertisement beginning, 'At the Desire of the Portugall Pimpassador . . .' appeared in the *Daily Post*, and resulted in the printer, Samuel Nevill, admitting under examination that it had been brought to him by John ('Orator') Henley's servant.[93] Newspapers sometimes named booksellers' shops or coffee-houses where advertisements would be accepted, but the simplest way was to take them to the printing house and pay for them on the spot. That printers sometimes took advantage of their favourable situation is suggested by a jocular letter (obviously editorial) in Mist's *Journal* of 30 April 1720, where a correspondent writes to say that he wanted to insert an advertisement in the *Daily Courant* or the *Daily Post*, but 'the Rogues the Printers would not oblige me under Three and Sixpence a-piece, and half a Crown to drink if I expected it in the Front of their Paper'. The day of the advertising manager on a newspaper was still to come; but a document among the State Papers suggests that by 1729 at least one newspaper had a man particularly in charge of advertisements.[94]

With the under-secretaries constantly harassing authors and publishers for what appeared in their papers, it is not surprising to find them taking precautionary steps to absolve themselves of responsibility. Notices like the following in the *St. James's Journal* of 3 May 1729 are not uncommon: 'The Author of the first Part of this Paper is not accountable for any other Part of it, being entirely a Stranger to all the rest, till it appears publickly in Print.' The first part of the *Journal* was usually an essay on some matter of literary or general interest. Abel Boyer, who appears to have been in effective control of the *Post-Boy* for some years in the early eighteenth century, had an uneasy relationship with the proprietor, Abel Roper, and took care to safeguard his own interests. Bearing in mind Roper's 'innate love of Scandal and Defamation' he got him to agree to pay all the fines he might incur through Roper's rashness.[95]

Defoe, in view of his more complicated relations with Mist, went to great lengths to conceal his contributions to the *Weekly Journal*. Mist had a reputation for not betraying his authors, and when word first got about that Defoe was writing for him, he stated publicly that he had done nothing for him except that formerly he had sometimes translated some foreign letters in the absence of the person usually employed. But when confronted by both Secretaries of State on 1 November 1718 he admitted that Defoe had usually written part of his newspaper, and in particular the letter signed 'Sir Andrew Politick' of 25 October, which was the cause of the present enquiry. He further told the Secretaries that 'because it should not be known who was the Author he always destroyed the Copy'.[96] When it came to the turn of the publisher, Thomas Warner, to be examined, he said that Mist had admitted to him that Defoe had given him the letter, 'thô at the same time [he] pretended to give him a Caution not to print it'. It was part of Warner's business to pay contributors to the journal, and Defoe had asked that his payments should be made 'to the order of Samuel Moorland, Esqr',[97] but of late he had been putting the money into his own hands. It is strange that so experienced a journalist as Defoe should have persuaded himself that even such elaborate precautions would have concealed his activities for any length of time from the prying eyes of his fellow journalists. On 22 November Mist's arch-enemy Read added a new detail to the record by disclosing that Defoe was in the habit of leaving his copy in a hole in Mist's 'back-shop', so that if challenged he could say that he had not given it into anyone's hands to be published.[98]

Publishers also took their own precautions. When Warner was giving evidence against Defoe in the examination just cited, he tried to minimise his own connection with Mist's *Weekly Journal*. He denied, in fact, that he was the publisher. In the words of the minute taken at the time,

Mist by himself or his Servants delivereth out the said Paper and at the Month's end gives the Examinant an Account of what Papers he has disposed of and to whom, by which this Examin^t collects the money due for the same and accounts to Mr. Mist.

On 28 August 1714, when John Morphew was cited as publisher of Roper's *Post-Boy*, he admitted that he received copies of the paper three times a week from the printer, Lucy Beardwell, but he did not know the name of the author, nor whether the copy then produced was one of those he had sold. (Three days earlier Mrs Beardwell had stated that the paper was mostly written by George James, and that she accounted with Mr Morphew for the charge of printing it.)[99] Asked whether Abel Roper was not the proprietor of the paper called the *Post-*

Boy, Morphew said he did not know. The explanation he offered for his ignorance is worth quoting in full:

He saith he formerly accounted with Abel Roper for the profits of the said paper, but that for a long time pass't nobody has call'd to him for money on that account. He saith that it is a very usual thing for persons to leave books and papers at his House and at the Houses of other Publishers, and a long time after to call for the value thereof without making themselves known to the said Publishers, and if the Government makes enquiry concerning the Authors of any books or papers so left, in order to bring them to punishment, it often happens that nobody comes to make any demand for the value of the said Books.[100]

If this practice was as widespread as Morphew's testimony seems to suggest, the danger of government prosecution must indeed have weighed heavily on the minds of those involved in producing and selling newspapers.

Some of the precautions taken by authors and publishers to conceal themselves may strike us as being still more naive. When the *Impartial Protestant Mercury* began to appear in April 1681 the imprint read: 'Printed for H.V. and T.C. Published and to be Sold by R. Janeway.' The publisher was prepared to give his name, but the two authors, Henry Care and Thomas Vile (H.C. and T.V.) were taking no chances. The transposition of the initial letters of their names was made for purposes of concealment. Similarly, when Langley Curtiss began publishing Care's *Weekly Pacquet of Advice from Rome*, the imprint read: 'Printed for C.L.' and continued so for the first 13 numbers, when it became: 'Printed for L.C.' For Nos. 21 and 22 the initial letters reverted to 'C.L.', but thereafter remained 'L.C.' By No. 23 Curtiss may have thought he was now so generally known to be the printer of the *Weekly Pacquet* that any further attempt at concealment would be futile. If the attempt may seem to the modern reader to have been doomed from the start, it can be answered that lawyers in the seventeenth and eighteenth centuries did sometimes succeed in obtaining a verdict for their client on terminological minutiae. At the trial of John Matthews in 1719, when the jury had returned a verdict of guilty, his counsel, Mr Hungerford, rose and moved for an arrest of judgement. In the indictment, he told the court, the word '*impressit*' had been used to mean 'printed'; but this Latin verb had other meanings, as, for example, 'stamped'.[101] A long argument followed, but Mr Hungerford was playing his last card, and on this occasion his objection was overruled. Yet it had apparently been worth trying.

At the lower end of the newspaper hierarchy came those men who provided the brief paragraphs of home news that formed a part of most newspapers. As we have seen, it was not until the nineteenth century that they were commonly known as 'reporters'. In the seventeenth and eighteenth centuries the men whose business it was to pick up news were usually referred to as news-gatherers or collectors of news, and they varied in number and quality from one newspaper to another. Specific information about news-gatherers and their activities is hard to come by; but some of them appear to have been regularly employed by a newspaper, and others to have been freelances. When, on 8 March 1681, Harris published a long and incriminating account of 'one Jolly' who had been surprised while saying mass to a secret gathering of about thirty papists,* Thompson exposed the story as utterly false, and added that it had been forged by one William Beckett, who supplied Harris with such stories, 'and had 2*s.* 6*d.* for every paragraph of news he brought him, true or false'. According to a writer in the *London Journal* of 15 October 1719, William Bond 'was lately for a considerable time a *Runner,* or *Devil,* or *Footman* (I know not what you Printers call them), to one Mawson a Journalist, to collect Paragraphs of Street News for him, at seven shillings a Week Wages'.[102] Bond, who had been quarrelling with most of his fellow journalists (partly, perhaps, to get enough copy to fill his *Weekly Medley*), was being taunted here with his humble journalistic origins. This contemptuous dismissal of him may have been written by John Trenchard or Thomas Gordon, in which case the gentleman writer was repudiating what he would consider to be the mere hack: but it may have been the work of Defoe's son, Benjamin Norton Defoe, if he was already writing for the *London Journal,* in which case one hack was looking for mud with which to bespatter another.

If it was his lucky day, the news-gatherer might find himself on the spot where a house was on fire, or where there had been a street accident; but the greater part of his news would be picked up in coffee-houses or the Exchange, or from communicative strangers, and would often contain the barest minimum of identification or authentication. In his *Commentator,* No. 5, Daniel Defoe has some sarcastic advice to offer newswriters. They must not be too circumstantial:

I discovered this Caution lately in a Brother-Writer, who informs the Publick that *A Man dropp'd down dead in the Street,* without any other Particulars. Here is the Surprize of a sudden Death, to keep up the Attention of the Reader; and yet, in Case it were not Fact, I would be glad to know which way you would go about to confute it.

* Cf. p. 100.

In a similar vein the *Grub-Street Journal* notes the man employed to frequent coffee-houses, 'in order to pick up Articles of News, and, in a scarcity, to make some; which are always introduced with *We hear*, or *We are informed*'; and another man employed 'to collect such News as is generally talked of, and of greater certainty, which is either directly affirmed, or begins with *We are assured*'.[103]

The fullest contemporary account of news-collectors at work is to be found in *The Case of the Coffee-Men of London and Westminster* (1728). For some time the coffee-men had been complaining bitterly about the cost of the growing number of newspapers they were expected to provide for their customers, and they now set out their proposals for publishing a morning and an evening paper of their own. But first they made a rousing attack on the existing papers, and subjected their methods of collecting news to a ruthless examination. This is so well written that the coffee-men almost certainly employed a journalist to do it for them:

Persons are employed (One or Two for each Paper) at so much a Week, to haunt Coffee-Houses, and thrust themselves into Companies where they are not known; or plant themselves at a convenient Distance, to overhear what is said, in order to pick up Matter for the Papers . . .

But this leads to false news being published; for 'persons of discernment' often spot those 'sons of Mercury', and deliberately utter some 'rouzing falshood', which appears in print next day 'upon credible information'. Other news-gatherers 'scrape acquaintance with the footmen and other servants of the Nobility and Gentry'; and so family secrets are betrayed, and 'matters sacred to Privacy and the fireside made the talk of the World'. Some talk with carmen and porters in ale-houses, and are often imposed upon. Others get in touch with the 'death-hunters', men employed by the Company of Undertakers to make enquiries and give them notice 'when Death knocks at the doors of the nobility and gentry who can afford to go to their Graves genteely, and be interr'd à la Mode'. The collectors of news arrange to meet those death-hunters, who 'for a treat and a little money tell them what they hear . . . But how often is the Publick imposed on in this Article!' Worse still, those news-gatherers will sometimes 'rummage old Chronicles, Histories of Antiquity, and other pieces recording accidents and remarkable occurrences of times long since gone, for old forgotten Stories; which they publish as relations of matters just happen'd, only changing the scenes'. An example of this happening occurred in the *Daily Post* of 26 February 1720, where the reader was told that Mrs Honeywood, mother of Robert Honeywood of Markes Hall in Essex, had lately died there at the age of 93, leaving 367 children lawfully descended from her. On the following day Mist's *Weekly Journal* had the pleasure of pointing out that Mrs Honeywood had not died 'lately', but a hundred years earlier in 1620. To complete their indictment, the coffee-men also charged the newspapers with inventing some of their news; with stealing from one another; and with sometimes giving as much space to advertisements as to news, so that 'they are paid on both hands; paid by the advertisers for taking in advertisements, and paid by the Coffee-men for delivering them out'. The aggrieved coffee-men's criticisms were all just; but when they started their own two newspapers in January 1729 (and presumably stopped taking in any others) they must have met with a hostile response from their customers, for no copies of *The Coffee-House Morning Post* or of its evening issue appear to have survived.

When a new paper was started it was common practice to send a free copy of the first number to all the coffee-houses in London, and in some instances to follow it with the second and third number. The well-financed *Daily Post*, founded in 1719, sent the coffee-houses free copies of the first six issues. Gentlemen would in this way become accustomed to reading the new paper, and would expect it to be regularly available when they turned up for their dish of coffee. Others might call for a new paper that was not yet provided, and the proprietor would have to give an order for it or risk losing their custom. This arrangement had been working satisfactorily in the days of Charles II, and that it then suited the coffee-men may be seen from the notices they occasionally inserted in the newspapers. In the *Impartial Protestant Mercury* of 30 July 1681 there appeared an advertisement for a new coffee-house

which is commonly called by the name of the Plot and Counter-plot Coffee-House; for that Dr. Oats's Man who married Mrs. Cellier's Maid, keeps the said House, and invites all People, as not only having the best Coffee, Chocolate, and Tee to be sold there, but also all sorts of News Pamphlets, lying ready upon the Table, for any Persons to read that will spend their penny, whether they be Papists, Bromidgham Protestants, Tories, or Tantivy Men.

But what was profitable in 1681, when newspapers were comparatively few in number, had become a burden forty years later. When Nicholas Amhurst started his essay paper, *Terrae Filius*, in January 1721, he found that the attitude of the coffee-men was hardening. In his issue for 4 February he printed an advertisement they had put in the *St. James's Post* complaining about the 'insipid and useless Papers, which weekly multiply upon the Publick', and calling a meeting of all masters of coffee-houses 'to consult on proper Measures to prevent this growing Evil'. Another unfortunate author who started, two days later, a paper called *The Projector* to discuss the affairs of the South Sea company, was informed that 'it cou'd not, tho' given, be suffer'd to lye on the Coffee Tables', and when enquiring the reason, was told that 'the Coffee-Men have met in Form and agreed to receive no New Papers'. *Terrae Filius* may have beaten the ban, for it survived for 52 numbers, but *The Projector* appears to have collapsed after its eighth issue. Two years later the author of another essay paper, *The Visiter*, designed to be non-political, and addressed to the ladies, who would be his 'most peculiar care', found that he had got off to a poor start. He had made the mistake of starting in June, and was inclined to blame 'the thinness of the Town'; but on 7 July he issued an appeal: 'If gentlemen wou'd oblige the Coffee-houses to take it in, they might all of them read it there.' The logic of this appeal is not easy to follow: since coffee-houses were a male preserve, the ladies would be unable to read his paper there, and since it was for them that it was particularly intended, their fathers and brothers were unlikely to call for it. None the less, it lasted for 51 numbers, with or without the co-operation of the coffee-men. It remains true, however, that the relationship between the newspapers and the coffee-houses was beneficial to both, and to the newspapers especially in their first few weeks, when they had still to find a public willing, and eventually accustomed, to reading them.

There were, of course, other outlets for the sale of newspapers. Copies could be obtained at the shops of certain named booksellers; and, as the years passed, newspapers became available at a growing number of pamphlet shops. One of these shops was kept by Mrs Anne Dodd, who occupies an unearned niche in literary history by being the reputed publisher of Pope's *Dunciad Variorum*. She was described in 1721 as 'a retailer of Newspapers and Pamphlets commonly called a Mercury'. She had been in trouble for selling copies of the *Post-Boy* at her pamphlet shop at the sign of the Peacock near Temple Bar, and again in 1731 for selling the *Craftsman*.[104] The 'mercuries' were commonly, if not exclusively, women. When John Wilford, a bookseller, was examined in August 1728 about the publication of Mist's *Journal*, his answer made clear the part played by the mercuries in the process of distribution:

The said Libel was publisht in the usual manner by sending it out to the Mercurys as they are called, who make a Trade of selling News papers and pamphlets and retailing them out to the hawkers.[105]

The hawkers, male and female, who added their quota to the street cries of London, were sometimes guilty of dishonest practices. On 29 February 1724 Mist announced that they were giving people a look at his journal for 'a third part of the price' (that is, for ½*d*.), and that 'henceforth no Returns will be allowed, and no more Papers can be given out than are paid for'. There is also evidence that hawkers were sometimes subjected to bribery or intimidation, and refused to cry a paper that for one reason or another was disliked in the trade. The short-lived *General Postscript*, the dialogue paper that specialised in sarcastic and dismissive observations on all the other papers, was victimised and probably snuffed out in this way. In its issue for 17 October 1709 it appears that 'some Fellows, under the Pretence of Officers' had stopped its hawkers 'to search their Aprons upon the Exchange', but this must have been 'only a Phanatical Stratagem, to frighten the poor People from carrying our Papers'. In its next issue those 'fellows' were said to have pretended to be the Lord Mayor's officers. In 1718 the author of another paper found a new reason to blame the hawkers. He had received complaints that his paper was not on sale in the streets, and he attributed this to 'the Negligence of the Hawkers, to whom the name of it may be difficult to be cry'd'. No doubt it was, for he had revived an old title and called the paper *Heraclitus Ridens*, which must have been more difficult for hawkers to cry than 'Post-Boy!' or 'Evening Post!' Even so, they seem to have coped with the difficulty in 1681, when the original *Heraclitus Ridens* ran for 82 issues.

3

In the short survey given above of the part played by proprietors, publishers, printers and newswriters, it has not been possible to establish a clear pattern of responsibility, either for what went into a newspaper, or for the way in which the news was presented. The apparent absence of effective editorial control over the make-up of so many of those early newspapers has already been noted, and it now remains to offer an explanation. What cannot fail to strike the modern reader is the frequently disconnected, and at times chaotic, juxtaposition of the various items in the day's news. Home and foreign, London and country news are often jumbled together in the same column on no rational principle. The reader of a modern newspaper knows at once where to turn for the news most likely to interest him, but the seventeenth-century reader got little such guidance.

In its issue of 1 November 1681 the *Impartial Protestant Mercury* started off with a short account of the new Lord Mayor being sworn in. The reader was then taken abroad for 'advice' from Constantinople, and then home again for a quarrel among some Irishmen at the Rose Tavern near Temple Bar; abroad again for news from Brussels; home again to London for a report that Slingsby Bethel, one of the late sheriffs, had deposited several hundred pounds in good hands 'for the Releasing Poor Prisoners in the two Compters and Ludgate'; and then abroad again to learn that the Spanish ambassador to Holland had presented a fresh memorial to the States. Next came an indignant denial of Nathaniel Thompson's assertion in 'his last Intelligence' that Stephen Dugdale, the informer, was suffering from venereal disease. This was followed by some news about the Common Council; an advertisement from 'the Gentlemen concerned in the Insurance Office behind the Royal Exchange'; news of a prisoner for debt in Southwark who had offered to turn informer; and finally foreign news from Frankfurt and Amsterdam. The last of the four columns was filled with advertisements.

To understand why intelligent men could produce such a rag-bag we must consider the difficulties facing the seventeenth-century printer. In 1681, and for many decades later, every book and every newspaper was printed on a hand-press, 'in design and method still the press of Caxton'.[106] The printer had to pick each letter for each word out of its appropriate 'box' in the 'case' or receptacle in which the type was kept, place it on his composing stick, and then go through the same movements with the next letter, and the next. While the process was the same for a newspaper as for a book, the newspaper had to appear on time at regular weekly, twice-weekly, thrice-weekly or daily intervals, and the copy for the current issue was coming in all the time the printer was at work. In reckoning the period available, we have to allow not only for the manual type-setting, but for the inking, the pulling of each sheet, and the time required for the wet sheets to dry. In addition, some time might be lost in correcting printer's mistakes. (Edward Rawlins, the putative author of *Heraclitus Ridens*, was described as a 'Corrector to the Press'; and when James Read was accused of having the man known as Burridge the Blasphemer as the author of his *Weekly Journal*, he emended the wording of the charge to 'Corrector, but not the Author of this Paper'.)[107]

In practice the low speeds that could be attained and sustained in manual type-setting meant that no sooner was a paper selling on the streets than the printer had begun to set the next issue. He could not wait until all the news was assembled and arranged in an orderly and systematic manner by himself or by someone else; he had to start with what he had, or he would never keep ahead of the clock. What was already set would normally have to be left standing; no printer of a seventeenth-century newspaper would willingly put up with time-wasting cancellations because a piece of news he had already set was superseded by later information, and still less because it would be more appropriately placed beside news of the same general kind (for example, home news or foreign news). In such circumstances the printer would probably have given short shrift to any busybody who asked him to make the necessary alterations. No doubt the contemporary reader had become conditioned to those grasshopper leaps from the Common Council to Frankfurt and back again, and would have seen nothing odd in them.

If, however, that reader also subscribed to a news-letter, he might have been more critical. The handwritten news-letters were better able to deal with the problem of arranging the news, and to cope with any late news that might come in. Before handing over his news to be copied, a man like Henry Muddiman had time to present the various items in a methodical fashion. A scrivener could then make a number of fair copies, and from those he and his fellow scriveners would transcribe the letters to be sent to the various subscribers. When an important piece of late news came in, it could be inserted without difficulty in the appropriate section of home or foreign (and even at the most appropriate point in either section) in all subsequent copies. If it was important enough, it could be added at the end of a letter already copied, and catch the evening post along with those that had been copied later. Such flexibility was not available to the printed newspaper.

It is fair to add that although the haphazard make-up of the *Impartial Protestant Mercury* in the number cited was fairly typical of that paper, and of those conducted by Harris, Thompson and Benskin, they were not always quite so disconnected. In general, the most methodical presentation is found in papers that concentrated on foreign news, such as the *Gazette*, the *Post Man* and the *Daily Courant*. If the packet boats arrived more or less at the expected hour with the Dutch and French newspapers, an experienced man like De Fonvive or Buckley would have time to translate, digest and select from the foreign news, and give it to the printer in an orderly form. Apart from the *Gazette*, the only Restoration paper that consistently attempted to keep the foreign news in one continuous section was Smith's *Currant Intelligence*, and even it had occasionally to break the pattern. By the time we reach the eighteenth century, the presentation of the news begins to show some improvement in the better-run newspapers. In the late 1720s the *London Evening Post* normally opens with a section from the foreign mails, goes on to 'Country News', and finishes with a section headed 'London'. In general, it is true, it was easier for an evening paper to set out the news rationally, since much of it had been lifted from the morning papers and could therefore be more easily arranged by the newswriter before it was given to the printers.

It might be thought that the weekly journals were exempt from the problems facing the daily and thrice-weekly papers. Admittedly they did have more time between each issue, but then they had six pages to fill instead of two, and the fact that they were setting for one and a half sheets presented typographical problems of its own. Examination of almost any weekly journal in the 1720s will quickly show that type-setting of the news must have begun quite early in the week, and continued from day to day. It may be relevant here to note that on 18 April 1724 James Read, whose *Weekly Journal*, like almost all the others, came out on Saturdays, announced to potential contributors: 'We also desire to receive whatever is design'd for the Week following, on the Saturday preceeding, at least.' On 25 February 1716, a printed weekly called *The News Letter* carried several paragraphs, appearing at intervals over two pages, about the six peers condemned to death for their part in the 1715 rebellion. On the first of those pages in columns one and two, we learn that on 'Saturday night last' (i.e. 18 February) the writs had been 'carried down' for the execution of the six condemned lords, together with some other news about them. In the first column of the next page we are told that they had received the sacrament, but in the second column the news is that they had sent petitions to both Houses of Parliament, and that the House of Lords had interceded for them. Lower down in the same column, we are given a fourth and final item about the peers: two of them had been executed. This way of doling out the news was the inevitable result of setting it as soon as it came in, and then proceeding to a new line with the next item, whatever that might be.[108] A piece of news in an eighteenth-century paper is where it is because that is where the printer had got to when it reached him. Once it was set, there it had to remain, unless the printer was to go through the disturbing and even exasperating process of removing the type from where it stood and re-setting it somewhere else when later news on the same subject was brought to him and had to be incorporated with the original statement. Printers have always had an inclination to be their own masters, and this must have been especially so in the eighteenth century, when the actual content of a newspaper was often left in the last resort to the printer's own judgement. No doubt the relations between newswriter and printer varied from one paper to another. If the newswriter did his work properly and set out his news in as methodical a fashion as the circumstances allowed, the result was a well-run newspaper; if he dribbled it to the printer in bits and pieces, the printer was not responsible for the consequences. At times, however, circumstances defeated both newswriter and printer.

A further complication occasioned by the hand-press remains to be noted. There was a limit to the number of sheets that could be run off in a given period, and in newspapers with a large circulation a second simultaneous setting might be required, and additional presses brought into use. That point may not have been reached by Restoration periodicals, although there is some evidence for two settings of *Heraclitus Ridens*,[109] and one would expect to find similar evidence for L'Estrange's *Observator*, but in the early eighteenth century a number of papers had certainly a high enough circulation to make more than one setting necessary. It has been shown conclusively that many copies of Steele's *Tatler* have significant typographical differences, and that every number probably appeared in at least two different settings.[110] Some more or less reliable figures exist for the circulation of newspapers in the reign of Queen Anne. In what appears to be a well-informed estimate in 1704, the writer puts the circulation of the *Flying Post*, the *London Post* and the *English Post* at 400; the *Post-Boy* at 3,000; and the *Post Man* at 3,800 on Mondays and Wednesdays and 4,000 on Saturdays. The figures for the *Daily Courant* are 800, and those for the *London Gazette*, 6,000.[111]

Fortunately it is possible to test this estimate by a more reliable one obtained from official figures, based on the returns from the recently imposed stamp duty. For seven weeks in August and September 1712 the *Post Man* had an average sale of 3,812 copies, the *Post-Boy* of 3,659, the *Flying Post* of 1,350, and the *Daily Courant* of 859. Corresponding figures in June and July 1713 show that the sale of the *Post Man* had dropped by almost one half to 1,992, and that of the *Post-Boy* by over 1,000 copies to 2,243.[112] Those official figures must be related to the political situation. In 1712 Marlborough's military successor, the Duke of Ormonde, had received secret 'restraining orders' not to engage the French in battle, and negotiations for peace were now under way. The expectancy of a peace treaty must have kept up the circulation of the newspapers, particularly those favoured by the Tories. But by 31 March 1713 the Treaty of Utrecht had been signed, and the country was no longer at war: peace had brought about an inevitable decline in the demand for foreign news. The sharp decline in the circulation figures for the *Post Man* is no more than might be expected; it had for long been looked upon (apart from the *Gazette*) as the most reliable and well-informed paper for foreign news. While it had a circulation verging on 4,000 the *Post Man* would probably require to be set more than once, and this would be even more necessary with the *Gazette*. In a notice in the *Post Man* of 17 January 1712 the reader is asked to 'correct a mistake of the Press in some of our last Papers . . . occasioned by an Accident in one of the Forms'. This is not, however, conclusive evidence for separate setting: there would be a form for the front page and another for the reverse in a single setting. It is worth remembering, too, that the first concern of a morning paper was to print enough copies to cover the sale in London and the suburbs; copies required by country readers could be run off up to an hour or so before the mails left for the country in the evening.

The weekly journals in their heyday reached heights of circulation hitherto unknown, and must have been driven to adopt multiple setting. On 15 January 1715 the *British Mercury*, in a drive to increase its revenue from advertisements, claimed a circulation of 'near 4,000'. But much higher figures were reached by some journals that were primarily political, and boldly attacked the government. On 25 April 1722 Edmund Curll drew attention to the *Freeholder's Journal* of the date, and stated roundly that 'Eight Thousand of these Libels are Printed'. Since Curll was on friendly terms with the publisher, the figures, for that issue at least, were probably correct.[113] When Elizee Dobree, the proprietor of the *London Journal*, claimed for it a sale of 15,000 copies,* it was then at the height of its popularity, but in any case he had an interest in putting the figure as high as possible since he was about to sell his paper to the government. The circulation may well have fluctuated considerably from one issue to another: the *Daily Journal* of 27 March 1721 reported 'such a Demand for the *London Journal* last Saturday, on account of that most excellent Piece relating to the scandalous Detention of Mr. Knight [Robert Knight, Cashier of the South Sea Company], that twenty Thousand were dispos'd of before the Evening'. When, however, its publisher, John Peele, was examined about an issue published in August 1721 he agreed that 'the parcel of such papers . . . he received last night might amount to Ten Thousand in Number', and this may have been nearer the normal sale.[114] All the contemporary evidence suggests that Mist's *Weekly Journal* and the *Craftsman* reached circulations comparable to that

* Cf. p. 214.

of the *London Journal* before it became a government organ, i.e. in the region of 10,000 copies. With such circulation figures it would be impossible to escape multiple setting. When Mist's premises were raided in November 1718, his entire work force was arrested: it amounted to eleven journeymen and apprentices. Since Mist engaged in comparatively little general publishing, most of these men would have been available for printing his newspaper.[115]

It is unnecessary to enlarge upon the limitations imposed on newspapers that enjoyed none of the resources of modern technology. Those resources have revolutionised not only the printing and distribution of newspapers, but the speed and efficiency with which the day's news is transmitted to them from all parts of the world. We have moved from the days of sailing-ships and the post-boy on his horse to instant communication. Yet it would be wrong to assume that the spirit of enterprise was lacking in those early newspapers, or that there was not a constant endeavour to be first with the news. The conditions were different, but the determination was there. As a final example of early enterprise we may consider an attempted scoop in August 1681 by Thomas Benskin, which, through no fault of his own, unfortunately miscarried. On 8 July Stephen College, the 'Protestant joiner', had been indicted at the Old Bailey on a charge of high treason, but the bill had been thrown out by a Whig grand jury. College, who had identified himself with the Shaftesbury faction and was an ardent opponent of a Catholic succession, was the real or reputed author of several seditious ballads and other pieces; he may have spoken some indiscreet words against the King, and when the parliament met at Oxford, he had turned up there in a suit of armour and carrying his 'Protestant flail'.[116] In spite of the *ignoramus* verdict of the London jury he had not been released, and a fresh indictment against him was drawn up at Oxford, where, as Sir Leoline Jenkins put it, the government might count on obtaining a jury of 'men rightly principled for the Church and the King'.[117] College's trial was fixed for Wednesday 17 August, and this gave Benskin his big chance; for, among the twice-weekly papers then being published in London, his *Domestick Intelligence* was the only one to appear on Thursdays. The renewed attempt to secure the conviction of College had aroused the greatest concern among all good Whigs, and if Benskin could obtain an account of the trial in time for his Thursday edition the following morning, he would get the better of all his rivals, whose papers came out on Friday. Meanwhile he had arranged to have someone in Oxford to cover the trial, and he kept open the first column of his first page for the expected report.

The trial began at 8 a.m., and in normal circumstances might have been concluded at some time in the afternoon. Unfortunately, the proceedings stretched out to an inordinate length. College (as was customary in a treason trial) was not allowed counsel for his defence, and spent many hours questioning points of law that he did not understand, asking for a copy of the indictment that he was not permitted to see, calling for the return of some papers that had been taken from him, stubbornly going over the same points again and again, and getting nowhere. The court adjourned till 2 p.m. before any witnesses had been called for the crown; but in due course its first witness, Stephen Dugdale, made his appearance, to be followed by many others equally suspect, and then it was the turn of witnesses for the defence, Titus Oates among them. Towards 2 a.m. on Thursday morning, two bottles of sack were called for and drunk by the jury 'for their Refreshment in the Presence of the Prisoner', and after a short retirement they brought in the expected verdict of guilty. Sentence of death was pronounced at 10 a.m. by Lord Chief Justice North.[118]

Benskin's enterprise had been defeated by College's brave and stubborn fight for his life. All was not lost, for Benskin was able to publish a report of 36 lines; but what he was able to tell his readers on the morning of Thursday 18 August, fell far short of what he must have hoped for. The report ended by stating that College had pleaded not guilty,

but the Witnesses being many, and swearing to several horrid Treasons, and Trayterous designs that they had heard him express, and several other circumstances too tedious to Recite; at the coming away of this Advice, most People concluded he would be cast for his Life.

It seems clear from this that whoever sent Benskin the account he printed had been unable to wait for the testimony of College's own witnesses. What arrangements Benskin had made for the account to reach him in London we can only guess; but since mail from the country got to the London Post Office on Monday, Wednesday and Friday evenings he probably received the report by a letter posted on Wednesday afternoon at Oxford. The more expensive alternative would have been to hire a man to ride post to London, a journey of about 60 miles, and this might have allowed for a later departure. In the circumstances, however, it would have been money wasted, for he, too, would have had to leave Oxford long before the trial was concluded. Benskin was unlucky, but at least he had tried.

Modern historians of the Restoration period have begun to show an increasing interest in its newspapers; and although they know better than 'to believe all they read in the papers', they may still find ample and reliable evidence of what people were thinking and what they were being told to think. It is clear that the Restoration newspapers were not written for ladies and gentlemen, the Millamants and the Mirabells who had the leisure, but not the inclination, for such reading. They were written for the middle-class reader who wished to hear the latest gossip from the Court and the City, to learn how the foreign news was likely to affect his commercial ventures, and who was also intelligent enough to take an interest in politics and political controversy. It may be a tribute to the dramatists of the day that life in the Restoration period is usually equated with the time-killing activities of such characters as Sir Frederick Frollick and Sir Fopling Flutter, but the Restoration newspapers can provide the social historian with a broader view of contemporary society, not only among the middle class but also among the lower orders.

The seventeenth-century newspapers have not been considered in these pages as 'literature'; but it would not be difficult to demonstrate their influence on the development of English prose style, not least because their very shortage of space encouraged the newswriter to express himself in a way that is at once succinct and fluent. Since the papers frequently gave their news in the actual words used by their correspondents, we are sometimes surprised by an elegant or learned turn of phrase, but the prevailing style is plain, workaday and forthright.

In the end, however, two quite different motives have kept this book going to the end. The first is an admiration (at times reluctant) for the way in which those early journalists resisted all attempts to suppress their papers and their right to express an opinion, and the way in which they suffered for the freedom of the press. Their motives, no doubt, were not always of the highest, and at times they showed a total disregard for the truth; but there can be no questioning their reckless courage, and their readiness to get on their feet again and fight on. The other motive has been a growing conviction that the last decades of the seventeenth century, and more especially the heady years from 1679 to 1682, were a formative period in the long history of the English newspaper. In those years many of the essential features of the English periodical press (waiting, to be sure, for development) were already there in embryo or plainly visible:

> And in such indexes, although small pricks
> To their subsequent volumes, there is seen
> The baby figure of the giant mass
> Of things to come at large.

Notes and references

ABBREVIATIONS

Applebee   *The Original Weekly Journal*, pbd J. Applebee, Oct. 1714 – Dec. 1737

Benskin   *The Domestick Intelligence; Or, News both from City and Country impartially related*, pbd Thomas Benskin, May 1681 – Nov. 1682

Boyer's Case   Mr. Boyer's Case: And His undoubted Right and Title to the Writing of the 'True Post-Boy', Asserted, (1709)

C.S.P.D.   *Calendar of State Papers, Domestic Series*

Currant Intelligence   *The Currant Intelligence: Or An Impartial Account of Transactions both foreign and domestick* (as *Smith's Currant Intelligence*, Nos. 10–24), pbd John Smith, Feb. – May: 1680; revived as *The Currant Intelligence*, Apr. – Dec. 1681

Defoe, *Letters*.   *The Letters of Daniel Defoe*, ed. George H. Healey (Oxford, 1953)

D.N.B.   *Dictionary of National Biography*

Haley   K. H. D. Haley, *The First Earl of Shaftesbury* (Oxford, 1968)

Handover   P. M. Handover, *A History of The London Gazette 1665–1965* (H. M. Stationery Office, 1965)

Hanson   Laurence Hanson, *Government and the Press 1695–1763* (Oxford, 1936)

Harris   *The Domestick Intelligence; Or News both from City and Country* (later, *The Protestant (Domestick) Intelligence*) pbd Benjamin Harris, July 1679 – Apr. 1681

Hart   W. H. Hart, *Index Expurgatorius Anglicanus* (London, 1872–8)

H.M.C.   *Reports of the Historical Manuscripts Commission*

Howell   *A Complete Collection of State Trials. . . .*, compiled by T. B. and T. J. Howell (1809–26)

I.P.M.   *The Impartial Protestant Mercury*, pbd Richard Janeway (Nos. 1–5 as *The True Protestant Mercury*) Apr. 1681 – May 1682

Jones   J. R. Jones, *The First Whigs: The Politics of the Exclusion Crisis* (Oxford, 1961)

Kitchin   George Kitchin, *Sir Roger L'Estrange* (London, 1913)

Loyal Prot.   *The Loyal Protestant and True Domestick Intelligence*, pbd Nathaniel Thompson, Mar. 1681 – Nov. 1682 (revived, Feb. – Mar. 1683)

Luttrell   Narcissus Luttrell, *A Brief Historical Relation of State Affairs*, (6 vols. Oxford, 1857)

Mist   *The Weekly Journal; Or, Saturday's Post* (later, *Mist's Weekly Journal*) Dec. 1716 – Sept. 1728

Morison Stanley Morison, *The English Newspaper: Some Account of the Physical Development* . . . (Cambridge, 1932)

Muddiman J. G. Muddiman, *The King's Journalist, 1659–1689* (London, 1923)

Ogg David Ogg, *England in the Reign of Charles II* (2 vols. Oxford, 1934)

Popish Plot Catalogues Narcissus Luttrell's Popish Plot Catalogues, Blackwell, Oxford, for the Luttrell Society, with an Introduction by F. C. Francis, 1956. (References are to the separately paginated section, 'A Continuation of the Compleat Catalogue'.)

P.R.O. Public Record Office

Read *The Weekly Journal; Or, British Gazetteer* (later, *Read's Weekly Journal*) Feb. 1715 – May 1761

S.P.D. State Papers Domestic.

State Trials A Compleat Collection of State Tryals (4 vols. London, 1719)

Steele Robert Steele, *Tudor and Stuart Proclamations* (2 vols. (*Bibliotheca Lindesiana*, vols. V–VII) 1910)

Thompson *The True Domestick Intelligence; Or, News both from City and Country*, pbd Nathaniel Thompson, Aug. 1679 – May 1680

T.P.M. *The True Protestant Mercury; Or, Occurrences forein and domestick*, pbd Langley Curtiss, Dec. 1680 – Oct. 1682

Note: newspapers appearing twice or three times a week were normally dated from the day of the previous issue to that of the current one; e.g. *The Impartial Protestant Mercury*, 17–21 June, 21–24 June 1681. The single date cited in the text and in the notes is always the day of publication.

1 ORIGINS AND DEVELOPMENTS

1. See P. W. Thomas, *Sir John Berkenhead 1617–1679: a royalist career in politics and polemics* (Oxford, 1969).
2. *C.S.P.D. 1661–2*, p. 282; *C.S.P.D. 1663–4*, p. 240.
3. *State Trials*, I. 974; Howell, VI. 526. *State Trials*, I. 988; Howell, VI. 564.
4. *The Statutes at Large*, ed. Danby Pickering, 1762–1807, VIII. 141–6.
5. *State Trials*, IV. 663, 673; Howell, XIV. 1105, 1128.
6. *The Parliamentary Intelligencer*, 2 Apr. 1660.
7. Muddiman, p. 130.
8. Henry Muddiman, who is not to be found in *D.N.B.*, was brought to general notice in 1923 by J. G. Muddiman's *The King's Journalist*. The author of this work was a man *plus royaliste que les royalistes*, whose political judgements are almost everywhere those of a twentieth-century Dr Sacheverell. But he had read carefully through the file of Henry Muddiman's news-letters in the library of the Marquess of Bath, and his book contains items of information unobtainable, or not easily to be found, elsewhere.
9. *The Diary of Samuel Pepys*, ed. Robert Latham and William Matthews (12 vols. London, 1970–8) I. 12.
10. Muddiman, pp. 130, 145. According to a reliable modern scholar, Mud-

diman depended on Sir Joseph Williamson for the foreign news he printed (Peter Fraser, *The Intelligence of the Secretaries of State . . . 1660–1688* (Cambridge, 1956) pp. 35–6). When Muddiman's official newsbooks came to an end, it is unlikely that the same assistance was available for his news-letters.

11. Muddiman, pp. 145–6, 147.
12. Ibid. p. 166.
13. *Journals of the House of Commons*, VIII. 74.
14. Muddiman, pp. 229–31; *C.S.P.D. 1676–7*, pp. 354, 356, 368.
15. Steele, I. 439; Ogg, II. 101–2.
16. *C.S.P.D. 1663–4*, p. 240; *C.S.P.D. 1665–6*, p. 22.
17. *The Diary of John Evelyn*, ed. E. S. de Beer (Oxford, 1955) IV. 38.
18. Brief summaries of L'Estrange's correspondence will be found in *C.S.P.D. 1665–6*, pp. 15, 17, 20, 22, and a fuller account in Muddiman, pp. 174–8.
19. *H.M.C. Ormonde Mss. New Series*, III. 351–2; Muddiman, p. 180
20. 17 May 1680; Steele, I. 450.
21. Handover, pp. 14, 16–18.
22. Muddiman, p. 193.
23. Handover, p. 23.
24. *Currant Intelligence*, 4 May 1680. For a fuller account of Harris's troubles, see pp. 186–90.
25. *London Gazette*, 6 May 1680.
26. Ibid. 20 May 1680; Steele, I. 450.
27. Muddiman, p. 227; *Votes of the House of Commons, Perused and Signed to be Printed . . . 1680*, 19 Nov., 23 Dec.
28. *C.S.P.D. 1680–1*, p. 181.
29. Roger North, *The Lives of the Right Hon. Francis North, Baron Guilford. . . .* (3 vols. 1826) I. 320–1.
30. For the authorship of *Heraclitus Ridens*, see T. F. M. Newton, 'The Mask of Heraclitus', *Harvard Studies and Notes in Philology and Literature* (1934) XVI. 145–60.
31. Robert South, 'Ecclesiastical Policy the best Policy', a sermon preached at Lincoln's Inn, 1660 (Irène Simon, *Three Protestant Divines* (Paris, 1976) II. Pt 1, p. 58).
32. *The Debates in the House of Commons assembled at Oxford*, 1681; Haley, p. 633. As Secretary Jenkins told the House, 'There is no great Assembly in Christendom does it. 'Tis against the gravity of this Assembly'.
33. 'Written permission was signalised by the word *Licensed . . .* The phrase *With Allowance* was used wherever the permission was verbal. *Published by Authority* implied almost a command to publish' (Ogg, p. 510).
34. *Macaulay's History of England* ('Everyman' edition) III. 534–5.
35. The characteristically reasonable views of John Locke on the Licensing Act of 1662 and on its various undesirable consequences are given in an appendix to *The Correspondence of John Locke*, ed. E. S. de Beer (Oxford 1976, in progress) V. 785–91. See also Raymond Astbury, 'The Renewal of the Licensing Act in 1693 and its Lapse in 1695', *The Library*, XXXIII (1978), pp. 296–322.

36. *Macaulay's History*, IV. 123.
37. 'On the Liberty of the Press', *Grub-Street Journal*, 26 Oct. 1732.
38. For an account of the early history of the *Post Man*, see Morison, pp. 57–60.
39. Robert Mawson, *The Supplement to the Weekly Journal*, 3 May 1715; Richard Burridge, *A New Review of London*, 1722, p. 34.
40. *Boyer's Case*. (This is a half sheet printed on one side in double columns.)
41. Morison, p. 63. Morison's account of the postscripts is the best so far available.
42. British Library, Add. Ms. 4295, fos 49, 50; printed in Hanson, pp. 135–8.
43. Defoe, *Letters*, p. 263.
44. S.P.D. 35/18/117.
45. *Daily Journal*, 23 Feb. 1728.
46. Pickering, *Statutes at Large*, XII. 369–70; F. Knight Hunt, *The Fourth Estate* (1850) I. 188.
47. R.M.Wiles, *Freshest Advices: Early Provincial Newspapers in England* (Ohio State University Press, 1965) pp. 47–8. Wiles also supplies useful information on the various sizes of sheet used to evade the Stamp Acts of 1712 and 1725. See also Morison, pp. 103–5, and G. A. Cranfield, *The Development of the Provincial Newspaper 1700–1760* (Oxford, 1962) pp. 42–7.
48. In his 'Proposal' Toland stated that the contrivance of publishing in a sheet and a half was 'first set on foot by a paper call'd the Daily Benefactor since dropt', and that it was 'straight imitated by St. James's Evening Post' (Hanson, p. 136). But Toland was not well-informed: the *Daily Benefactor* (2 May – 9 June 1715) was far from being the first. (*supra*, pp. 32–4.)
49. Michael Shugrue, 'The Rise of the Weekly Journal', *Notes and Queries*, CCVII (July 1962) 246–7. Shugrue's evidence for the dating of Mawson's *Journal* is based on 'microfilm of the holdings of that Journal in the Library of the University of Edinburgh', and, for dating Applebee's *Journal*, on the file in the University of Illinois, which has 'patiently pieced together a unique microfilm of the entire run of the periodical'. In his pioneering lists of English newspapers in the *Cambridge Bibliography of English Literature* (1940), Graham Pollard, using square brackets to indicate his dependence on 'authorities which do not give any recent accessible location, and, in some cases, on the dubious expedient of reckoning backward from extant issues', had to record the earliest date of publication for Applebee's *Journal* as '[1713?]', and that for Mawson's *Journal* as '[No. 1, 2 Jan. 1714]'. In the case of Mawson, 'reckoning backward' produced a date only four days off the mark. When Pollard was compiling his bibliography in the late 1930s, microfilm was in its infancy, not much more than a word that one was gradually growing accustomed to hearing.
50. G. A. Cranfield, *Provincial Newspaper* p. 44.
51. For those changes, see Morison, pp. 104–5.
52. In 1729 it was claimed that all the considerable coffee-houses 'find their Account in taking constantly, some two, some three, some four of a Sort

of the Leading Papers every Day, besides Duplicates of most of the others' (*The Case between the Proprietors of Newspapers and the Coffee-men . . .*, (1729) p. 9).

53. *D.N.B.* s.v. 'NATHANIEL MIST' (by G. A. Aitken).
54. *An Historical View . . .* pp. 2, 13.
55. Hanson, pp. 55, 65–6.
56. S.P.D. 35/30/52.
57. The terms proposed by the proprietor of the *London Journal* will be found in S.P.D. 35/30/34, 35. Cf. Hanson, pp. 106–7, 144–5.
58. According to the *Craftsman*, 31 July 1731, the government also paid for the printing and distribution of Read's *Weekly Journal*, the *Weekly Register*, the *Flying Post* and Henley's *Hyp-Doctor*. Cf. Hanson, pp. 109, 114–15.
59. Those figures were given added publicity by Pope in a note on William Arnall in *The Dunciad*, 1743, II. 315.
60. *Memoirs of the Society of Grub-Street*, 1737, I. xiii–xiv.

2 LONDON NEWS

1. In his *Domestick Intelligence* of 30 March 1680 Thompson declared that Oates denied speaking the words attributed to him, but on 3 April the *Currant Intelligence* repeated its original statement, and added that it had witnesses to prove it. The upshot was that John Smith was prosecuted at the King's Bench as 'a pernicious person, and contriving and maliciously intending to excite discord and scandal between the King and his people' (Hart, p. 269). The new penny post was well advertised in the contemporary press; e.g. in *Mercurius Civicus*, 22, 24, 29 Mar., 6 Apr. 1680. The number for 3 Apr. carried a notice that the undertakers 'will give 5 pounds to be inform'd of any Papist they imploy either as messenger or bearer'. For contemporary literature on the penny post, see T. Todd, *William Dockwra and the Rest of the Undertakers* (Edinburgh, 1952). On behalf of the Duke of York, who had been granted the revenue from the Post Office by the King, actions were brought against Dockwra, culminating in 1682 with one for damages of £5,000, 'yet only £100 was found against Mr. Dockwra at the desire of the King's counsel, and that was forgiven'. His penny post was taken over by the government on 11 Dec. 1682 (Todd, *William Dockwra*, pp. 28–9, 50, 151).
2. *Heraclitus Ridens*, 25 Oct. 1681.
3. *State Trials*, II. 355, 367, 396; Howell, VII. 596, 620, 686.
4. Harris, 22 July 1679.
5. *State Trials*, II. 743; Howell, VIII. 333.
6. *C.S.P.D. 1681*, p. 310; *Loyal Prot.* 7 June 1681.
7. In his evidence at the trial Oates stated that Everard had told him the pamphlet 'was to be printed, and to be sent abroad by the Penny-Post to the protesting Lords, and the leading Men in the House of Commons, and they were to be searched, and to have it found about them' (*State Trials*, II. 755; Howell, VIII. 362).

8. Haley, p. 630.
9. Among those called for the defence by Fitzharris were the Duchess of Portsmouth and Mrs Wall her woman. Both were unwilling to give specific answers to his questions, and the court did little to elicit any information from them. The Duchess finally dismissed herself from further questioning by saying she had nothing to tell that could do Mr Fitzharris any good, 'and so can't see that I am any ways more useful here' (*State Trials*, II. 756–8, 761–2, 764; Howell, VIII. 365 ff., 377).
10. *Memoirs of Sir John Reresby*, ed. A. Browning, 1936, pp. 249 ff.
11. *State Trials*, III. 9; Howell, IX. 22.
12. *I.P.M.* 21 March 1682.
13. *C.S.P.D. 1679–80.* p. 308.
14. *Mercurius Anglicus*, 13 Dec. 1679.
15. *London Gazette*, 3 Aug. 1714. The Gazetteer at this time was Charles Ford, who owed his appointment (on 1 July 1712) to the influence of his friend Jonathan Swift. For Ford's embarrassment on the unexpected death of the Queen, when he 'had no body to consult with [on a Sunday], and therefore chose to say too little than any thing I doubted might be proper', see *The Letters of Jonathan Swift to Charles Ford*, ed. D. Nichol Smith (Oxford, 1935) p. 47.
16. *Commentator*, 4 Jan. 1720.
17. *The Historian*, No. 1, 2 Feb. 1712.

3 COUNTRY NEWS

1. Brian Austen, *English Provincial Posts 1633–1840* (1978) pp. 8, 20.
2. Thomas Delaune, *The Present State of London* (1681) p. 346.
3. Thomas Gardiner, *A General Survey of the Post Office 1677–1682* (Postal Historical Society, Special Series, No. 5, 1958) pp. 58, 61, 20, 13; Delaune, *The Present State of London*, pp. 345–6.
4. *The Kingdomes Intelligencer*, 25 Aug. 1662.
5. *Mercurius Publicus*, 11 Sept. 1662.
6. Ibid. 27 Feb., 29 May 1662.
7. Ibid. 24 Apr., 26 June, 29 May 1662.
8. Pepys, *Diary*, V. 348; VI. 127, 128.
9. Country news in the *Gazette* was mainly shipping intelligence from the seaports, but visits of the royal family to the two universities, to Bath, Newmarket, Windsor, etc. were officially recorded.
10. Harris, 28 July 1679.
11. Benskin, 21 July 1681.
12. Harris, 26 Mar. 1680. A satirical comment on Harris's whales had been made by Thompson on 19 March. It is not impossible that he planted the story on Harris.
13. On 22 March, giving his own account of how he had been imposed upon, Harris turned defence into attack by suggesting it was most probable 'that Letter was originally Forged by some Popish Priest, who set on Beckett to put the Story upon us, that they might have the greater pretence to

Clamour against our Intelligence'.

14. Harris, 19 Sept. 1679.
15. Ibid. 28 Nov. 1679.
16. Ibid. 12 Apr. 1681.
17. Ibid. 18 Nov. 1679. The Pope-burning processions of 1679 were on an exceptional scale, 'a tribute to the quite unprecedented political showmanship and capacity for organization of Shaftesbury and the Whigs' (Jones, pp. 112–13).
18. Harris, 24 Feb. 1680. In Harris's account the student who abused the Mayor's daughter was a scholar of Queen's College, and 'the Towns-Men were so enraged thereat, that they broke into the Hall where they were at Dinner, and killed sixty-three of the Students: since which time, upon the tenth of February yearly, the Scollers of that Colledge dine very privately, the door being locked and no Person being admitted to come in, and there all sit with their faces toward the door, as if to prevent any mischief intended against them'. In 1680 this may have become the accepted version of the slaughter of some Oxford students on St Scholastica's Day more than 300 years earlier; or, alternatively, Harris's correspondent may have been the victim of some Oxford joker.
19. Harris began publishing election results on 8 August 1679, and was still giving late returns on 10 October.
20. Harris, 11, 15 Mar. 1681.
21. If Harris's Edinburgh correspondent was a Scot, it is within the bounds of possibility that he was George Ridpath, later to become the writer of the *Flying Post*. In 1679 he was still a student at Edinburgh University, but he was also the ringleader in the Pope-burning riots of Christmas 1680 (*infra*, pp. 149–50). For this he was arrested, kept in irons, but spared 'the boot', and banished from Scotland in March 1681 (Will Laick [i.e. George Ridpath], *The Scots Episcopal Innocence* (1694) pp. 53–6). See also *Miscellany of the Abbotsford Club* (1837) I. 356–7, 363.
22. On 12 Sept. 1681 Benskin had published two reports from Newmarket, the second of which mentioned the King's being 'divertized' with a match of cock-fighting and a foot-race. On 17 Sept. the *Loyal Protestant's* Newmarket correspondent asserted that there was 'not one word of Truth in that Relation'.
23. *Loyal Prot.* 12 July 1681.
24. Ibid. 27 Dec. 1681.
25. *Popish Plot Catalogues*, p. 21.
26. Smith may have had a special interest in horses and horse-racing: in June 1683 he began publishing an advertisement paper, *The Jockey's Intelligencer*.
27. *Calendar of Treasury Books 1685–1689*, ed. William A. Shaw (1922) VIII. 1848.
28. Gardiner, *General Survey*, p. 27.
29. *C.S.P.D. October 1683 – April 1684*, p. 54.
30. Gardiner, *General Survey*, p. 53. Searle's salary was £30. In April 1687 he is referred to as 'second clerk for the Kentish Road' (*Calendar of Treasury Books 1685–1689*, p. 1284).

31. *The Case between the Proprietors of Newspapers and the Coffee-men* (1729) p. 7.

32. Sir F. D. Mackinnon, 'The Law and Lawyers', *Johnson's England* (Oxford, 1933) II. 303n.3.

4 FOREIGN NEWS

1. The materials for this paragraph come mainly from Peter Fraser, *The Intelligence of the Secretaries of State 1660–1688* (Cambridge, 1956) pp. 35–8, 54, 66–70, 156–8.

2. Ibid. p. 65.

3. *The Correspondence of Richard Steele*, ed. Rae Blanchard (Oxford, 1941) p. 23.

4. *H.M.C. Polwarth Mss.* I. 58; II. 236–7.

5. *H.M.C. Portland Papers*, VIII. 187.

6. Steele, *Correspondence*, p. 22.

7. Ibid. pp. 26–7n. (quoted by Rae Blanchard from *Mr. Steele's Apology for Himself and his Writings* (1714) p. 81).

8. *C.S.P.D. 1682*, p. 200.

9. *The General Postscript*, 31 Oct. 1709.

10. *The Post Man*, 8, 11 Jan. 1704.

11. Handover, p. 50. In a letter to Charles Ford from Horace Walpole, 24 Sept. 1714, Ford was thanked for his services, and told that it was thought fit Mr Buckley should begin writing the *Gazette* 'next Tuesday' (S.P.D. 44/147).

12. *London Gazette*, 18 Dec. 1679.

13. *Daily Courant*, 22 Oct. 1702.

14. Defoe, *Review*, 19 Sept. 1706.

15. Harris, 12 Sept. 1679.

16. See Brian Austen, *English Provincial Posts*, p. 23: 'Deal had a particular importance because of the need to provide for letters to and from shipping in the Downs.'

17. Rumours in 1681 that a new parliament was to be called were particularly obnoxious to the King and his ministers, and Richard Janeway was to suffer for this indiscretion in due course. See p. 202.

18. Defoe, *The Anatomy of Exchange-Alley* (1719) p. 16.

19. *Boyer's Case.*

20. *An Account of the Surrendring of the Castle of NAMUR* was published as a postscript to the *Post-Boy* later in the day of 29 Aug. 1695.

21. G. M. Trevelyan, *England under Queen Anne: The Peace and the Protestant Succession* (London, 1934) pp. 130–2.

22. *Currant Intelligence*, 3 Dec. 1681; ibid. 21 May 1681.

23. *Dunton's Whipping-Post* (1706) p. 94.

24. *The General Postscript*, 27 Aug. 1709.

25. *Boyer's Case.*

26. *The St. James's Post*, 4 May 1716: 'Tho' we have receiv'd no Letters from Norway, we are inform'd by a West-India Ship, which sail'd the 30th of

April from Staverne in Norway, That Brigadier Budde, on the 28th, at 7 of the Clock in the Morning, had attack'd 900 Swedes by Land and Water; [and] that he had killed 3 or 400 . . .'

27. *The Thursday's Journal*, 6 Aug. 1719. The original Genoa correspondent was an Italian with an imperfect command of English. In his report published on 20 August he writes of ships 'which are ready to sail downwards'. In an editorial note the reader 'is desired to make Allowance in this Letter for the Italian English'.

28. *Daily Journal*, 19 Aug. 1728 (1½ columns); 20 August (2 columns).

29. *The Spectator*, ed. Donald F. Bond (Oxford, 1965) IV. 92.

30. Nicholas Rowe, *The Fair Penitent* (1703) Prologue.

31. *The Poems of Alexander Pope* ('Twickenham' edn) V. 165.

32. *Spectator*, IV. 93. For Addison's joke about 'Boat News', cf. Defoe's contemptuous evaluation of 'ship news' (*supra*, p. 131).

5 POLITICS

1. *London Gazette*, 4 Dec. 1679.

2. Harris, 5 Dec. 1679.

3. Thompson, 5 Dec. 1679.

4. *Currant Intelligence*, 30 Sept. 1681.

5. For a long and interesting account of a Pope-burning procession, see *Mercurius Anglicus*, 20 Nov. 1679.

6. *London Gazette*, 2 Feb. 1682. In the epilogue to *Venice Preserved* Otway referred to 'the Picture-mangler at Guildhall' and others of 'the Rebel-Tribe' who mutilated the Duke's portrait 'as they before had massacred his Name'.

7. For the unexpected return of Monmouth, see Haley, pp. 574–5.

8. The only newspaper man to become involved with the black box was John Smith, who published a pamphlet called *The Protestant Massacre* (based on materials collected by Israel Tonge) in which one Richard Greene asserted that Bishop Cosin had married Charles to Monmouth's mother. An informer found the pamphlet on display in Smith's shop, and he was summoned to appear before the Council on 6 May 1680 (*C.S.P.D. 1679–80*, p. 466).

9. On 11 April 1682 the *Loyal Protestant* described the scenes in the City when the King and his brother returned together from Newmarket. Some cried for Monmouth, but the majority were for the King and the Duke of York. Most of the bonfires had been built to consume 'the Rump, the Covenant, Association and Green Ribbons' (worn by Monmouth's supporters). Thompson dwelt with particular satisfaction on a bonfire in which an effigy of Shaftesbury was burnt, 'a little meagre-fac'd wither'd Conjurer, with a Tap and Spiggot in his side'. The *Impartial Protestant Mercury* saw things rather differently, and noted that 'whereas it was noised that abundance of people would go forth in a particular respect to his Royal Highness, we do not hear of any extraordinary number besides the usual Guards that waited on them into Town'. The King's Protestant

subjects were happy to express their joy at his safe return in good health; but a number of apprentices shouted, 'No Papist, no Papist, God bless the king and the Duke of Monmouth!' (*I.P.M.* 11 Apr. 1682.)

10. Harris's report of what was discussed on 26 March may be verified from *Debates in the House of Commons* (1681). See also Haley, pp. 635–6. Other fragments of the Oxford debates were published in *Smith's Protestant Intelligence* and the *True Protestant Mercury*.

11. Hanson, pp. 76–83. The right to print parliamentary reports was 'silently conceded', and was never made the subject of a resolution by the House of Commons (D. Nichol Smith, 'The Newspaper', *Johnson's England* (Oxford, 1933) II. 355–6).

12. E. R. Turner, *The Privy Council of England in the Seventeenth and Eighteenth Centuries* (Baltimore, 1927–8) I. 398–9.

13. Ogg, II. 621–2.

14. *London Gazette, I.P.M.* and *Loyal Prot.* of 4 July; *Currant Intelligence,* 5 July 1681.

15. *C.S.P.D. 1680–1*, pp. 482–3. Netterville was apparently an Irishman, and a cousin of Edward Fitzharris (*C.S.P.D. Jan.–June 1683*, p. 219). Shortly after Fitzharris was hanged, questions were asked about Netterville's 'transactions with Mrs. Fitzharris, where she is and who supports her' (*C.S.P.D. 1680–1*, p. 483). On 12 Nov. 1681 the Irish correspondent of the *Currant Intelligence* reported that a Mr Netterville (possbily the same man) had been apprehended for trying to tamper with the evidence of a prisoner in the Marshalsea Prison in Dublin.

16. *C.S.P.D. Oct. 1683 – Apr. 1684*, pp. 51, 53.

17. Harris, 9 Dec. 1679. In his *Loyal Protestant* of 17 May 1681 Thompson gives a memorable account of the King's way of dealing with petitions. When, on 15 May (a Sunday), a deputation from the City, unbidden and unwelcome, arrived at Windsor Castle to deliver a petition for the calling of a parliament, the King chose not to appear, but sent a message that the Council would sit on Thursday at Hampton Court, and 'if they had anything of moment to communicate to him', they could deliver it there. Unwilling, perhaps, to antagonise his subjects by too abrupt a dismissal, or his natural affability reasserting itself, the King was pleased to add, 'But if they had a mind to see the House, they were welcome.' On the following Thursday, when they reappeared at Hampton Court and presented their strongly-worded petition for a parliament that would redress 'the people's grievances', the King told them that 'this was beyond their Sphere to meddle into, and that they should mind their own Business and Trade at home'. The power of calling his parliament 'when and where he thought convenient was one of the greatest Trusts lodged in the King', and it was 'dangerous for them to incroach upon his Prerogative' (*Loyal Prot.* 21 May 1681).

18. *Loyal Prot.* 12 July 1681.

19. Jones, p. 166. For an illuminating discussion of the instructions given to Whig members of parliament, see Jones, pp. 166–73.

20. What the cooks and chandlers really did is probably expressed more

accurately by Narcissus Luttrell: 'The company of cooks and chandlers of the citty of Salisbury returned thankes to the magistrates of that citty for their addresse to his majestie thanking him for his declaration' (Luttrell, I. 92).

21. The Grand Jury had referred to the Norwich address as a 'scandalous libel' (*Currant Intelligence*, 24 May 1681).

22. John T. Evans, *Seventeenth-Century Norwich 1620–1690* (Oxford, 1979) pp. 252, 266–7, 272.

23. The dinner for the apprentices was held at Saddlers' Hall. The government evidently attached some importance to the occasion, for the guests included the Duke of Grafton, the Earl of Arlington and other distinguished persons (*Loyal Prot.* 6 Aug. 1681). Thompson's report took up most of his front page.

24. In the end two different addresses were sent to the King (*Currant Intelligence*, 24 May 1681).

25. *T.P.M.* 25 June 1681.

26. Luttrell, I. 94.

27. It is only fair to Thompson to record that he gave almost the whole of his issue of 26 November to the trial of Shaftesbury and honestly reported that in the evening 'more Bonfires were made in the City than ever yet was seen on the 29th of May' (the anniversary of the day in 1660 when Charles arrived back in London, and was met by both Houses of Parliament).

28. Ogg, II. 617. On 4 February 1682 the *True Protestant Mercury* reported that a Grand Jury presented a number of conventicles, but that the presentments had not been accepted, since 'it was the declared Opinion of the Commons, and a Vote had passed in that House, That the Presentation of Protestant Dissenters upon the Penal Law is at this time grievous to the Subject, a weakning of the Protestant Interest, and dangerous to the Peace of the Kingdom'. See *Journals of the House of Commons*, IX. 703–4; Ogg, II. 606.

29. As might be expected, reports in the Whig press of the disturbing of conventicles were normally indignant, while in the Tory press they were often facetious. When a conventicle was raided, the dissenting minister sometimes escaped by some ingenious mechanical contrivance. The *Loyal Protestant Mercury* of 4 July 1682 reported a disturbance in a Bristol meeting-house from which the preacher 'vanished by the assistance of a trap-door made under the Pulpit, and could by no means be found'.

30. *C.S.P.D. 1682*, pp. 520–1.

31. *Observator*, 26 Aug. 1682.

32. On 16 July 1681 the *Currant Intelligence* published a letter from 'a person of quality' giving an account of those proceedings much more favourable to the Bishop, and controverting 'the scandalous passage in Janeway's Intelligence, falsly reflecting upon the Bishop of Chichester'.

33. David Ogg, *England in the Reigns of James II and William III* (Oxford, 1955) pp. 428–9.

34. Hanson, pp. 65 ff.

35. Applebee, 18 Feb. 1721. The writer was probably Defoe.
36. Abel Boyer, *Political State* (1716) XII. 85–7, 94, 105, 652–3. While Flint was carrying on *The Shift Shifted* in Newgate, he had a visit from his wife, 'who, under pretence of bringing him a Pudding baked in an Earthen Pan, there was found at the bottom of it a Tin-Pot stuff'd with Treasonable Letters and Papers, being Materials for the said Paper, which were presently sent to the Ld. Townshend's Office' (Read, 15 Sept. 1716). Later, Flint made his escape from Newgate 'in the Habit of a Footman, and run as fast as the best of that Denomination, 'till he got over to France, and so escaped the Gallows' (*The Secret History of the Rebels in Newgate*, n.d. p. 30).
37. *The Humourist* ('The Second Edition', 1735) pp. 96–105.

6 THE NEWSPAPER MEN AND WOMEN

1. *The Life and Errors of John Dunton*, ed. J. Nichols (1818), I. 177.
2. Hart, p. 220.
3. *State Trials*, II. 476.
4. Muddiman, p. 218.
5. Luttrell, I. 36.
6. *State Trials*, II. 477; Howell, VII. 928. The Recorder was Jeffreys.
7. Harris, 17 Feb. 1680.
8. See Timothy Crist, 'Government Control of the Press after the Expiration of the Printing Act in 1679', *Publishing History*, V. (1979), pp. 70–1, 77. See also David Knott, 'The Booksellers and the Plot', *The Book Collector*, XXIII. pp. 202–4.
9. *State Trials*, II. 477; Howell VII. 929.
10. *State Trials*, II. 477–8; Howell, VII. 929–30, 931.
11. *State Trials*, II. 477; Howell, VII. 929. When summing up at the trial of Henry Care (*State Trials* II. 560; Howell, VII. 1126) Lord Chief Justice Scroggs reverted to the case of Harris, whose misfortune it was that 'he hath no place of Mercy left from the King because he was attended by such a Rabble', and 'it hath turned this man's Cause into a publick Cause . . . and the Government is hereby concerned much more'. Harris, it would seem, was given a severer sentence because of the provocative support of his friends. According to Muddiman (p. 244) the King remitted his fine 'upon promise of his better behaviour', but no date is given for this act of clemency.
12. Luttrell, I. 34.
13. *State Trials*, II. 560; Howell, VII. 1125–6.
14. *State Trials*, II. 476; Howell, VII. 931.
15. A puzzling statement that no sooner was the Oxford parliament dissolved on 29 March 1681 than 'Harris was arrested on a charge of being present at the Southwark election for parliament' (on 12 March), and of 'being frequent with Sheriff Bethel' seems to rest upon the confusion of Benjamin Harris with Samuel Harris, who had been active in the petitioning movement and was a friend of Slingsby Bethel. (See Kitchin, p. 275.)

16. *C.S.P.D. 1680–1*, pp. 335, 481.
17. The paper in question was *Intelligence Domestick and Foreign*, re-named by Harris on 2 July 1695 *The Pacquet-Boat from Holland and Flanders*. 'The Privy Council was able to intimidate Benjamin Harris, and the last number of his newly born *Pacquet Boat from Holland and Flanders* appeared on 9 July . . .' (Raymond Astbury, 'The Renewal of the Licensing Act in 1693 and its Lapse in 1695', *The Library*, XXXIII (1978) p. 317.
18. S.P.D. Entry Book 77; P. C. Webb, *Copies taken from the Records of the Court of King's Bench* (1763) p. 17. Mrs Popping was arrested on 3 December She was replaced by J. Baker (*Protestant Postboy*, 8 Dec. 1711).
19. Muddiman, pp. 230, 255.
20. *T.P.M.* 21 Feb. 1682.
21. *A Choice Collection of 180 Loyal Songs* ('The Third Edition, with many Additions') 1685.
22. Thompson, 30 Mar. 1680. Several of the apprentices were brought before the Council. Their ringleader, Thomas Alford, was sent to Newgate on a charge of 'conspiring to levy war against the King' (*London Gazette*, 25 Mar. 1680).
23. Thompson, 3 Feb. 1680. For Thompson's sarcastic comments on Waller's treatment of Mr Christian, the former steward of the Duke of Buckingham, see his *Domestick Intelligence* of 3, 6, 10, 13 Feb. and 5, 12 Mar. 1680.
24. Thompson, 30 Mar. 1680.
25. *C.S.P.D. 1679–80*, p. 425.
26. Thompson, 15 June 1680; Hart, p. 236.
27. *T.P.M.* 26 Feb. 1681; *Presentation of Nathaniel Thompson at the General Sessions of the Peace, 31 August 1681* (Bodleian Library, Ashm. 1677, No. IX); *C.S.P.D. 1680–1*, p. 517.
28. *T.P.M.* 4 Mar. 1682.
29. At the end of March 1682 Thompson was brought before the Lord Mayor for saying that the murder of Godfrey was *felo de se* (*I.P.M.* 24 Mar.), and was then examined by the Council on the same charge (Luttrell, I. 175). On 5 April he was committed to Newgate along with Paine and Farwell, and obtained bail on 7 April (ibid. I. 176).
30. *State Trials*, III. 50; Howell, VIII. 1386.
31. *State Trials*, III. 51; Howell, VIII. 1389.
32. Kitchin, pp. 303–4n. (quoting from Henry Care's 'Popish Courant').
33. Luttrell, I. 207, 233; Muddiman, p. 243 (from a news-letter).
34. Leona Rostenberg, *Literary, Political, Scientific, Religious & Legal Publishing* . . . (New York, 1965) II. 341–2. (This work supplies useful summaries of the careers of several newspaper men and women.)
35. Luttrell, I. 75, 92, 109.
36. Ibid. I. 62, 64; *London Gazette*, 14 Nov. 1681; *Loyal Prot.* 15 Nov. 1681.
37. *State Trials*, II. 479, 480, 481: Howell, VII. 936, 937.
38. *State Trials*, II. 481; Howell, VII. 937, 939.
39. *Loyal Prot.* 8 July 1682.
40. *State Trials*, II. 481; Howell, VII. 937.

41. *C.S.P.D. 1680–1*, p. 310; *Loyal Prot.* 4, 11 June 1681. In November Lord Danby brought an action of *scandalum magnatum* against Curtiss (*Loyal Prot.* 10 Nov. 1681), and some time later Lord Berkeley obtained a warrant against him for 'printing base and scandalous words of his Lordship' (ibid. 10 Dec. 1681).

42. Jane Curtiss was indicted for publishing the *T.P.M.* of 10 June 1682 (Hart, p. 254).

43. Kitchin, p. 322.

44. In his valedictory statement Curtiss announced that he would 'forbear publishing this Intelligence, to see whether Thompson, *Observator* and Others will follow my Example'. In his *Observator* of 25 October L'Estrange made it clear that he had no intention of laying down his paper.

45. Hart, p. 283; *Poems on Affairs of State 1682–1685*, ed. Howard H. Schless (Yale University Press, 1968) pp. 498–9.

46. *Loyal Prot.* 4 June, 27 Oct. 1681; *London Gazette*, 17 Oct. 1681; *I.P.M.* 18 Oct. 1681; *C.S.P.D. 1682*, p. 211.

47. Muddiman, p. 242.

48. *London Mercury*, 13 June 1682.

49. *Loyal Prot.* 2 Aug. 1682.

50. Luttrell, I. 138.

51. *Loyal Prot.* 25 May 1682.

52. Hart, pp. 213–14, 240–1.

53. *Loyal Prot.* 31 Oct. 1682.

54. Kitchin, pp. 323–4.

55. *State Trials*, III. 125; Howell, IX. 551.

56. *Publick Occurrences Truely Stated*, 21 Feb. 1688.

57. S.P.D. 79A.

58. S.P.D. 35/19/3, 31.

59. For a fuller account of John Matthews, see James Sutherland, *Background for Queen Anne* (1939) pp. 182–200.

60. *Flying Post*, 24 Mar. 1716; Read, 31 Mar. 1716; *Postscript to the Weekly Journal*, 27 July 1715.

61. *Thursday's Journal*, 22 June 1719. For Pittis, see T. F. M. Newton, *Modern Philology* (1935) pp. 169–86; ibid. (1936) pp. 279–302.

62. S.P.D. Entry Book 79A, pp. 246–7.

63. S.P.D. 35/18/122.

64. S.P.D. 35/20/57.

65. S.P.D. 35/22/32.

66. S.P.D. Entry Book 79A.

67. *C.S.P.D. Oct. 1683 – Apr. 1684*, pp. 53–4.

68. *Popish Plot Catalogues* p. 20.

69. Hart, p. 278; Dunton, *Life and Errors*, I. 435.

70. *The General Postscript*, 27 Sept. 1709.

71. Muddiman, p. 215. Since Crouch was prosecuted for a paragraph in the number for 12 March 1680, he was presumably in charge of the *Domestick Intelligence* while Harris was in prison.

72. *C.S.P.D. 1680–1*, p. 481.
73. Cf. the statement by Thompson when he was imprisoned in the Gatehouse, that he had the use of pen, ink and paper, and would continue with 'the same faithful account' (*supra*, p. 194).
74. Muddiman, p. 240.
75. *C.S.P.D. 1682*, pp. 199, 200.
76. Benskin, 4 Apr. 1681.
77. *Loyal Prot.* 12 and 14 Jan. 1682.
78. *The General Postscript*, 27 Sept. 1709.
79. Berrington appears to have been both compiler and printer of the *Evening Post*. When shown a copy of the paper dated 17 July 1729 and asked to name the author, he said he collected his news out of the other papers, and had taken the paragraph in question from the *Daily Post* of the same date (S.P.D. 35/13/118–19).
80. *The Scots Episcopal Innocence* (1694) p. 67.
81. S.P.D. 79A, p. 324.
82. S.P.D. 35/13/32.
83. S.P.D. 35/18/113. For further evidence of newspapers being owned by a group of booksellers, see two useful articles by Michael Harris: 'The Structure, Ownership and Control of the Press, 1620–1780', *Newspaper History*, ed. G. Boyce *et al.* (1978) pp. 82–97; and 'The Management of the London Newspaper Press during the Eighteenth Century', *Publishing History*, IV (1978) pp. 95–112. See also the same author's 'Periodicals and the English Book Trade', *Development of the English Book Trade 1700–1899*, eds. R. Myers and M. Harris (1981).
84. S.P.D. 35/31/39.
85. Hanson, pp. 65, 66.
86. S.P.D. 35/30/34, 35.
87. Mist, 11 Jan. 1724.
88. *Daily Courant*, 6 Sept. 1718.
89. S.P.D. 35/34/78b. Gaylard also stated that he 'was to have one half of the profitts of printing the Journal, but had no Share in the Property or Profitts of the said Paper'. For some months between 1721 and 1722 Mist's *Journal* was 'Printed by Doctor Gaylard for N. Mist'.
90. S.P.D. 36/13/116–17.
91. S.P.D. 36/11/85, 89.
92. *Some Memoirs of the Life of Abel, Toby's Uncle* (by 'Dr. Andrew Tripe'), 1726, pp. 36–7.
93. S.P.D. 36/15/91.
94. S.P.D. 36/5/93–6.
95. *Boyer's Case.*
96. S.P.D. 35/13/32.
97. S.P.D. 35/13/33.
98. Read, 22 Nov. 1718.
99. S.P.D. 35/1/28(2).
100. S.P.D. 35/1/28(9).
101. Howell, xv. 1394–1400.

102. William Bond (d. 1735) collaborated with Aaron Hill in a periodical called *The Plain Dealer*, 1724–5. According to Dr Johnson, Richard Savage called Hill and Bond 'the two contending powers of light and darkness': each wrote six essays by turns, 'and the character of the work was observed regularly to rise in Mr. Hill's weeks, and fall in Mr. Bond's' (Samuel Johnson, *Lives of the English Poets*, ed. G. B. Hill (1905) II. 341n. 7).

103. *Grub-Street Journal*, 4 Nov. 1731.

104. S.P.D. 35/1/28 (8, 9); *Calendar of Treasury Books and Papers 1731–1734*, p. 51.

105. S.P.D. 36/8/157.

106. D. Nichol Smith, 'The Newspaper', *Johnson's England*, II. 331.

107. *T.P.M.* 28 Dec. 1680; Read, 8 Mar., 1718. For Richard Burridge, see James Sutherland, *Background for Queen Anne*, pp. 3–32.

108. The first number of *The News Letter*, 7 Jan. 1716, carried a recommendation from Robert Mawson: 'Those Gentlemen who have encouraged the Weekly Journals by Subscription, and their Quarters are not up till after Christmas, are desired to pay them to Mr. Nathaniel Storer, the Proprietor of this Paper, who will make up their Quarters with his WEEKLY NEWS-LETTERS . . . and lay infinite Obligation upon their most obedient Servant – ROBERT MAWSON.' Mawson may have been in fresh trouble. His *Weekly Journal*, the last number of which recorded in the Cambridge *Bibliography* is that for 14 Dec. 1715, may have been carried on for him by friends since his arrest in April 1715 (*supra*, p. 34). It is to his friends that we owe the two short-lived papers, *Robin's Last Shift* (No. 1, 18 Feb. 1716), and *The Shift Shifted* (No. 1, 5 May 1716).

109. R. T. Milford and D. M. Sutherland, *A Catalogue of English Newspapers and Periodicals in the Bodleian Library* (Oxford, 1936) pp. 62–3.

110. D. Nichol Smith, 'The Newspaper', *Johnson's England*, II. 334. Similar results have been obtained by Donald F. Bond for the *Spectator* ('The First Printing of the *Spectator*', *Modern Philology* (1930) XLVII. 164–77).

111. James Sutherland, 'The Circulation of Newspapers and Literary Periodicals 1700–30', *The Library* (1934) XV. 111–12.

112. J. M. Price, 'A Note on the Circulation of the London Press 1704–14', *Bulletin of the Institute of Historical Research*, XXXI. 220–1. (The figures for the circulation of the *London Gazette* in Aug. – Sept. 1712 averaged 5,143.) See also H. L. Snyder, 'The Circulation of Newspapers in the Reign of Queen Anne', *The Library*, 5 Series, (1968) XXIII. 206–35; Michael Harris, 'Figures relating to the Printing and Distribution of the *Craftsman*, 1726–1730', *Bulletin of the Institute of Hisorical Research*, (1970) XLIII.

113. S.P.D. 35/31/39.

114. S.P.D. 35/28/9.

115. *Whitehall Evening-Post*, 4 Nov. 1718. How low the circulation of an unsubsidised six-page weekly could drop without its having to close down may be indicated by a hostile comment in Read's *Weekly Journal*, 29 Nov. 1718. The writer was attacking William Bond's *Weekly Medley*, and

remarked that it was now being printed by Francis Clifton, 'a poor Papist, who must quickly drop it for want of Money to pay Journeymen, or else because publishing the small Number of printing but 1,200 will not quit the Costs for carrying on that seditious Paper'. Subsidies of one sort or another were certainly needed to secure the survival of some periodicals. When Defoe was about to lay down his *Review*, he told his readers on 6 June 1713 that he had 'kept this Paper up for the sake of the few Friends I have left, who from the beginning have been Benefactors to the Work, and without whom I could not have supported the Expence of it'. He managed to produce two more numbers, but closed it down on 11 June with the Words, *EXIT REVIEW*. His own need for financial backing had not kept him from making several snide comments on Charles Lesley's High Church periodical, *The Rehearsal*; most explicitly on 9 Oct. 1705, when he stated that it was 'promoted by the Non-Jurors, and not being able otherwise to force its Way, is handed by Gift, and presented to the People's Reading *gratis*'.

116. *D.N.B.* s.v. 'STEPHEN COLLEGE'; Haley, p. 632.
117. Haley, p. 658.
118. *State Trials*, II. 826; Howell, VIII. 714.

The more important London newspapers
from 1660–1720

This list is restricted to papers that were chiefly concerned with publishing the day's or the week's news, and it does not therefore include such periodicals as *Heraclitus Ridens*, L'Estrange's *Observator*, or Defoe's *Review*, which were mainly engaged in commenting on the news. A comprehensive list of all the periodicals of the period (many of them short-lived) will be found in Vol. II of the *Cambridge Bibliography of English Literature*. Where no copy of the first number of a newspaper has so far been located the date of that number is supplied by reckoning backward from the earliest extant issue. Where there is reason to believe that a paper may have survived beyond the terminal date given, this is indicated by the sign —[?].

The Parliamentary Intelligencer (continued from 7 Jan. 1661 as The Kingdome's Intelligencer) 26 Dec. 1659 – 31 Aug. 1663. By Henry Muddiman and Giles Dury. Weekly.

Mercurius Publicus, Comprising the sum of forraign Intelligence with the affairs now in agitation in England, Scotland and Ireland, 5 Jan. 1660 – 3 Sept. 1663. By Henry Muddiman and Giles Dury. Weekly.

The Intelligencer. Published for the Satisfaction of the People, 31 Aug. 1663 – 29 Jan. 1666. By Sir Roger L'Estrange. Weekly.

The Newes, 3 Sept. 1663 – 25 Jan. 1666. By Sir Roger L'Estrange. Weekly.

The London Gazette (from 16 Nov. 1665 – 29 Jan. 1666 as The Oxford Gazette) 5 Feb. 1666 (still in progress). Twice a Week; later, for a period in the early eighteenth century, three times a week.

The Current Intelligence, 7 June – 23 Aug. 1666. By Henry Muddiman. Weekly.

The Domestick Intelligence; Or, News both from City and Country, 7 July 1679 – 13 Jan. 1680. Continued as The Protestant (Domestick) Intelligence, 16 Jan. – 16 Apr. 1680, and, after some months' suspension, from 28 Dec. 1680 – 15 Apr. 1681. Pbd Benjamin Harris. Twice a week.

The Domestick Intelligence; Or, News both from City and Country, No. 15 (i.e. No. 1) 26 Aug. – 5 Sept. 1679. Continued as The True Domestick Intelligence, 9 Sept. 1679 – 14 May 1680. Pbd Nathaniel Thompson. Twice a week.

Mercurius Anglicus; Or, The Weekly Occurrences faithfully transmitted (continued from 27 Dec. 1679 as True News; Or, Mercurius Anglicus) 10 Nov. 1679 – 15 May 1680. Pbd Robert Hartford. Twice a week.

London newspapers 1660 to 1720

The Currant Intelligence; Or An Impartial Account of Transactions both foreign and domestick (continued from 16 Mar. 1680 as Smith's Currant Intelligence) 14 Feb. – 4 May 1680. Pbd John Smith. Twice a week.

Mercurius Civicus; Or, A True Account of affairs both foreign and domestick, 22 Mar. – 6 May 1680. Twice a week.

The True Protestant Mercury; Or, Occurrences forein and domestick, 28 Dec. 1680 – 25 Oct. 1682 (with a lapse of two weeks in April 1681). Pbd Langley Curtiss. Twice a week.

Smith's Protestant Intelligence, domestick and foreign, 1 Feb. – 14 Apr. 1681. Pbd Francis Smith. Twice a week.

The Loyal Protestant and True Domestick Intelligence; Or, News both from City and Country, 9 Mar. 1681 – 20 Mar. 1683 (suspended from 16 Nov. 1682 – 20 Feb. 1683). Pbd Nathaniel Thompson. Twice a week; three times a week from 3 Nov. 1681.

The Protestant Oxford Intelligence; Or, Occurrences foraign and domestick (continued from 4 Apr. 1681 as The Impartial London Intelligence), 10 Mar. – 14 Apr. 1681. Twice a week.

The Impartial Protestant Mercury; Or, Occurrences, Foreign and Domestick (from 27 Apr. – 5 May 1681 as The True Protestant Mercury [etc.]) 27 Apr. 1681 – 30 May 1682. Ptd for H.V. and T.C. (i.e. H.C. and T.V., viz. Henry Care and Thomas Vile) and sold by Richard Janeway. Twice a week.

The Currant Intelligence, 30 Apr. – 24 Dec. 1681. Pbd John Smith; revival of his 1680 paper above. Twice a week.

The Domestick Intelligence; Or, News both from City and Country impartially related, 13 May 1681 – 16 Nov. 1682. Pbd T. Benskin. Twice a week.

The London Mercury, 6 Apr. – 17 Oct. 1682. Pbd Thomas Vile. Twice a week.

The Loyal Impartial Mercury; Or, News both foreign and Domestick, 9 June – 17 Nov. 1682. Pbd E. Brooks; ed. Thomas Vile (?). Twice a week.

The Loyal London Mercury; Or, The Moderate Intelligencer (continued from 23 Aug. 1682 as The Moderate Intelligencer) 14 June – 23 Oct. 1682. Twice a week.

The Conventicle Courant. Setting forth the proceedings against unlawful meetings, 24 July (?) 1682 – 14 Feb. 1683. By John Hilton. Weekly.

The Loyal London Mercury; Or, The Currant Intelligence, 23 Aug. – 15 Nov. 1682. Twice a week.

Publick Occurrences Truely Stated, 21 Feb. – 2 Oct. 1688. By Henry Care and Elkanah Settle. Weekly.

The Universal Intelligence, 11 Dec. 1688 – 18 Feb. 1689 (suspended from 12 Jan. – 13 Feb. 1689). Twice a week; three times a week from 1 Jan. 1682.

The London Courant, 12 Dec. 1688 – 9 Jan. 1689. Twice a week.

The English Currant, 12 Dec. 1688 – 9 Jan. 1689. Twice a week.

The London Mercury; Or, Moderate Intelligencer, 15 Dec. 1688 – 18 Feb. 1689. Ptd George Croom. Twice a week.

The Orange Gazette, 31 Dec. 1688 – 9 Mar. 1689. Twice a week.

The London Intelligence, 15 Jan. – 16 Feb. 1689. Twice a week.

An Account of the Publick Transactions in Christendom. In a Letter to a friend in the Country (continued as An Historical Account. . . .), 11 Aug. – 8 Sept. 1694. No further issues appeared until 4 May – 17 June 1695, when An Historical Account was incorporated with the Post-Boy, and later with the Post Man.

The Post-Boy, Foreign and Domestick, 14 May 1695 – 30 Sept. 1728. Ed. Abel Roper, with the assistance of E. Thomas, Abel Boyer and George James. Three times a week.

The Flying Post; Or, The Post-Master, 7 May 1695 – 25 Dec. 1733. Ed. George Ridpath. Twice a week from 7 May – 8 June 1695; then three times a week.

The Post Man and the Historical Account . . ., No. 72 (i.e. No. 1) 24 Oct. 1695 – 21 Feb. 1730. Ed. John de Fonvive. Three times a week.

Dawks's News-Letter, 23 June 1696 – 22 Dec. 1716. Pbd I. Dawks. An evening paper. Three times a week.

Lloyd's News, 1 Sept.(?) 1696 – 23 Feb. 1697. Pbd Edward Lloyd. Three times a week.

The Protestant Mercury. Occurrences Forein and Domestick, 9 Mar. 1697 – 18 Dec. 1700. Pbd I. Dawks. Three times a week.

The Foreign Post, 17 May 1697 – 31 Jan. 1698 – [?]

The London Post, With Intelligence Foreign and Domestick (No. 1 as The London Slip of News) 6 June 1699 – 8 June 1705 – [?]. Pbd Benjamin Harris and B. Bragg. Three times a week.

The English Post, Giving an Authentick Account of the Transactions of the World, Foreign and Domestick, 14 Oct. 1700 – Oct. 1709. (This paper was still appearing in Sept. – Oct. 1709, when it was referred to sarcastically in The General Postscript.) Ed. Nathaniel Crouch. Three times a week.

The Daily Courant, 11 Mar. 1702 – 28 June 1735. Ed. Samuel Buckley.

The Supplement, 19 Jan. 1708 – 30 July 1712 – [?]. Ed. George James as a supplement to The Post-Boy on the three days when that paper did not appear.

The Evening Post, 6 Sept. 1709 – 29 Aug. 1740. Ed. E. Berrington, B. Berrington. Three times a week.

The British Mercury. Published by the Company of London Insurers, 27 March 1710 – 2 May 1716. Three times a week until 2 Aug. 1712, when it changed to weekly publication. On 15 Jan. 1715 the title was altered to The British Weekly Mercury.

The Protestant Postboy, 4 Sept. 1711 – 12 July 1712 – [?]. Ptd Benjamin Harris; pbd Sarah Popping. Three times a week.

The Weekly Packet, 12 July 1712 – 29 July 1721 – [?]. Pbd H. Meere.

The Weekly Journal, With Fresh Advices Foreign and Domestick, 6 Jan. 1714 – 4 Jan. 1716. Pbd Robert Mawson.

A Weekly Journal, With Fresh Advices, Foreign and Domestick (continued from 11 June 1715 as The Original Weekly Journal, and from 16 July 1720 as Applebee's Original Weekly Journal) 9 Oct. 1714 – 24 Dec. 1737. Pbd J. Applebee.

The St. James's Post, 21 Jan. 1715 – 30 July 1722 – [?]. Pbd J. Baker. Three
times a week.

The Weekly Journal; Or, British Gazetteer, Being the Freshest Advices
Foreign and Domestick (continued from 22 Aug. 1730 as Read's Weekly
Journal; Or, British Gazetteer) 5 Feb. 1715 – 2 May 1761. Pbd James
Read.

St. James's Evening Post, 22 June 1715 – 16 June 1757 – [?]. Three times
a week.

Robin's Last Shift; Or, Weekly Remarks (continued from 5 May 1716 as The
Shift Shifted) 18 Feb. – 29 Sept. 1716. Carried on by the friends of
Robert Mawson; edited by George Flint, and printed by Isaac Dalton.

The General Post (continued from 5 Apr. 1716 as The Evening General Post)
15 Mar. – 6 Dec. 1716 – [?]. Three times a week.

The Whitehall Courant, 2 May – 30 July 1716 – [?]. Three times a week.

The Weekly Journal; Or, Saturday's Post, with freshest Advices foreign and
Domestick (continued from 1 May 1725 as Mist's Weekly Journal) 15
Dec. 1716 – 21 Sept. 1728. Ed. Nathaniel Mist.

The London Post; Or, The Tradesman's Intelligence. Being a Collection of the
Freshest Advices, Foreign and Domestick (continued as The Original
London Post; Or, Heathcote's Intelligence) 31 Mar. 1717 – 12 June
1723 – [?]. Pbd W. Heathcote. Three times a week.

The Whitehall Evening-Post, 18 Sept. 1718 – 10 Apr. 1739 – [?]. Three
times a week.

The London Journal (from No. 1 – No. 21 as The Thursday's Journal) 6 Aug.
1719 – 17 Mar. 1744. Ed. (in the early years) by John Trenchard and
Thomas Gordon. Weekly.

The Daily Post, 3 Oct. 1719 – 14 Feb. 1746.

The Daily Journal, 23 Jan. 1720 (i.e. 1721, New Style) – 9 Apr. 1737 – [?].
As the file of this paper shows, the printer used the Old Style of dating
up to 24 March, when the old year ended. The number for 25 March
is therefore the first to bear the date 1721.

Index

Note. When newspapers in this index are merely quoted in the text, page references have not been entered.

Index

Index

Index

Paine, William, 196–7
Parkyns, Sir William, 178
Parliamentary Intelligencer, The, 5
Parliaments of Charles II, 12–13, 156; their debates reported, 7–8, 157–9; petitions to the King for a parliament, 162–7, 169; petitions against holding one in Oxford, 167.
Partridge, John, astrologer, 193
Pemberton, Sir Francis, Lord Chief Justice, 55, 57, 196–7
Pembroke, Philip Herbert, seventh Earl of, 68
penny post, The, 48–9, 80, 237 *n*.1
Pepys, Samuel, 5–6, 96–7, 100–1
Perrot, Charles, 11
Pilkington, thomas, sheriff, 174
pillory, The, 189–90, 197, 202
Pitt, James, journalist, 215–16
Pittis, William, journalist, 206
Plague of London, the (1665), 9, 10
Plunket, Oliver, Archbishop of Armagh, 54–5, 112
politics, 146 ff.; changes in political climate, 169–71, 174–5, 180–3; city politics, 19, 174–5
political comment, 3–4, 28, 38–9, 112, 146–7, 196; use of innuendo, 183–4
Political State of Great Britain, The, 159
Polwarth, Alexander Campbell, Lord, 124
Pope, Alexander, 145, 223
pope-burning, 74, 149–50
Popish Plot, The, 12, 50–9, 67, 112, 180, 196–7
Popping, Sarah, printer and publisher, 192
Post-Boy, The (Abel Roper), 26, 27–8, 29, 31, 87, 88, 128, 134, 139–41, 180, 212, 217, 218, 228
Post-Boy, The, (Abel Boyer), 139–40
Post Man, The, 26, 27, 29, 31, 44, 127, 131, 139, 212, 228–9
postal services, 26–7, 91–2, 116–18; postmasters, 40, 116–17, 132; *see also* penny post.
Powell, Elizabeth, 205, 206–7
Powell, Nathaniel, Muggletonian, 150
Prance, Miles, 195–6
Pratt, Charles (later Earl Camden), Lord Chief Justice, 3
press control, 1–5, 7–8, 15–16, 19–20,

23–4, 25, 38–40, 55, 181–3, 189, 198–204, 205–7
Pretender, the 'Old' (James Francis Edward Stuart), 142, 147, 183, 215
printers: left in charge of newspapers, 215; blamed for mistakes, 215–16; their effect on the make-up of newspapers, 224–8
Privy Council, The, 80–1, 159–62
Projector, The, 223
propaganda for the government, 41, 92–3, 94, 95–8, 170, 193–4, 204
Protestant Courant, The (Richard Baldwin), 203
Protestant Mercury, The, 118
Protestant Oxford Intelligence, The, 157
Protestant Postboy, The, 180, 192–3
protestant succession, 12–13, 17, 19, 59, 147, 151–2, 162, 169, 178, 181–3
public disorder, 72–7
Public Intelligencer, The, 4
Publick Occurrences, Both Foreign and Domestick, (Benjamin Harris), 26
Publick Occurrences Truely Stated (Henry Care and Elkanah Settle), 22
publishers of newspapers, 209–13; precautions taken by, 217–19
Pulteney, William (later Earl of Bath), 184

Ralph, James, 145
Rawlins, Edward, 35, 225
Read, James, printer and publisher, 34, 35, 213, 215, 227; his son, Thomas Read, 215
Rehearsal, The (Charles Lesley), 180, 249 *n*.115
Reresby, Sir John, 59
Review, The (Daniel Defoe), 180, 249 *n*.115
Richardson, Samuel, 41
Ridpath, George, 26, 28, 89, 179, 184, 212, 239 *n.* 21
Robin's Last Shift, 183
Roper, Abel, 26, 29, 134, 139–40, 181, 212, 239 *n.* 21
Rothes, John Leslie, first Duke of, 90, 115
Rowe, Nicholas, 144
Rye House Plot, The, 202, 204

Saint James's Evening Post, The, 34

Index

Index